Adult Safeguarding and Homelessness

also in the Knowledge in Practice series

Working with Domestic Abuse across the Lifecourse
Understanding Good Practice
Edited by Ravi K. Thiara and Lorraine Radford
ISBN 978 1 78592 404 0
eISBN 978 1 78450 758 9

Safeguarding Adults under the Care Act 2014
Understanding Good Practice
Edited by Adi Cooper OBE and Emily White
Foreword by Lyn Romeo
ISBN 978 1 78592 094 3
eISBN 978 1 78450 358 1

Adult Safeguarding and Homelessness

Edited by **Adi Cooper**
and **Michael Preston-Shoot**

Jessica Kingsley Publishers
London and Philadelphia

First published in Great Britain in 2022 by Jessica Kingsley Publishers
An imprint of Hodder & Stoughton Ltd
An Hachette Company

1

Copyright © Jessica Kingsley Publishers 2022

Front cover image source: Cover photographs © Research in Practice

All rights reserved. No part of this publication may be reproduced, stored in a retrieval system, or transmitted, in any form or by any means without the prior written permission of the publisher, nor be otherwise circulated in any form of binding or cover other than that in which it is published and without a similar condition being imposed on the subsequent purchaser.

A CIP catalogue record for this title is available from the
British Library and the Library of Congress

ISBN 978 1 78775 786 8
eISBN 978 1 78775 787 5

Printed and bound by CPI Group (UK) Ltd, Croydon, CR0 4YY

Jessica Kingsley Publishers' policy is to use papers that are natural, renewable and recyclable products and made from wood grown in sustainable forests. The logging and manufacturing processes are expected to conform to the environmental regulations of the country of origin.

Jessica Kingsley Publishers
Carmelite House
50 Victoria Embankment
London EC4Y 0DZ

www.jkp.com

Acknowledgements

We would like to thank all the speakers for their presentations during the four national conferences on adult safeguarding and homelessness held in late 2019 and the eight webinars held between December 2020 and March 2021, and all participants. Their contributions informed the two briefings on adult safeguarding and homelessness published in March 2020 and summer 2021 through the Care and Health Improvement Programme (Local Government Association (LGA) and the Association of Directors of Adult Social Services (ADASS)). We also acknowledge the support provided by colleagues at ADASS and the LGA.

We have benefited enormously from members of an expert reference group, set up to develop the initiatives described above. The members were drawn from across statutory and third sector organisations, but also comprise academics, representatives of Safeguarding Adults Boards (SABs) and civil servants. This expert reference group has become a community of policy and practice, contributing to our understanding of adult safeguarding and homelessness and also disseminating the evidence base about positive practice.

SAB Independent Chairs and Business Managers have also contributed to our understanding of adult safeguarding and homelessness, provided examples of how their Boards have developed policies and procedures for this field of practice, and informed us of the outcomes of Fatality Reviews and Safeguarding Adults Reviews.

Finally, we would like to thank Professor Christine Cocker and Professor Suzy Braye, who have sustained us personally and offered important insights as we have sought to bring together the best examples of policy and practice concerning adult safeguarding and homelessness.

Our hope is that this book will make a positive difference for people experiencing homelessness and the practitioners and services working with them.

Adi Cooper and Michael Preston-Shoot
Editors

Contents

1. Introduction 9
   Adi Cooper and Michael Preston-Shoot

2. The Policy Framework 23
   Karl Mason

Part 1: Best Evidence on Working with Individuals

3. Seen But Not Heard: Why Challenging Your Assumptions about Homelessness Is a Matter of Life and Death 40
   Gill Taylor, Carl Price and Sharon Clint

4. Using Curiosity: A Psychologically Informed Approach to Adult Safeguarding and Rough Sleeping 59
   Sione Marshall, Tim Robson, Nathan Servini and Barney Wells

5. Health, Homelessness and Housing Supply 79
   Susan Harrison

6. Understanding Assessments and Protection Planning Duties for Adults Experiencing Homelessness 95
   Fiona Bateman and Bruno Ornelas

Part 2: Best Evidence for Multi-Agency and Multi-Disciplinary Teams around the Person

7. Working Together to Safeguard Individuals at Risk: Bristol Creative Solutions Board – A Case Study 114
   Kate Spreadbury and Paul England

8. Sustainable Housing 131
Imogen Blood

9. People with No Recourse to Public Funds Experiencing Homelessness. 152
Catherine Houlcroft and Henry St Clair Miller

Part 3: Best Evidence for Leadership and Strategic Partnerships

10. Learning from Safeguarding Adults Reviews and Fatality Reviews 174
Michael Preston-Shoot and Gill Taylor

11. Safeguarding Adults Boards and Multiple Exclusion Homelessness: The Challenges for System Leadership 195
Adi Cooper

12. Multiple Exclusion Homelessness and Safeguarding: Supporting Practitioners 212
Katy Shorten

13. Commissioning Services: Safeguarding and Homelessness . . 232
Rebecca Pritchard

References 256

Author Biographies 275

Subject Index 279

Author Index 285

Chapter 1

Introduction

Adi Cooper and Michael Preston-Shoot

Human Stories

[I want] people to listen to me and not make me feel like a bad person.

(see Chapter 3)

When asked what he needed, Terence replied: 'Some love, man. Family environment. Support.' He wanted to be part of something real, part of real society and not just 'the system'.

(Worcestershire Safeguarding Adults Board 2020)

I lost everything all at once: my job, my family, my hope… [W]ithout [this help in Leeds], I'd already be dead. I've no doubts about that. If the elements hadn't got me, I would have got me. Sometimes I have rolled up to this van in a real mess and they have offered help and support and got my head straight.

(Leeds Safeguarding Adults Board and Safer Leeds 2020)

Ms I's partner commented that at times 'she could not help herself' because of the feelings that were resurfacing; access to non-judgemental services was vital and helpful, and that support is especially important when individuals are striving to be alcohol and drug free. It was during these times that stress, anxiety and painful feelings could 'bubble up', prompting a return to substance misuse to suppress what it was very hard to acknowledge and work through.

(Tower Hamlets Safeguarding Adults Board 2020)

These words from individuals who have been homeless remind us why we need to listen to the voices of people with lived experience and why safeguarding is so important. Listening is key to understanding and being able to respond appropriately, whatever role we take. People with lived experience tell us time and time again that they 'want to be listened to, believed and trusted, informed and involved, and not to be judged' (Cooper and White 2017, p.12). Everyone has the same human rights, regardless of whether or not they are experiencing multiple exclusion homelessness (Mason *et al.* 2018). This includes when we are working with people to feel safer and more secure in their lives and reduce risks of abuse or neglect.

Human stories, such as those summarised above and those captured in Safeguarding Adults Reviews (SARs), remind us that there are multiple reasons why people become and remain homeless. They also remind us of the importance of relationships, of demonstrating emotional connection and of offering respectful and timely engagement that fits with the person's own perception of their needs.

Why Homelessness? Why Multiple Exclusion Homelessness? Why Adult Safeguarding?

There is evidence of growing numbers of people experiencing homelessness who are more likely than people who are not living street-based lives to experience abuse, exploitation and neglect, escalating health and care needs, and premature mortality (Bradley 2018; St Mungo's 2018; Office of National Statistics 2019a). In response to rising concerns, media publicity and the increased visibility of homelessness as an issue across the country, the government issued its Rough Sleeping Strategy (Ministry of Housing, Communities and Local Government (MHCLG) 2018a). This raised the profile of people sleeping rough and the government's stated commitment to end this by 2027. The strategy proposed three core pillars, namely prevention, intervention and recovery. Under prevention were included the new duties in the Homelessness Reduction Act 2017 and commitments to provide secure and affordable housing, longer and more secure private rented sector tenancies, and access to timely support to tackle mental health and substance misuse issues. There were commitments also on targeted support for women and for people discharged from prison, and to improve understanding of the needs of the LGBTQ+ communities.

On intervention, the strategy focused on secure and affordable housing, the sufficiency and quality of supported housing, and funding for 'somewhere safe to stay' pilots and rough sleeping navigators. The strategy recognised the importance of access to mental health and substance misuse treatment, and of support to resolve the immigration status of non-UK nationals. On recovery, the strategy included 'Housing First' to support people with complex needs.

One thematic SAR (Leeds Safeguarding Adults Board and Safer Leeds 2020) uses their three pillar metaphor to highlight the key components of the framework for addressing homelessness locally. However, as SARs and researchers also observe, financial, legislative, policy and institutional barriers remain, despite the aforementioned strategy (Dobson 2019a; Preston-Shoot 2020a).

The Covid-19 pandemic and accompanying lockdowns have brought a new focus on the needs of people sleeping on the streets and experiencing multiple exclusion homelessness, which has had a substantial impact on their lives and practice in this area of work. The 'Everybody In' initiative in 2020 has demonstrated what can be achieved when there is government investment and a coordinated intervention aiming to meet people's accommodation, physical and mental health, and care and support needs (see Chapter 5). The pandemic, however, has also illustrated the diversity of routes into homelessness, as people have lost their jobs and found themselves at risk of being unable to retain their homes.

Multiple exclusion homelessness comprises extreme marginalisation that includes childhood trauma, physical and mental ill-health, substance misuse and experiences of institutional care (Mason *et al.* 2018). Adverse experiences in childhood can include abuse and neglect, domestic violence, poverty and parental mental illness or substance misuse (Public Health England 2018). However, there are also other negative circumstances in childhood that are associated with poor adult outcomes, including economic disadvantage, discrimination, poverty and deprivation. Thus, trauma-informed approaches should guard against over-individualisation at the expense of a focus on structural inequalities (Asmussen *et al.* 2020). For many of those who are rough sleeping, homelessness is a long-term experience and associated with tri-morbidity (impairments arising from a combination of mental ill-health, physical ill-health, and drug and/or alcohol misuse) and premature mortality (Mason *et al.* 2018).

The government's Rough Sleeping Strategy (MHCLG 2018a) made an explicit link between homelessness and adult safeguarding in respect of individuals who die whilst sleeping on the streets. The strategy cites Safeguarding Adults Reviews as 'powerful tools, which unfortunately are rarely used in the case of people who sleep rough' (MHCLG 2018a). This criticism of Safeguarding Adults Boards (SABs) for their failure to review all deaths of people living on the streets or in temporary accommodation is countered by evidence that reviews have been completed and models of good practice identified (Martineau *et al.* 2019; Preston-Shoot 2019).

A Whole System Approach

Working with people experiencing multiple exclusion homelessness is a complex area of safeguarding adults' practice. It requires an integrated whole system response but, perhaps, has been consigned to the 'too difficult' box for a long time. There is certainly evidence to suggest that social care practitioners can feel ill-equipped to support people with housing-related needs (Public Health England 2018). This emerging or new area of practice may not actually be 'new'; rather it takes forward and rearticulates longstanding tensions in public policy (see Chapter 2).

It is a truism, but 'adult safeguarding is everyone's business'. Moreover, there is an emerging evidence base relating to policy, service development and practice in this area of work (Preston-Shoot 2020a). That evidence base spans five domains, as captured in Figure 1.1: direct work with individuals; how the team around the person work together; how organisations support the practitioners and operational managers who comprise the team around the person; governance by SABs working alongside Health and Wellbeing Boards, Community Safety Partnerships and Homelessness Reduction Boards; and, finally, the legal, policy and financial context within which adult safeguarding and responses to people experiencing homelessness are situated. The structure of the book mirrors these domains, and to varying degrees each chapter in this book focuses on one or more of these domains, and/or explores the interfaces between them. The authors contribute to reviewing, consolidating and building on the evidence base for positive practice.

Figure 1.1 Whole system understanding

Each domain is an essential component of a jigsaw or mosaic for preventing homelessness and for responding to its impact in terms of safeguarding risks; the six adult safeguarding principles (Department of Health and Social Care 2020, section 14.13) reflect this. When applied to working with people who experience multiple exclusion homelessness, there are core messages for all of us who work in this area in any role (see Chapter 5):

- *Empowerment (the domain of direct practice)*: Look beyond the presenting 'problem' to the backstory; Make Every Adult Matter (MEAM 2019); listen, hear and acknowledge; Make Safeguarding Personal.

- *Prevention (the domain of direct practice)*: Commission to provide integrated wrap-around support and to avoid 'revolving doors'; see transitions as opportunities for change.

- *Protection (the domain of direct practice)*: Address the risks of premature mortality for people experiencing homelessness; recognise and address experiences of abuse and neglect.

- *Partnership (the domains of the team around the person and of organisational support)*: Ensure that there is 'no wrong door' and 'make every contact count' (Public Health England and Health Education England 2018).

- *Proportionality (the domain of direct practice)*: Minimise risk; judge the level of intervention required.

- *Accountability (the domain of governance)*: Get the governance right; provide mechanisms to support practice.

The chapters in this book are clustered to reflect the domains outlined above. Chapters 3–6 focus on working with individuals; Chapters 7–9 examine multi-agency working; and Chapters 10–13 explore leadership and strategic partnerships. Zooming in on each domain separately illustrates the necessity of a whole system response. The domain of direct practice begins with a person-centred approach that comprises proactive rather than reactive engagement, and a detailed exploration of the person's wishes, feelings, views, experiences, needs and desired outcomes (see Chapter 3); work to build motivation with a focus on a person's fluctuating and conflicting hopes, fears and beliefs, and the barriers to change (Ward and Holmes 2014; NICE 2018a). Not just listening but hearing and understanding what people say is fundamental to good practice; identifying and recognising our unconscious bias is key (see Chapters 3, 4, 5, 6 and 12). Self-awareness of unconscious bias, awareness of use of language and developing professional curiosity mitigate negative, unproductive and damaging behaviours for all of us undertaking any role in the system (see Chapters 3 and 4). Contact should be maintained rather than the case closed so that trust can be built up; use of advocacy services might assist a person to engage with assessment processes, service provision and treatment.

A core requirement of best practice, underpinned by the Equality Act 2010 and the Human Rights Act 1998, is to counteract discrimination. Unfortunately, SARs often fail to consider whether sufficient consideration was given to a person's race, culture, religion, language, ethnicity and heritage (see Chapter 10) (Preston-Shoot *et al.* 2020). A focus on the impact of poverty on wellbeing is also a noticeable omission. Promoting equalities, diversity and inclusion has particular features in this area of work, across the range of protected characteristics. Appreciating the personal histories of the people we work with requires an understanding of structural discrimination and systemic inequalities. Not only is cultural competence required knowledge for frontline staff, but also legal literacy, particularly when working with non-UK nationals (see Chapter 9). Needs of different homeless communities, such as LGBTQ+, have not necessarily been addressed (see Chapters 3 and 10). There has been some limited acknowledgement and addressing of gender-specific and sex-specific risks (see Chapters 4 and 5). Research has found that the causes of homelessness are multi-faceted and impact differently on men and women (Cameron *et al.* 2016). Routes into homelessness can have a gendered dimension, founded in abuse and violence towards women in close relationships. Support is often fragmented, available across separate agencies, with budget cuts intensifying this picture. The research has found positive appreciation of keyworker and women-only provision but frustration at having to engage with multiple services at the same time and with provision that was not personalised to their needs. Women who are homeless are found to experience a complex range of social and health needs. Homelessness can sometimes result from previous experiences that may include abuse in childhood, and in turn being homeless can expose them to risk of further abuse (Cameron *et al.* 2016).

When someone declines an assessment or refuses a service, there should be a full exploration of what may (inaccurately) be described as 'lifestyle choice', with detailed discussion of what might lie behind a person's apparent refusal to engage. Failing to explore 'choices', and the constraints within which those perceived 'choices' are being made, prevents deeper analysis, and it is helpful to build up a picture of the person's history and to address this 'backstory' (NICE 2018a; Alcohol Change UK 2019). This may include recognition of and work to address issues of loss and trauma in someone's life that can underlie refusals to engage or manifest in repetitive patterns. However, the narrative of 'lifestyle choice' should also be carefully scrutinised to guard against over-individualisation of responsibility. An apparent 'failure to engage' may be the result of services being inaccessible, exclusive rather than inclusive, and inflexible.

SARs have identified how loss and trauma can resurface to undermine a person's determination to move forward (see Chapter 10). Moreover, a person may be at greater risk when their situation is beginning to improve, either because they are even more acutely aware of what they have experienced and/or because they may feel prematurely that the challenges they have experienced have been resolved and there is no further need for support. It is equally important to recognise that the presenting problem may be a way of coping (Satir *et al.* 1991). However dysfunctional, there is a logic behind behaviour, a positive function. Working with people to adapt their behaviour without understanding its survival function will prove unsuccessful (see Chapter 4). It is responding to symptoms and not causes. What is being highlighted here is the need to explore beyond the presenting problem and to consider what wrap-around support is necessary in order to support those who are trying to recover from the impact of trauma and adverse experiences, and endeavouring to manage their emotional responses. People's lives may be too complex, or their survival strategies incompatible, to enable them to routinely keep appointments at designated times and places without support (see Chapters 3 and 5).

Thorough mental health and mental capacity assessments can be essential means of understanding a person's abilities and capabilities to protect themselves. This includes consideration of executive capacity, and assumptions should not be made about people's capacity to be in control of their own care and support (NICE 2018a). Especially where there are repetitive patterns, it is essential to assess executive capacity as part of mental capacity assessment. Guidance has commented that it can be difficult to assess capacity in people with executive dysfunction[1] and recommends that assessment should include real-world observation of a person's functioning and decision-making ability (NICE 2018b), with subsequent discussion to assess whether someone can use and weigh information. Chapters include case studies illustrating the complexities and challenges in this area of practice. SARs (see Chapter 10) have also highlighted the importance of thorough mental capacity assessments, including a focus on executive dysfunction, when individuals demonstrate addictive and compulsive behaviours, possibly indicative of impulse control disorder or alcohol dependence syndrome. SARs have also reported access issues in relation to mental health assessments and treatment, especially when individuals are not experiencing a psychotic crisis, with views expressed that more resources here are necessary to meet demand, for example for outreach, and to respond to mental distress and trauma (Preston-Shoot *et al.* 2020).

Comprehensive risk assessments are advised, especially in situations where people appear to refuse support services, or 'don't

---

1 The inability to perform tasks of daily living even when the person understands the need for them; the inability to realise when a decision needs to be implemented and to execute it at the appropriate moment.

engage', using recognised indicators to focus work on prevention and mitigation (Parry 2013; Ward and Holmes 2014). Also essential are thorough assessments, care plans and regular reviews (see Chapters 4 and 6), and comprehensive enquiries into a person's rehabilitation, resettlement and support needs (Ministry of Justice 2018), taking into account the negative effect of social isolation and housing status on wellbeing (NICE 2018a). The final component of the evidence base relating to direct work with individuals focuses on points of transition, especially hospital discharge (see Chapter 10) and release from prison. The importance is emphasised of enquiring about people's accommodation needs, recognition of the vulnerabilities of homeless attendees at A&E departments, and the duty to refer people who are homeless or threatened with homelessness.

The second domain focuses on the services around the individual and how they work together to support the person experiencing homelessness (see Chapter 7). The first component of this domain is inter-agency communication and collaboration, working together (Parry 2014; Ministry of Justice 2018), coordinated by a lead agency and key worker in the community (Whiteford and Simpson 2015; NICE 2018a) to act as the continuity and coordinator of contact, with named people to whom referrals can be made (Parry 2013). The emphasis is on integrated, whole system working, linking services to meet people's complex needs (Ward and Holmes 2014; Public Health England 2018; MEAM 2019).

Collaboration requires a comprehensive approach to information-sharing, so that all agencies involved possess the full rather than a partial picture of someone's circumstances. One mechanism for improving how services work together and share information is the use of multi-agency meetings that pool information and assessments of risk, mental health and mental capacity, agree a risk management plan, consider legal options and subsequently implement planning and review outcomes (Ward and Holmes 2014). Another mechanism that can facilitate multi-agency collaboration and also address risks of abuse and neglect is the use of the duty to enquire (under section 42 of the Care Act 2014), sometimes referred to as safeguarding literacy. The focus on section 42 is one part of an evaluation of the relevance of diverse legal options to assist with delivering better outcomes for people, sometimes referred to as legal literacy (see Chapters 2, 6, 8 and 12). People experiencing multiple exclusion homelessness often have care and support needs, which should be assessed (under section 9, Care Act 2014). For individuals with no recourse to public funds (see Chapter 9), a Human Rights Act 1998 assessment may be required to determine whether support is necessary to prevent a breach of their human rights, especially the right to live free of inhuman and degrading treatment (Article 3, European Convention on Human Rights and Fundamental Freedoms). In the context of homelessness, this might require consideration of whether the decision to withhold accommodation-based support, social care or health care would result in actual bodily harm or intense mental suffering and physical harm (Preston-Shoot 2020a).

One feature of positive inter-agency practice is when detailed referrals from one agency request the assistance of another in order to meet a person's needs. Research (Mason *et al.* 2018) has spotlighted the challenge of different workforce sectors understanding the powers and duties available to different statutory agencies. Thus, adult social care practitioners and managers have the challenge of exploring the fit between vulnerability, as defined by the Housing Act 1996 and subsequent case law, and the duty in the Care Act 2014 to assess anyone who appears to have care and support needs. Staff working directly with people experiencing homelessness similarly have to know about how the Care Act 2014 conceptualises wellbeing and eligible needs, and to map people's stories and needs accordingly to secure access to adult social care support. The final component of this domain emphasises the importance of clear, up-to-date (Parry 2013) and thorough recording of assessments, reviews and decision-making; recording should include details of unmet needs (Ward and Holmes 2014).

The third domain focuses on the organisations around the team. There are five components to this domain – namely:

- Supervision and support that promote reflection and critical analysis of the approach being taken, especially when working with people who are perceived or experienced as hard to engage, resistant and sometimes hostile (see Chapter 4).

- Access to specialist legal, mental capacity, mental health and safeguarding advice (see Chapter 6).

- Oversight of work being done, including comprehensive commissioning and contract monitoring of service providers (see Chapter 13).

- Agreed indicators of risk that are formulated into a risk assessment template that will guide assessments and planning.

- Attention to workforce development (Whiteford and Simpson 2015; MEAM 2019) and workplace issues, such as staffing levels, organisational cultures and thresholds (see Chapter 12).

The fourth domain focuses on governance (see Chapter 11). This includes ensuring that multi-agency agreements are concluded and then implemented with respect to working with individuals at risk of significant harm, abuse and neglect, with clear pathways into multi-agency risk management meetings or other multi-agency panel arrangements. Other features in this domain include:

- Development, dissemination and auditing of the impact of policies and procedures regarding self-neglect and multiple exclusion homelessness.

- Reviewing the interface between housing/homelessness and adult social care, mental health and adult safeguarding, and including housing in multi-agency policies and procedures (Parry 2013).

- Working with Community Safety Partnerships, Health and Wellbeing Boards and partnership arrangements for safeguarding children and young people to coordinate governance, namely oversight of the development and review of policies, procedures and practice.

- Clear procedures for commissioning mandatory and discretionary SARs and also drawing on learning from Homelessness Fatality Reviews and reviews of drug- and alcohol-related deaths (see Chapter 10).

- Providing or arranging for the provision of workshops or equivalent, to improve practice and the management of practice with adults who experience multiple exclusion homelessness (see Chapter 12).

Getting governance right is important. Clearly the SAB holds the statutory mandate for governance of adult safeguarding. However, there is no one model for where governance of multiple exclusion homelessness might reside – the SAB, Health and Wellbeing Board, Community

Safety Partnership or Homelessness Reduction Board may all be appropriate choices for 'holding the ring', for providing strategic leadership and holding partners to account. What works may vary, depending on local government and local governance structures.

The fifth and final domain, the legal, policy and financial context within which adult safeguarding is situated in England, presents challenges for practitioners, managers and agencies striving to prevent or counteract homelessness (see Chapter 2). Government policy with respect to 'no recourse to public funds' undeniably presents challenges to those working with people who are homeless with care and support needs (see Chapters 9 and 10). The processes to secure settled status and habitual residency are slow and complex. Adults at risk, including people experiencing homelessness, can find it difficult to apply for settled status, especially if they have limited ability to speak and understand English, limited access to online technology, and difficulty in obtaining documentary evidence from High Commissions and/or Embassies. The impact of this policy, the hostile environment, has left individuals isolated and destitute, and added considerable difficulty to finding a long-term means of helping these individuals.

Research (Cornes *et al.* 2016; Mason *et al.* 2018) has also shone the spotlight on the financial context, noting the impact of financial austerity on the capacity of all agencies (not just adult social services) to absorb the workload arising from recognition of the health, care and support needs and safeguarding concerns of people sleeping on the streets.

The Homelessness Reduction Act 2017 is silent with respect to two of the main contributing factors towards homelessness, namely the lack of supply of affordable housing and affordability of available accommodation. Welfare reforms have had a negative impact by creating landlord mistrust of Universal Credit and by failing to assist people renting in the private sector due to the rise in rents not being matched by the level of assistance available. Reducing support for people to help them maintain tenancies (Pleace 2013) and changes in housing benefit have rendered some people homeless.[2] It is not unusual to remark that the achievement of one government policy, here the prevention of homelessness,

---

2   *The Impact of Welfare Reform on Homelessness in London.* Undated report, accessed 23 August 2020 at www.london.gov.uk/what-we-do/housing-and-land/housing-and-land-publications/impact-welfare-reform-homelessness-london.

is undermined by another, namely welfare benefit changes (Butler and Drakeford 2005).

That said, it is important to acknowledge what has been achieved with respect to people experiencing homelessness as a result of the response to the Covid-19 pandemic (see Chapter 5). Derogation of legal rules and the injection of financial resources have made a marked difference for people previously homeless. It has demonstrated what can be achieved when the financial, legal and policy context changes, and supports good practice locally. It has demonstrated what recent research (Cream *et al.* 2020) has advised when outlining five principles – find and engage people, build and support the workforce to go beyond existing service limitations, prioritise relationships, tailor local responses to people sleeping rough and, finally, use the full power of commissioning to meet people's health, housing and social care needs.

Building Hopeful Futures

This book aims to bring together the voices of people with lived experience, best research evidence, service development knowledge and practice expertise. The purpose is to collate and make accessible the best available evidence for safeguarding people experiencing multiple exclusion homelessness, for multi-agency and multi-disciplinary teams working with people who are homeless, for organisations supporting these teams and responsible for commissioning services, and for senior leaders and elected members responsible for governance and strategic partnerships.

The book is designed to provide information and insight to senior leaders, such as members of SABs, as well as commissioners, practitioners and operational managers who are working across relevant sectors and agencies, including statutory and non-statutory, homelessness, housing, health and social care, to support people who are at risk of or are experiencing abuse or neglect.

Safeguarding adults and homelessness has been prioritised in sector-led improvement work by the safeguarding workstream of the Care and Health Improvement Partnership (CHIP) programme. The CHIP programme is funded by the Department of Health and Social Care and delivered by the Local Government Association, in collaboration with the Association of Directors of Adult Social Services. The editors developed the proposal for this book whilst working with colleagues in delivering four national workshops in 2019/2020, in recognition that there was an appetite for information, insight and understanding in this complex area of work. The outcome of the contributions and discussions at the workshops was a briefing on best practice in adult safeguarding and homelessness (Preston-Shoot 2020a).

Before the Covid-19 pandemic the intention had been to disseminate the briefing through regional workshops which would support local discussion and debate about taking this work forward. However, due to the pandemic, a series of eight webinars on various themes was delivered from December 2020 to March 2021. The recordings and presentational materials are available on the Local Government Association website.[3] A second briefing has been developed from the eight webinars (Preston-Shoot 2021).

This book, then, adds to the knowledge base about adult safeguarding, about working with people who are experiencing homelessness, and about the interface between the two. In opening this book, we hope that readers will prioritise spending time on Chapter 3, which places centre-stage the voices of experts by experience. As a whole, the book outlines what can be achieved when practice and services align around what has been learned through research and reviews. Each chapter presents part of what can be transformative in adult safeguarding and homelessness work, capturing what matters deeply within a social justice and human rights framework. The chapters are variously questioning and challenging, facilitating thoughtfulness, stimulating a capacity to imagine and envision. UNESCO refers to this as 'futures literacy'.[4] The chapters look forward to a desired world and highlight what is needed to get there.

---

3   www.local.gov.uk
4   https://en.unesco.org/futuresliteracy

Chapter 2

The Policy Framework

Karl Mason

Introduction

Homelessness has increased across the United Kingdom over the last decade, with rough sleeping increasing by 141% between 2010 and 2019 (Wilson and Barton 2020). In the same period, a range of policy responses have been directed at addressing homelessness, but these have drawn on very different ideas about what homelessness is and how the state should respond. These ideas can be crudely mapped to Gowan's (2010) three-part typology, referred to here as persistent policy discourses on homelessness – 'sin talk' (moralistic/punishment), 'sick talk' (vulnerability/treatment) and 'system talk' (rights/system change). To illustrate these discourses, we can track their progress historically and continued relevance today.

Starting with 'sin talk', homelessness has been subject to continued punitive and moralistic responses with the development of anti-social behaviour approaches and the continuing threat of the Vagrancy Act 1824 – under debate in parliament at the time of writing (Pyper *et al.* 2019) – and the continued importance placed on the intentionality of homelessness (Reeson 2019). At the same time, 'sick talk' has maintained our attention on the precarity of homelessness and its association with severe health inequalities (Rogans-Watson *et al.* 2020), multiple forms of exclusion (Fitzpatrick *et al.* 2011a) and the importance of a welfare orientation to homelessness (Maseele *et al.* 2013). Severe weather emergency protocols and the recent Covid-19 clinical homeless sector plan (MHCLG 2020a; Pathway 2020) are examples of health- and welfare-oriented policy, influenced by 'sick talk' discourses, as are the integration responses of the Homelessness Reduction Act 2017 and the Care Act 2014 (Dobson 2019a). It is also reflected in the increasing attention to the interplay between homelessness, health care and hospital discharge (for example, Whiteford and Simpson 2015; Dorney-Smith *et al.* 2018). Meanwhile, 'system talk' emphasises rights, including housing rights, foregrounded by recent Housing First interventions, rather than emphasising punishment or welfare (Bretherton and Pleace 2015). There is overlap between these discourses, for example 'sin' and 'sick' discourses both provide individualistic accounts of homelessness rather than attending to structural issues. The discourses also operate alongside each other – housing first emphasises rights and 'system talk', whilst wider welfare reforms have had the opposite effect on rights, driving homelessness statistics higher (O'Leary and Simcock 2020) and emphasising the 'sin talk' of individual responsibility. It is notable that 'system talk' underpins academic scholarship in relation to the particular disadvantages faced by women, people identifying as LGBTQ+ or those from Black, Asian or other minoritised communities, but this has not yielded particular ground in policy. Whilst referring to policy discourses, it is recognised that these ways of framing homelessness exist in wider public discourses – but the point here is the impact on policy and, consequently, on practice. As such, Gowan's three-part typology provides a useful basis for considering the discourses that inform contemporary policy initiatives, including those relating to safeguarding adults.

Safeguarding adults processes and policies with people who are homeless have recently been spotlighted in Safeguarding Adults Reviews where homelessness was a feature (Martineau and Manthorpe 2020; Preston-Shoot *et al.* 2020). Failings in these reviews highlight approaches that ignored risks and emphasised 'problematic attitudes' concerning risk and homelessness, including an emphasis on 'individual responsibility' and 'poor lifestyle choices'. The findings emphasise significant health and welfare issues (mental health, chronic physical health and substance misuse in particular) that reflect broader trends in the deaths of people experiencing homelessness (Aldridge *et al.* 2018). Additionally, attending to the views, wishes and human rights of adults (including those who are homeless) who may be at risk of abuse and neglect is a cornerstone of safeguarding policy (DHSC 2020). This chapter begins by setting out the policy context for safeguarding adults with people experiencing homelessness. Next, the chapter argues that homelessness has been presented as a 'new' challenge for safeguarding policy following the 'discovery' that people who are homeless may fall under the remit of safeguarding adults (the 'discovery' approach). The chapter continues by challenging this 'discovery' approach (and the idea of this problem being 'new'). Instead, the chapter argues that safeguarding responses are constructed within existing and persistent discourses, which can be illustrated using Gowan's (2010) three-part typology. The concluding discussion draws out the importance of recognising these persistent discourses in policy and practice in order to call out problematic professional attitudes, which may be rooted in 'unconscious bias' and which contribute to risk.

Overviewing Safeguarding Policy

Safeguarding adults is, in relative terms, a new policy and practice endeavour. The move to establish a legislative footing for safeguarding adults can be seen in the context of growing societal awareness of abuse and neglect of adults who may be 'vulnerable' or 'at risk'. Policy in this area is devolved in the UK with significant differences of approach across its constituent countries (see Mackay 2018). Taking England as an example, high profile cases, such as the murder of Steven Hoskin in 2006 or the highlighting of abuse operating in Winterbourne View in 2011, have contributed to calls for these policy changes. 'No Secrets' was introduced in 2000 as guidance to highlight the ways in which some adults may be 'vulnerable' or 'at risk', and integrated, multi-agency responses required ('everybody's business') (DHSC 2000). This was replaced with the enactment of the Care Act 2014 and its accompanying statutory guidance (DHSC 2020), which integrated safeguarding duties into primary legislation for the first time.

The Care Act 2014 introduces a duty for a local authority to make a 'safeguarding enquiry' when an adult, who has care and support needs, experiences, or is at risk of, abuse or neglect and cannot protect themselves from this due to their identified care and support needs (section 42). There is a duty to establish strategic Safeguarding Adults Boards (section 43), with responsibility to commission Safeguarding Adults Reviews (section 44) where there is concern about how agencies worked together to safeguard an adult with care and support needs, particularly where the adult has died or significant abuse or neglect has been experienced. There are further duties to supply information to the Safeguarding Adults Board (section 45) and to provide advocacy services for an adult taking part in a safeguarding enquiry who may have significant difficulty engaging with the process and does not have anyone appropriate to support them (section 68). Interestingly, the English legislation abolishes a provision (National Assistance Act 1948) which allowed for the removal of an adult from their home (note Scotland retains some provisions for the removal of adults from their homes in certain situations). Any safeguarding action under the Act needs to take the adult's 'wellbeing' into account (section 1), and wellbeing is defined broadly according to nine components, including suitability of living accommodation and social and economic wellbeing. The Care Act 2014 and its safeguarding provisions do not necessarily constitute a 'new deal' for people experiencing homelessness, but certainly can be seen as 'good news' (Mason *et al.* 2018). Indeed, the Rough Sleeping Strategy (MHCLG 2018a) recognises the use of Safeguarding Adults Reviews as a potential tool to highlight learning and practice issues in this field.

Homelessness has increasingly been recognised as a risk factor for the development of care and support needs as a result of the experience of being homeless or coinciding with the process of becoming homeless (Preston-Shoot 2020a). For example, homelessness is associated with multiple exclusions and forms of health inequality. For these reasons, it is not surprising that people experiencing homelessness may come under the purview of safeguarding policies where they have developed some level of care and support need and are at risk of, or experiencing, some form of abuse or neglect (Mason *et al.* 2018). The first national analysis of Safeguarding Adults Reviews notes that a small group of these reviews (25 of 231) involved people who are homeless, including abuse occurring within hostel settings (Preston-Shoot *et al.* 2020). Indeed, two recent studies have reviewed a number of Safeguarding Adults Reviews across England which have involved the deaths of homeless adults as a result of abuse or neglect (Martineau and Manthorpe 2020; Preston-Shoot *et al.* 2020). Highlighted themes include missed opportunities to safeguard, inadequate involvement of the person experiencing homelessness in the enquiry and limited 'professional curiosity' about the safeguarding issue. Nationally, self-neglect is the most common form of abuse arising in Safeguarding Adults Reviews (104 of 231 reviews). In Martineau and Manthorpe's (2020) study of Safeguarding Adults Reviews regarding people who are homeless, self-neglect was present in over half of the cases reviewed. However, the statutory guidance for the Care Act 2014 (DHSC 2020) states that self-neglect is only sometimes considered to be a safeguarding category and this ambiguity may lead to confusion about whether an enquiry is required (Mason and Evans 2020). Critically, problematic professional attitudes about homelessness, including the dismissal of homelessness as a lifestyle choice, are highlighted (Preston-Shoot 2020a). It is noteworthy that exactly the same theme arises in Safeguarding Adults Reviews in relation to self-neglect, showing the dominance of ideas and discourses about 'lifestyle choices' (Preston-Shoot *et al.* 2020).

These messages from Safeguarding Adults Reviews coincide with an important strand of research on statutory responses to adults who are homeless and have care and support needs (for example Whiteford and Simpson 2015; Cornes *et al.* 2016; Mason *et al.* 2018; Dobson 2019a). These research studies are premised on an argument that policy shifts and developments have created a need for new practice responses from adult social care towards adults who are homeless. These policy developments are identified as the ending of ring-fenced Supporting People funding for accommodation-related support and the enactment of the Care Act 2014 (Cornes *et al.* 2016; Dobson 2019a). The winding down of ring-fenced Supporting People funding meant that those deemed to have support needs were responded to within the homelessness sector, diverting the requirement for health and social care involvement (Dobson 2019a). Meanwhile, the enactment of the Care Act 2014 is important because it widened the eligibility criteria beyond personal and domestic care needs to stretch to social inclusion type domains, such as accessing the community or maintaining a habitable home. Further flexibility around the new safeguarding statutory guidance included the category of self-neglect which might apply to some adults who are homeless (Mason *et al.* 2018). Additionally, important developments have emerged at the intersection of homelessness or housing insecurity and care and support provision in case law.

The High Court case of R (SG) v London Borough of Haringey [2015] involved a woman living in accommodation provided as a result of her asylum claim, but the local authority assessment did not account for her accommodation-related support needs and the judge criticised the local authority for not providing advocacy services. Meanwhile, another High Court Judgment – R (Antoniak) v Westminster City Council [2019] – involved a man with intermittent psychosis and a history of homelessness who was temporarily housed following an accident. When he was assessed under the Care Act 2014, the assessor deemed him ineligible, incorrectly drawing on the fact that he had access to support in his temporary accommodation. The judge determined that the assessment had failed to include all of this man's needs, whether met or not. Both pieces of case law show some unfamiliarity among social care staff with the issues that occur at the interface of housing and social care. Therefore, this growth in attention to safeguarding practice with adults experiencing homelessness is recent and contextualised within recent policy changes, case law and Safeguarding Adults Reviews.

Discovery or Construction: Thinking Through This 'New' Phenomenon

Hidden amidst the emerging research base, case law, policy shifts and practice responses on the care and support needs of people experiencing homelessness lies the idea that this is a 'new' phenomenon that requires innovative steps to stretch the existing safeguarding framework (see also Dobson 2019b). The seemingly logical and linear development of policy and practice responses to apparently 'new' social problems is associated with a 'discovery' approach. Such an approach conceals the idea that policy and practice have been filtered through existing and historical societal understandings, political and ideological norms and organisational frameworks (Sherwood-Johnson 2016). Therefore, the categorisation of homelessness as a potential safeguarding issue is not a logical and innovative response to a 'new' problem, but a constructed outcome based on existing ways of thinking about and framing the abuse and neglect of adults. This construction occurs within the context of the political and ideological successes of neoliberalism, which emphasises market solutions rather than public spending, here realised through cuts to housing support and homelessness services, such as the ending of ring-fenced Supporting People funding. This political and ideological backdrop has in fact contributed to these new vulnerabilities, rather than simply responding to them – the vulnerabilities that expose people who are homeless to abuse and neglect are, at least in part, caused by an absence of funding and 'sin talk' discourses of individual responsibility or 'sick talk' discourses of vulnerability. In summary, the development of safeguarding practices for and discourses around people who are homeless is a constructed response rather than a discovered problem. From this perspective, safeguarding policy for people who are homeless should be seen in the context of persistent policy discourses that shape and construct the state's response to homelessness.

It is important to note that the use of constructionism in homelessness research is controversial. Constructionism proposes that reality is a 'way of seeing' the world rather than actually constituting any materially real circumstance. This can lead to the idea that these ways of seeing can be reframed. For instance, a 'weak constructionist' approach might reveal that homelessness exists in different forms and problematises quantification of such a hidden phenomenon. However, there are clear ethical issues in reducing homelessness, or indeed abuse and neglect, to simply a construction or a 'way of seeing' (Fitzpatrick 2006). This is clearly inappropriate for significant social problems such as homelessness or abuse (Payne 2021). The point here is not to deny the material reality of either homelessness or abuse, but to contextualise the policy responses within existing discourses.

Persistent Discourses of Homelessness

Although safeguarding policy responses to the needs of people who are homeless may be 'new', the state has been responding to homelessness for centuries (Humphreys 1999) and therefore an emphasis on 'newness' conceals a number of shadows from existing policy discourses. Considering the discourses that have informed these policy responses across this particular social history can offer helpful insights into the ways in which contemporary safeguarding policy can be framed. Three particular discourses, identified by Gowan (2010), have significant coinage in the social history of statutory responses to homelessness and continue to linger in the ways in which safeguarding policy responds to this group.

Gowan (2010) identified three forms of discourse emerging from the ways in which homeless participants framed their situations – 'sin talk', 'sick talk' and 'system talk'. These can usefully be mapped to the social history of policy responses to homelessness. These discourses reveal dominant ideas about how homelessness is conceived and how different proponents of these positions see the state's role in responding. The terms – sin, sick and system – are rather emotive but generally provide an insight into dominant ways of framing homelessness and the state's response. 'Sin talk' emphasises the moral failure of individuals who are homeless and their responsibility for their situation, leading to punitive state responses. 'Sick talk' emphasises vulnerability and promotes treatment or welfare responses. 'System talk' underlines a rights-based approach and advocates system change. There are some commonalities between these approaches, based on the extent to which individuals are seen as active or passive and the degree to which they are credited with some sense of agency. These discourses also oppose one another in their framing of homelessness and appropriate state responses, but they have existed alongside each other and they can all still be found in policy responses today. This includes the 'new' stretching of safeguarding responses to people who are homeless, and therefore a necessarily brief historical sketch will be provided for each of these discourses before discussing their relevance and implications for safeguarding policy. Humphreys (1999) provides a more comprehensive review of historical state responses to homelessness.

'Sin Talk'

The emergence of travelling labour from the freedom of serfs in 14th century England coincided with punitive responses to the 'wandering poor', underpinned by the desire among the ruling class to stifle the movement of labour. Various contemporary statutes prohibited movement beyond certain geographical limits in order to stifle the leakage of labour supply, suiting the interests of land-owners. Vagrancy was the subject of an increasing range of laws in the Tudor era, punishments for which included branding, slavery, the removal of children and even the death penalty. Houses of correction and industry began to be established and physical punishments (such as flogging) or resettlement policies (foreshadowing modern ordinary residence rules) were enacted (Humphreys 1999). The 17th and 18th centuries introduced the deportation of vagrants, while resettlement and removal laws were reinforced. At the same time, the Vagrancy Act 1824 was enacted to suppress rootless people, allowing for the punishment of idle and disorderly rogues and vagabonds. Vagrancy imprisonments increased in the early decades of the 19th century and casual wards with a required work task were developed to prevent vagrants from using the workhouse. The Charity Organisation Society (COS), whose caseworkers are often seen as precursors to the formalisation of the social work profession, severely restricted the availability of outdoor (community) relief to vagrants where they did not see potential for rehabilitation (Humphreys 1999).

'Sin talk' declined in the 20th century with the decriminalisation of rough sleeping in 1935, although causing a nuisance through rough sleeping was created as a new offence. The Vagrancy Act 1824 remains in force (though it is being debated in parliament at the time of writing) and has seen a resurgence in recent years. Court cases relating to vagrancy have increased significantly in recent years and there has been a corresponding growth in the use of Public Space Protection Orders (Cooper and McCulloch 2017). Even in the era of housing rights for the most vulnerable people, intentionality remains a key principle in moderating the duties owed to people who are homeless by local authorities (Reeson 2019), reminding us that ideas of homelessness as a 'reckless' choice are not submerged too deeply (Crowson 2012).

'Sick Talk'

'Sick talk' can be traced back to alms-giving in the pre-Reformation era to support those who were seen as incapacitated rather than immoral. Humphreys' (1999) review of the 15th and 16th centuries provides some insight into the Poor Law provisions for those who travelled beyond their parish for work, but in sickness or old age lacked protections. The Old Poor Law of 1601 provided for places of habitation for poor, incapacitated or old people who could not fend for themselves. Later, in Victorian times, emerging societal values acknowledged diverse causes of poverty, splitting away from the 'sin talk' imagery of simply being 'work-shy'. The Workhouse Visiting Society noted that those visiting casual wards should remember the humanity of those they visit and the mental health and physical health issues that those residents might face (Humphreys 1999). Soup kitchens, night shelters and free dormitories were set up outside of the workhouse system by philanthropic organisations. The Charity Organisation Society (COS) aimed to rehabilitate those seen as 'helpable' (Humphreys 1999). In 1908, the 'Commission on the Feeble-Minded' reported that those discharged from the mental institutions of the day had no option but to wander the street or enter the workhouse, in some way recognising the vulnerability of this group. The emergence of the welfare state after the Second World War abolished the Poor Laws and saw the reinforcement of a welfare approach. A system of rehabilitation hostels was developed following the enactment of the National Assistance Act 1948 and casework methods were employed in growing recognition of the prevalence of mental health conditions in the homeless population (Humphreys 1999). Meanwhile in the USA, the development of clinical social work, 'armed with the language of disease and dysfunction' (Gowan 2010, p.49), led to the development of interventions for developing client life skills in the context of substance misuse, poor parenting experiences or budgeting problems.

The discourse of 'sick talk' went into decline in the context of a social justice, rights-based 'system talk' discourse in the 1960s and 1970s, where personal inadequacies or incapacities were no longer seen as appropriate and a (limited) right to housing was inserted into the Housing (Homeless Persons) Act 1977. However, 'sick talk' prevailed through soup kitchens, food banks and similar welfare agencies and we see an increase in calls for social work action (Manthorpe *et al.* 2015; Mason *et al.* 2018), psychologically informed environments in hostels (Haigh *et al.* 2012) and evidence from the medical community about tri-morbidity, frailty and a significantly lower life expectancy than housed people of the same age (Rogans-Watson *et al.* 2020). Annual Severe Weather Emergency Provision policies and the Covid-19-specific 'Everyone In' policy are justified on the basis of the increased vulnerability of those experiencing homelessness to the pandemic due to co-morbidities (Henderson 2020; Lewer *et al.* 2020; MHCLG 2020a), so this discourse continues to underpin policies responding to homelessness.

'System Talk'

This discourse is associated with current 'housing rights' approaches, which have been prevalent, though moderated by a resurgence in 'sin' and 'sick' talk discourses, in recent decades (Gowan 2010). However, there is evidence of an earlier appreciation that war, poor harvests and famine could result in dislocation across the centuries; for example, at the close of the American War of Independence in the 18th century, George III acknowledged the number of homeless people that peace-time would bring (Humphreys 1999). Social forces during the 19th century led to the emergence of 'system talk' as a more prevalent discourse, particularly with the growth of social movements like the Swing Riots in 1830, the Chartists in the 1840s and later Socialism in the 1880s, all making varying claims for political reform in favour of working people (Croley 1995). At the same time, workhouse reformers were expressing concern about poor conditions for the poor, including several journalists who went to casual wards, observing and critiquing the conditions there (Longmate 2003). At the end of the Boer War at the turn of the century, poverty rather than lifestyle choice was being discussed as the issue at hand for those in the 'casual ward' (Humphreys 1999). In the following decades, the introduction of the pension and an improved jobs market led to a decrease in those using the casual ward and in 1929–1930 the Ministry of Health Departmental Committee agreed that 'as a general rule it must be true that long periods of industrial depression swell the number of casuals' (cited in Humphreys 1999, p.132).

The post-war political consensus led to the development of a 'welfarisation' ('sick talk') of homelessness, but also demands for social justice. At a time when civil rights were being championed, the televised film *Cathy Come Home* (dir. Loach 1966) depicted a woman, her partner and her children being moved around the temporary hostel system, evicted and separated in traumatic circumstances. In the same year, the housing rights advocacy charities Crisis and Shelter were both established, calling for homelessness to be re-cast as a rights issue and related to an absence of housing, rather than personal inadequacy or moral failing. This culminated in the Labour government's 1977 Housing (Homeless Persons) Act with its statutory definition of homeless as encompassing the absence of a home. Although the Act retained the concept of 'intentionality', it marked a high point for 'system talk' in the UK, shifting the discourse from social pathology to the result of poverty and an absence of appropriate housing (Humphreys 1999; Crowson 2012). This 'system talk' has been subject to sustained attack through the New Right 'sin talk' of the 1980s and beyond (Gowan 2010), and 'system talk' has not resulted in policy taking account of the diverse needs of homelessness within Black and Asian or other racialised minorities, or for those who identify as LGBTQ+ whose needs are simply subsumed into 'homelessness'. Notwithstanding this, 'system talk' remains relevant as a discourse governing modern conceptions of homelessness, for example through 'Housing First' policies (Bretherton and Pleace 2015).

Safeguarding and Homelessness: Exploring the Underpinning Discourses

Following this review of Gowan's (2010) persistent discourses of homelessness, it is useful to interrogate the extent to which safeguarding responses are rooted in these approaches, rather than as a 'new' phenomenon, and what implications might arise as a result. On the surface, a safeguarding response feels substantially different to the moralistic 'sin talk' discourse. However, evidence from empirical research continues to highlight conditionality in social care responses and a 'ping-pong' approach where a person's needs are 'gamed'. 'Gaming' in this context has been used in research on adult social care and homelessness as a term to refer to agencies 'looking for ways in which individuals fall outside of their eligibility criteria' (Whiteford and Simpson 2015, p.130; see also Cornes *et al.* 2011; Mason *et al.* 2018). It pushes beyond the idea of gatekeeping as a 'legitimate' practice, necessitated by chronic resource issues, and frames this as an exclusion from access to statutory services, often underpinned by problematic attitudes about a particular group. Indeed, Safeguarding Adults Reviews have highlighted such problematic responses from practitioners charged with safeguarding duties, ignoring or failing to recognise risks as safeguarding issues and instead normalising such risks as part of the person's homelessness (Martineau and Manthorpe 2020; Preston-Shoot 2020a). This is often under the ambit of a person's 'lifestyle choice', used to responsibilise the individual for their homelessness rather than seek to assist. Johnstone *et al.* (2015) usefully point to 'highly legitimised forms of discrimination' faced by homeless people on the basis of the language of choice and the perception that housing status is something that can be controlled by the individual (see also Parsell and Parsell 2012). These responses show that the stretching of safeguarding response to homelessness has not elided the powerful and persistent discourse of 'sin talk'.

Meanwhile 'sick talk' discourses, with their emphasis on need, vulnerability and disability, are closer to the surface in terms of the ways in which safeguarding policy is discussed. Safeguarding under the Care Act 2014 depends on the identification of some level of need for care and support which might mean that an adult cannot protect themselves from the experience or risk of abuse or neglect. These needs are largely framed through an individualistic, medical model (the eligibility rules require a 'physical or mental impairment') rather than a social model of disability or structural factors (poverty etc.). Multiple exclusion homelessness provides a framework for acknowledging the frequently under-recognised frailties, mobility issues, substance misuse or mental health issues, learning disabilities or acquired brain injuries that are common in adults experiencing homelessness (Rogans-Watson *et al.* 2020).

In a somewhat contradictory way, an emphasis on need, vulnerability and deficit is both required and rejected in contemporary safeguarding policy. Recognition of needs is required because safeguarding is only open to adults with some level of need for care and support and where these needs may mean the person cannot protect themselves from abuse or neglect. On the other hand, safeguarding policy also appears to reject such an approach through an emphasis on strengths-based approaches. 'Making Safeguarding Personal' is a strengths-based approach discussed in the statutory guidance for the Care Act 2014, but also emerging from the sector as a values-driven perspective (Lawson 2017). It is a person-led approach to safeguarding and takes account of the outcomes the person who has experienced abuse or neglect wishes to achieve. It emphasises involvement, choice and control and seeks to move away from 'doing safeguarding to' people and instead improving their quality of life, safety and wellbeing (DHSC 2020). This approach can be seen within the lens of a 'system talk' approach, given the emphasis on rights and voice rather than morality or vulnerability. From another viewpoint, however, strengths-based approaches have been critiqued as a camouflage for spending cuts and the retreat of the state by emphasising self- or community-reliance, with potentially less statutory intervention (Slasberg and Beresford 2017; Payne 2021). It is important to acknowledge these tensions inherent in this work and their relevance to safeguarding with people who experience homelessness.

The 'Making Safeguarding Personal' approach certainly problematises too much emphasis on vulnerability and its potential to elicit paternalistic responses. Research findings from Mason *et al.* (2018) reveal discomfort amongst social work staff about the ways in which safeguarding may be used by homelessness practitioners as a heuristic for a demanded paternalistic response, moving away from strengths-based safeguarding principles of choice and control. This is delicate territory where human rights issues around the right to freedom from degrading treatment intersect with the right to liberty or private and family life. This suggests that 'sick talk' could be pejoratively associated with a paternalistic 'medical model' or gaze, and in fact there is evidence that the reality of chronic illness and disability have often been under-recognised rather than over-emphasised as part of a dominant discourse (Preston-Shoot 2020a).

Herring (2017) reminds us that in moving towards strengths-based policy imperatives, it is crucial not to lose sight of the vulnerability that brought the person to the attention of services in the first place.

Some of these presenting issues (substance misuse, acquired brain injury, mental health issues) are associated with impaired cognition and mental capacity issues relating to safeguarding risks. The recognition of heightened medical vulnerability in homelessness means that a large number of people experiencing homelessness might meet the criterion of having a care and support issue which could prevent the person from protecting themselves. Homelessness often arises due to an absence of choice and limited social networks (Neale and Brown 2016), which means that emphasis on independence, choice and control can collapse quickly into empty rhetoric. Importantly, all of this is happening within a service environment which has seen huge cuts in adult social care funding, big increases in homelessness and an increasing recognition of the intersections between homelessness and adult social care (Cornes *et al.* 2016; Mason *et al.* 2018). In such an environment it is not difficult to see how the potential of strengths-based work to achieve system change and social justice ('system talk'), with its emphasis on voice and participation, could morph into an over-emphasis on independence and the retreat of statutory support (Slasberg and Beresford 2017; Payne 2021). In a similar vein, a 'sick talk' emphasis on vulnerability and incapacity might quickly lead to a 'sin talk' discourse of responsibility, conditionality and 'lifestyle choices' if people are not seen to 'act responsibly', thereby ignoring the vulnerabilities that were being addressed through contact with statutory services in the first place (Whiteford and Simpson 2015; Cornes *et al.* 2016; Mason *et al.* 2018).

Conclusion

What is important here is not to choose between these strategies for thinking about homelessness, but to develop an ability to identify these in action and to reflect on how these three discourse types might link with 'unconscious bias' in the social care and inter-professional workforce. The term 'unconscious bias' has begun to emerge in the social care sector (Stuart 2016) but does not yet have a strong research base in relation to safeguarding work. However, it acknowledges that we all grew up with and hold certain social stereotypes about groups and people which may lead to discriminatory actions or influence our decisions about individuals from a particular group. Sometimes this term is used to describe racist or homophobic biases that we may not be aware of. Here, we have argued that social care professionals may also come to this work with unconscious biases about homelessness (particularly as a 'lifestyle choice'), which are underpinned by strong and persistent discourses and are common in society (Parsell and Parsell 2012; Johnstone *et al.* 2015). The above evidence confirms that viewing homelessness in such a way is problematic and has contributed to the most serious safeguarding cases picked up in Safeguarding Adults Reviews. Consequently, addressing these attitudes, potentially through the prism of unconscious bias, should be considered as a workforce development priority (see Chapters 3 and 10 for further discussion).

This chapter has particularly emphasised the problematic nature of 'sin talk' discourses such as moralising and responsibilising narratives about 'lifestyle choices'. However, there are other varieties of problematic views in this area of work, such as paternalistic calls for a service without consent through the piling up of vulnerabilities or taking an apparently strengths-based approach that over-emphasises independence at the expense of considering risk. Calling these problematic approaches out in practice depends on being able to recognise them for what they are: persistent discourses – each with a long history. Critically engaging with this idea of persistent discourses in social policy also helps to contextualise these views: we all are affected by dominant ideas in society. This may avoid unhelpfully splitting 'good' and 'bad' individual staff views about homelessness. Rather more helpfully, the identification of such discourses might facilitate a conversation that side-steps any entrenchment of moralising views and provide critical spaces in teams and classrooms that can surface these persistent policy discourses in their everyday professional contexts (see Chapter 10). In this way, reflecting on these persistent policy discourses can help to ensure that problematic attitudes about homelessness identified through Safeguarding Adults Reviews are avoided.

Part 1
BEST EVIDENCE ON WORKING WITH INDIVIDUALS

Chapter 3

Seen But Not Heard: Why Challenging Your Assumptions about Homelessness Is a Matter of Life and Death

Gill Taylor, Carl Price and Sharon Clint

Introduction

What workers don't get is that we've heard it all before. Most of us has never felt listened to in us whole lives and they wonder why we don't bother with them.

(Alan)[1]

This chapter was conceived, discussed and written by people with lived experience of homelessness. Our chapter attempts to highlight the transformative effect that lived experience can have on professional approaches to multiple exclusion homelessness (Fitzpatrick *et al.* 2011b) and safeguarding.

In conversation with 15 people, the chapter authors explored ideas of safety, professional relationships, risk, responsibility, prejudice, friendship and even pets. These are drawn out in a thematic analysis of five recurrent areas: knowledge, power, stigma, listening and relationships. The chapter concludes that subverting normative power dynamics, preconceptions, relationships and conversation styles between people and practitioners can enable meaningful and effective

---

1   All names used have been changed at the request of participants, in the interests of confidentiality.

responses to safeguarding concerns affecting vulnerable adults affected by homelessness.

Methodology

[I want] people to listen to me and not make me feel like a bad person.

(Sara)

This chapter presents findings from a series of semi-structured conversations between people (n=15) with lived experience of homelessness, between May and September 2020. Conversations were shaped around five broad questions about safety and the lack thereof, professional responses and potential improvements to practice.

Participants relayed varied and sometimes overlapping experiences of homelessness in adulthood, including rough sleeping (n=10), sofa surfing (n=7), hostel-living (n=12) and emergency accommodation provided via the government's March 2020 'Everybody In' directive (Hall 2020), to prevent the spread of the Covid-19 virus (n=5). Authors and participants are based in London and Birmingham, and although some have lived in rural towns and villages, experiences discussed were almost exclusively urban (n=13). As such, although findings describe a variety of homelessness experiences in two English cities, there is an opportunity to expand this enquiry in rural and seaside locations.

Participants were not asked to disclose personally identifiable information such as age, gender, sexuality, ethnicity, disability, religion or immigration status, although some participants alluded to or specifically mentioned these in their responses. Chapter authors elected not to ask for this to avoid emulating typical and outdated modes of professional-person interaction, and to assure people that their information and insights would not be shared with statutory agencies, which was requested by several participants. This choice limits the ability to meaningfully discuss gendered, racialised and other differences of homelessness experience, and this is a key gap and area for further exploration. All participants were over the age of 18, all consented to take part, and all remain anonymous by choice and design.

Half of participants identified having care and support needs (n=6) as defined in the Care Act 2014. However, everyone involved had experienced issues related to violence, abuse and neglect, concurrently with one or more health tri-morbidities – mental health, drug/alcohol dependency and physical health. As such, around 80% of participants could be defined as having at one time experienced multiple exclusion homelessness or multiple disadvantage (Bramley *et al.* 2015).

A thematic analysis was conducted by the chapter authors, who drew on 25 years' combined professional experience in the homelessness sector, as well as their own lived experiences of homelessness. Each section begins with a direct quote and concludes with a number of key messages, inviting the reader to consider how their work creates an environment that is conducive or not to these perspectives.

This chapter attempts to subvert the traditional format of academic writing, which discusses existing literature to corroborate or critique new and/or anecdotal evidence. It is the chapter authors' belief that the experiences, observations and recommendations of people affected by homelessness are inherently credible and insightful even as they are subjective, sometimes contradictory and often challenging. As such, direct quotes and reflections from participants provide the lens through which to consider a literature review, which can be found at the end of the chapter. Although this formatting choice does little to address the imbalance of authority given to different forms of data and intelligence, it is an invitation for the reader to begin as they mean to go on: listen to what people are actually saying, think about how it relates to your role and then draw on available literature to determine a person-centred course of action.

Making Safeguarding (Really) Personal

I thought safeguarding was just about taking people's kids away, not about people like me.

(Zainab)

Before embarking on the thematic analysis of our conversations, we first reflected on the term safeguarding itself and, with it, the importance of knowledge and information. Chapter authors discussed learning what the word meant only via our professional lives, even though all of us had been the subject of some form of safeguarding intervention before that. One chapter author reflected:

I didn't know there was this whole team of people involved in 'fixing' my life until I later became part of an MDT [multi-disciplinary team] as a professional. It made me wonder if maybe the team existed more to support each other, than to support me.

Of the people we spoke to, 73% (n=11) didn't recognise the term safeguarding, and when asked to describe what they thought it meant, most aligned it with the protection of children or an assumed relationship to the word safety. When asked, most people (n=9) didn't identify or recognise the role of safeguarding practice in their own lives unprompted, even where they had mentioned former social workers or other practitioners who could reasonably be assumed to have an array of safeguarding responsibilities in their work. It was a common occurrence for participants to speak of meetings taking place about and without them, often involving practitioners who they hadn't met or spoken to before. One person said, 'Imagine there's a room full of workers sat round a table talking about me, it must have been serious!' (Zainab). The use of the word 'must' suggests a significant gap in this person's involvement in and knowledge of their own care, not knowing what the 'workers' were talking about, and making the assumption that it must be something serious to warrant such an event.

Despite strategic and operational practice centring on ideas of personalised and accountable care and support, it appears that in its application further attention is needed to ensure people are at least equal partners with professionals when it comes to planning their care. Beyond this the higher prevalence of conditions affecting memory, cognition and executive function, such as acquired brain injury, learning difficulty and drug and alcohol dependency, means practitioners should be mindful of the need to repeat and reinforce information, and continuously emphasise service users' rights and entitlements. Not only is this strong and accountable practice, it is likely to encourage people to feel more confident and invested in support planning. Knowledge gaps suggest shortcomings in the implementation of the Making Safeguarding Personal (MSP) approach (Local Government Association 2020a), and thus an opportunity to examine how MSP relates to work with people facing multiple exclusion homelessness.

> **Key Messages**
>
> - Tell me what your role is and what I can expect from you.
> - Involve me and invite me to everything about me; if I don't come, don't give up.
> - Invite people experiencing homelessness to be part of a multi-agency discussion about embedding the MSP principles in local services.

Fight the Power!

They shouldn't have threatened me with sanctions or with taking things away from me when I couldn't do what they asked me to.

(Danny)

An advantage to acquiring knowledge is the way in which it can empower us to take action. Contemporary health and social care policy recognised this, introducing concepts and practices such as 'service user involvement', and then later 'co-production', to maximise the choice and control people have to determine their own goals and actions, to hold service providers to account and to have an equitable say in the way that services operate. However, our conversations suggest that the policy drivers around participatory and co-produced practice have not succeeded in empowering people with lived experience of homelessness to have this level of equitable input.

Although the word power itself was never used by those we interviewed, every participant recounted examples of professionals making decisions without their input, and about their choices being undermined by what professionals deemed suitable for them. For many (n=7), a perceived powerlessness in the face of professionals began in childhood. One person said poignantly, 'No wonder I dunno how to make decisions for myself anymore, they've been doing it for so long… I just leave em to it' (Alan). This quote not only speaks to problematic power relations between professionals and people. It highlights that as well as the likelihood of a life littered with statutory intervention and institutionalisation (Bramley *et al.* 2015), many people facing multiple exclusion have rarely been invited to make their own choices, let alone given the security to know that they will be supported to deal with any consequences that arise from making unwise ones. This makes the case for an urgent refocusing of how frontline and strategic practitioners understand the role of capacity-building, positive risk-taking and sharing responsibility for outcomes with the people they support.

As well as a sense of powerlessness, participants described how professionals withheld help as 'punishment' (n=5), or threatened eviction or statutory involvement if they failed to comply with a particular request (n=4). It was in light of these distressing stories that chapter authors reflected on professional and institutional abuse in residential settings, not to mention the contradiction of utilising punishment to encourage behavioural change with people whose historical trauma was often at the hands of people in authority. It is difficult to avoid the parallel with criminal justice and welfare benefits practice here, where sanctions act as a standard behaviour management practice (Silver and Nedelec 2018; Webster 2020; Williams 2020). Given the alarming prevalence of violence and suicide in custodial settings (Ministry of Justice 2019) and high recidivism rates (Ministry of Justice 2020a), punitive approaches to working with vulnerable people are not only highly contestable, they also contradict the idea of trauma-informed working foregrounded in this field. These reflections highlight the importance of flexible and psychologically informed approaches (Maguire *et al.* 2010; Mental Health Foundation 2017) when supporting people who don't always keep appointments or arrive on time, who use 'inappropriate' language or react 'disproportionately' to certain topics, as opposed to weaponising power as a means to achieve compliance. These reflections from participants also invite reflection on the critical role of appropriate supervision, observation and professional development opportunities for practitioners, to ensure safe and accountable practice is foregrounded in people-facing roles.

The concept of a homogenous and largely oppositional professional 'agenda' was frequently employed to describe feelings of powerlessness. Participants illustrated this agenda as paternalistic and self-serving; being told they were moving hostels without notice, referred to services they hadn't asked for, or asked to complete 'childish' activities that felt out of context and irrelevant. People spoke about how practitioners maligned or ignored risk-management mechanisms they had employed to survive the streets, such as owning a dog, staying in a harmful relationship, or choosing to refuse hostel accommodation; practitioners believed these to be poor *lifestyle choices*, made without proper insight.

This sense of powerlessness and erosion of agency was cited by several participants as a reason for avoiding support services and practitioners (n=5), and as a result was a factor in preventable health and housing crises occurring later. Latent in these conversations was a good-bad/right-wrong binary, and a sense that people were only good/right when following the path that professionals set out for them. These insights also complicate how concepts like *choice* and *engagement* really operate for people with so few genuine options, and whose behaviour and reasoning are rarely engaged with from a trauma-informed perspective.

Finally, it feels relevant to highlight the unequal distribution of power *between* professionals, recognising that some chapter participants were working in 'peer support' roles. As well as hierarchies of influence between public and voluntary sector services, and between managerial and frontline practitioners, 'peer support workers' in particular are rarely privileged with the authority to take a leading or valued role in safeguarding interventions. Although it is increasingly common to see peer support roles in homelessness services, and for these roles to be hugely successful in building relationships and engagement with people deemed 'hard to reach', it is also normal for these roles to have responsibilities perceived as largely pastoral, focused primarily on role-modelling and inspiration (Barker and Maguire 2017). Where people with lived experience work in other roles, as with the chapter authors, it is common for their lived experience to be less visible or drawn on only tokenistically, even perceived by some colleagues to be inappropriate to mention. This suggests that lived experience is a valued quality only in certain frontline roles, and less so in decision-making and senior positions. As such, exploring the organisational and systemic benefits of lived experience in the workforce could not only improve safeguarding outcomes, but could also be a route to challenging prejudice and bias, as the next section elucidates.

Key Messages

- How can you share power with me so that I can make my own decisions?
- How can you support me to access the help I want without creating an environment where I'm afraid of punishment or abandonment?

- How can you change your approach so that I feel safer and more validated, rather than me having to try to fit into what you think is appropriate?
- How can the visibility and value given to people with lived experience be amplified in your service or organisation?

Bias and Stigma Can Kill

I wish they hadn't made me feel like I deserved [to be hurt] cos I'd been drinking.

(Leroy)

Prejudice and stigma arise from socially generated biases about individuals or groups. Biases in themselves are not necessarily stigmatising or negative – in fact holding biases can be an effective way of understanding risk, by differentiating between something that is safe or unsafe based on previous experience or the views of people we trust. Unfortunately, bias is built on broad generalisations about different identities and behaviours, which we typically learn from pervasive cultural norms and our socialisation as children (Psychology Today 2020). Therefore, we can understand bias as both subjective and socially constructed, factors which are likely to result in unconscious decision-making that gives preference to the individuals most likely to be viewed as safe, good and/or deserving of care in a particular society.

Bias is often identifiable in professional language choices rather than in outward attitudes or behaviours towards someone. People who experience homelessness have been characterised as untrustworthy, anti-social and unclean since the 17th century Poor Laws, prejudices built into legislation such as the Vagrancy Act (1824) whose archaic powers are still used to criminalise individuals for the failures of society to protect its most vulnerable (Morris 2019). Not only are these stereotypical evocations of homelessness dehumanising, they are simply incorrect. Research shows clearly that homeless people are significantly more likely to be the victim of a crime than the housed population (Newburn and Rock 2006; Scurfield *et al.* 2009), and that experiences of crime are amongst the main causes of homelessness (ONS 2020).

Recognising the actors, sites and practices of power in homelessness and social care can shed light on the effect of bias on vulnerable adults affected by homelessness. In our conversations, more than half of respondents identified professional responses and behaviours linked to negative biases and social stigma about homelessness, mental health and addiction. People spoke about reporting violence to professionals and not being believed, about deep mistrust of police preventing them from reporting being a victim of crime, of being held responsible for incidents in hostels that had not been their fault. People expressed this by talking about 'assumptions' people made about them and how this would result in negative consequences. One participant recalled not being able to tell professionals about domestic violence because 'they hear what they want to anyway, and it wasn't worth losing my kids over' (Sara). It was notable that all the women we spoke to described not being believed and being held responsible for harm perpetrated against them, perhaps highlighting how domestic and sexual abuse campaigning has yet to benefit the most marginalised women in society despite its high profile in mainstream discourse. We can see the prejudice and responsibilisation described by our participants in now banned anti-begging posters (BBC 2016) and in safeguarding adults reviews (Martineau *et al.* 2019; Preston-Shoot 2020b). The prevalence of the attitude that further harm is inevitable for people experiencing homelessness not only highlights an inaccurate homogenisation of homelessness and the people who experience it, but also leads to decision-making and multi-agency planning that is cynical, lacking in both creativity and hopefulness.

The chapter authors reflected on the duality of their experience as practitioners and former service users, concluding that much of the language we use as practitioners is 'for us', which unchecked can perpetuate harmful characterisations of the causes, triggers and effects of homelessness. A contemporary example is the term 'rough sleeper', commonly used to describe someone who is experiencing street homelessness. But far from being an innocuous term describing the experience, its use inextricably links the personal and experiential, characterising the whole person by the (largely negative) connotations linked to that singular experience rather than the plethora of experiences, traits and strengths the person actually embodies. If this seems a bit far-fetched, imagine referring to someone with leukaemia as 'a cancer'. Thus, practitioners must be aware of the power and meaning behind the phrases they use in their work and should check in with people about how they would like to be described and referred to, a small act towards meaningfully embedding whole person approaches to homelessness and risk.

> **Key Messages**
>
> - If your preconceptions about me affect the help you offer, what happens if you're wrong?
> - Believe me when I tell you something has happened to me, make it feel safe and validating for me to share things with you.
> - If a colleague or service shows prejudice or bias towards me, how will you address this?

Asking and (Really) Listening

If they don't listen…I just give up cos they're showing they're just like all the rest, so what's the point?

(Patrick)

The most common theme in all our conversations was the role of asking and listening. Participants frequently mentioned practitioners are 'always writing everything down' whilst concurrently, and potentially contradictorily, 'writing down what they want to hear and making it sound like someone else's life'. These insights suggest a disconnect between the motivations of practitioners and the people they support when discussing or assessing risk, and the value of documenting what someone is actually saying about their experience and not just an interpretation which fits more neatly with professional expectations or the way documents are formatted.

One participant shared a candid insight into how he navigates the system. Having been homeless on and off for more than 20 years he described having learnt 'what you need to say to get [professionals] to give you what you need'. He described having learnt in prison and mental health wards how to emulate the symptoms of particular health conditions in order to access medication to help with insomnia. Notwithstanding the risks of deceptively acquiring medication, this anecdote speaks to the reality not only that people absolutely do understand the complex system they find themselves subject to, but also that its failure to understand and meet their needs has resulted in the development of a discrete form of expertise to navigate it. It also alludes to a listening imbalance; people are listening, observing and learning from practitioners about how to access help, often shaping what they say around what they think professionals need to hear. This irony is not lost on the chapter authors, but more importantly this anecdote highlights how safeguarding risks, for example the inappropriate use of medication, can occur as a direct result of the failure of services to adequately respond to individual experience, or to cultivate honest relationships that don't require deceit to fulfil someone's needs.

As well as highlighting the nuanced and complex modes of communication between practitioners and the people they support, our conversations foregrounded the well-documented rigidity of eligibility criteria, interview and assessment practices, hostel 'house rules' and engagement expectations. Participants frequently spoke to feelings of abandonment that arise from being told 'you don't meet the criteria', or that they'd been discharged for missing an appointment, or deemed not sufficiently in crisis to be offered help. One participant reflected powerfully, 'you basically have to be dead already before anyone will help you these days' (Leroy). The chapter authors reflected how frontline practitioners commonly share these frustrations, recognising that generic practice and arbitrary criteria significantly limit the scope and impact of their work.

One way of resisting this rigidity is to adopt and embed a commitment to 'professional curiosity' with homeless adults. Professional curiosity is the practice of enquiring beyond the obvious, seeking to understand who and why a person is the way they are by understanding their life story as they see it. It involves taking the time to build a picture of the person beyond a timeline of professional interventions or criminal convictions, into what and who gives them confidence and security, and conversely what is likely to trigger reactions based on previous trauma and professional failure. In our conversations, participants were aware of the time pressures faced by practitioners, but they also reflected that it's not easy to trust people 'just because you're supposed to'. They wanted to feel like practitioners were interested in hearing about more than what was required for their performance targets. The chapter authors reflected on noticeable differences in the tone of voice and animation of participants when they were talking about their pets, favourite possessions and hobbies, highlighting the importance and mutual enjoyment of seeing the whole person and establishing common ground when two people begin working together. Not only is professional curiosity a crucial mechanism for building rapport and meaningful relationships, it is also a tool through which to challenge unconscious bias and prejudice. Hafford-Letchfield and Carr (2017) note that participation in curious professional behaviour involves deconstructing stereotypes that prevent the inclusion of service users' voices within safeguarding adult practice.

Finally, participants alluded to, and spoke directly about, a disengagement with the words written about them on official forms. One said: 'I can barely recognise myself when I read that stuff, I sound like a fucking monster' (Ajay). People (n=3) described not understanding the language, never having read their own support plans (n=6), and told us that they found it upsetting that things which happened years before were still drawn on to make decisions about their care and support today. In short, their voice was nowhere to be found in the reams of documentation describing their lives, goals and histories. Practical ways to remedy this include inviting people to write the notes of your meetings together, or to include a reflection of their own at the end. Another is to write using 'I' statements in documents specifically about an individual, i.e. assessments and support plans, including the sections about practitioner observations, where the practitioner's input is often over-professionalised and without personality. This simple, accountable and personalised practice humanises and centres the personal over the professional.

Key Messages

- Listen to what is important to me, ask follow-up questions, act on what I say I need and not what you think I need.

- Ask about more than my 'needs' – conversation is more fun if we're both interested in it!

- Write down the words I actually say, not what you think I'm saying.

Relationships Really Matter

It's my friends and the homeless community that I stay with and see every day who make me feel safest.

(Patrick)

A concurrent theme in our conversations was the understanding that safety is relational and contextual, unequivocally entangled with childhood circumstances, intimacy, material security, loyalty and responsibility. Given longstanding (and contested) exploration into adverse childhood experiences (Herman *et al.* 1997), the social exclusion and segregation that can be both the cause and effect of homelessness, and the reflections of chapter participants about the inconsistency of professional approaches, the connection between safety and relationships is an interesting one to disentangle.

A commitment to relational models of care (Together Network 2019) is fairly commonplace within contemporary homelessness and social care practice. Indeed, the positive impact of strong relationships between workers and the people they support is what has driven the growth in peer-support roles, where shared experience with workers is understood to benefit people affected by long histories of professional failure and institutionalisation. Building trust can also be a challenge for practitioners, where workforce turnover, unmanageable workloads and budget pressures eat into the time available to invest in the softer, less immediately fruitful, aspects of working with people. To this end, adopting lead professional approaches is recommended as a useful and effective way to build trusting relationships between people and practitioners (Preston-Shoot *et al.* 2020). Although ideal, it is not necessary for all people working on someone's behalf to know them well and spend time with them. There is almost certainly someone that the person prefers to work with anyway. Identifying lead roles can give clarity about who is supporting someone and what they can expect from individual practitioners and services. A trusted relationship may take on aspects of advocacy, friendship, advice or any number of other roles that help to build a stable emotional environment for the person to make decisions about the help and support available. Identifying roles to practitioners within the multi-agency network around a person can also help reduce duplication, share workload and consistently ensure relevant information is shared about the person's changing needs and circumstances.

Coping is defined as the 'constantly changing cognitive and behavioural efforts to manage external and/or internal demands that were deemed to be taking or exceeding a person's resources' (Shangold 2003 in Sloane 2015, p.3). The practice of coping is necessarily made up of actions, thoughts and decisions that use the resources someone has available, to help them survive their situation. For people who are homeless, social subjugation and material deprivation mean that coping mechanisms are often limited and conditional, for example one participant spoke about choosing to stay in a volatile relationship because sleeping on the street alone felt more unsafe. Another spoke about not opening letters, because he was unable to cope with the anxiety that he might be evicted again. Other participants discussed the role of drugs, alcohol and sex as a means of feeling safer. Irrespective of the long-term consequences of some coping mechanisms, participants all described employing the resources available in the here and now. All participants talked about the value of friends and family in feeling safe, each finding their own way to stay connected with those they love in the knowledge that this gave them a reason to keep going. It's therefore reasonable to assume that people affected by multiple exclusion homelessness are highly attuned to risk, and draw on a toolbox of behaviours, routines and relationships to cope with a risk-laden life. As such, practitioners should take the opportunity to learn from the extensively experienced people they support, ask exploratory and non-judgmental questions about behaviour that seems unusual or harmful, enquire about the behaviours that *feel* risky versus those that seem so to the practitioner, and work together to develop an approach to taking and avoiding risks that is based on that individual's experience and capability.

Key Messages

- Be patient, remember my trust has been broken many times before.
- Help me build/rebuild relationships with people I care about.
- Involve people who are important to me in my support, not just professionals.
- Learn from me, I'm managing risks every day.

Literature Review

The body of academic work exploring legislation, public policy, the charity industry, so-called cultures of poverty and the behaviours and afflictions of people who sleep rough is so extensive it appears to tell an indomitable story of homelessness since the Poor Laws of the 17th century. However, precious little of this has been written by researchers with a declared lived experience of homelessness, and most user-led research is hosted by grassroots organisations, typically working on the peripheries of the homelessness system. Although this is far less than ideal, these groups benefit from being less inhibited by the political, contractual and reputational constraints of large charities and local councils.

In recent years, a growing number of user-led groups and organisations have made incisive contributions to adult homelessness and safeguarding. One such project, Dying Homeless, is a crowd-sourced investigation, memorial and campaign surrounding the deaths of people affected by homelessness. Originally conceived by the Bureau of Investigative Journalism and continued by user-led organisation the Museum of Homelessness (2020), this project invites individuals, charities and local authorities to share information about people who have died in order to memorialise their lives and to raise awareness of the injustice that results in almost 1000 people dying homeless every year at around half the age of their housed peers (ONS 2019a). The Dying Homeless project has gained significant sector support and media traction, highlighting that the vast majority of deaths go un-investigated, leading to missed opportunities for learning and the prevention of further deaths. This work directly influenced the Ministry of Housing Communities and Local Government (MHCLG) Rough Sleeping Strategy (MHCLG 2018a), which for the first time advised local authorities to record and review the deaths of people affected by street homelessness. This user-led project tells us that not only do people with experience of homelessness produce insightful and impactful research, but their approach is uniquely human and collaborative.

Another organisation that has pioneered user-led research is Groundswell. A health-focused organisation, Groundswell have been at the forefront of user-led research into homelessness since 1992. One co-produced research project, delivered in partnership with Crisis (2019), made recommendations for a homelessness strategy based on the priorities of people who are currently homeless. Whilst not specifically exploring safeguarding, the views expressed by participants mirrored the safety concerns and experiences that have come through in this chapter. In particular Groundswell participants highlight the crucial role of peer and mutual support as a means of developing self-respect and resilience and the need to reduce stigma associated with poverty and homelessness. Importantly this research was conducted by participants from across the country, suggesting our conversations broadly mirror the views of people across the UK.

Beyond insightful research, user-led groups have also made an impact on frontline practice. One such group, the Voices of Stoke, conduct research and develop practical tools to support professionals and service users to navigate the complexities of legislation, policy and practice around multiple exclusion and disadvantage. The creation of these tools, in particular their pioneering Care Act Toolkit (Ornelas *et al.* 2018), highlights how the experiences shared by participants of this chapter are mirrored by people who are homeless, and their supporters, nationally. In particular, the Voices toolkit seeks to break down knowledge hierarchies between professionals and service users, by accessibly articulating definitions, processes and entitlements under the Act. The inclusion of the Voices toolkit in the Local Government Association's recent briefing on positive practice in homelessness and safeguarding (Preston-Shoot 2020a) provides optimism for a shift in the value placed on experiential knowledge in practice development.

Despite this encouraging step to integrate lived experience within practice development, research by and for people who are homeless with protected characteristics (Equality Act 2010) is notable in its relative absence. Perhaps because of their historic and ongoing socio-economic marginalisation, awareness of the needs and homelessness experiences of women, Black, LGBTQ+ and disabled people arises predominantly from self-organising community campaigns and activist groups. As with the birth of the refuge movement in the 1970s, contemporary feminist collectives in the UK have been at the forefront of tackling the austerity-driven homelessness and safeguarding risks affecting women and non-binary folk. One example is the work of direct-action group Sisters Uncut who occupied a number of buildings, including the Holloway Prison Visitor Centre, to draw attention to homelessness and poverty affecting vulnerable survivors of gender-based abuse (Archer 2017). Their user-led actions highlight poor conditions in temporary accommodation, homelessness facing people leaving prison, the gatekeeping practices of key agencies and crippling financial cuts to specialist services. Another example is the work of The Outside Project, a grassroots organisation from North London who took matters into their own hands in 2018 to address the lack of safe accommodation and specialist support available to homeless LGBTQ+ people. Highlighting the absence of any dedicated LGBTQ+ night shelter in the city, The Outside Project embarked on a vibrant and counter-cultural approach to securing a safe, community-led shelter and social space for LGBTQ+ people affected by homelessness (Ecola 2018). Both these campaigns centre mutual aid, self-advocacy and knowledge-sharing as mechanisms to address harm and injustice. Their work follows the long tradition of user-led change in social care and housing, in which disabled people have led successful campaigns for greater choice, control and self-determination for all marginalised people for decades.

The degree of power and influence that an individual or group has in a given circumstance is altered by complex and interrelated factors, such as their identity, cognitive ability and social status. Additionally, the power a person is able to mobilise is both contextual and relational; it changes according to who is involved and what the situation is. Kwok-Fu Wong (2003) built on existing feminist analyses to frame four types of power:

- *Power-from-within*: Personal power that comes from self-respect, acceptance and value.

- *Power-to*: Power granted by an external person or agency, usually with limited scope and a specific context.

- *Power-with*: Invoked by engaging in a relationship with others towards a joint goal.

- *Power-over*: Exerted by someone or something, which could be positive, e.g. legal protection against discrimination, or negative, e.g. threat of eviction from a hostel.

Wong's framework elucidates the experiences described by chapter participants. It also invites the reader to think about the adoption of *power-with* strategies, which could be mutually beneficial for individuals, frontline safeguarding practice, and strategic decision-making, as well as helping to strengthen and encourage *power-from-within*. Advocacy is an attempt to draw on *power-with* and *power-from-within* by amplifying and centring the voices of people who use statutory care services so that they can secure the assistance they want and not the help professionals determine they need. Henderson and Pochin (2001) theorise that successful advocacy empowers individuals to fulfil three main purposes:

- The maximisation of personal *choice*.
- Enablement of *access* to relevant information and experiences.
- As a means to fight for *justice*.

Given the pre-existing recognition of advocacy in social care practice there is an opportunity for advocacy to be recognised and employed by people facing multiple exclusion homelessness.

In Teresa Gowan's ethnographic study of people experiencing homelessness in San Francisco (2010), she identifies three language typologies commonly used to articulate experiences of, and solutions for, homelessness. She posits that the language register organisations and services draw on indicates the broad ideological basis for their work, which inevitably shapes the practices which flow from it. Gowan describes three registers: *sick-talk*, *sin-talk* and *system-talk* (explored in detail in Chapter 2). Gowan's findings invite practitioners, commissioners and policy-makers to critique cultures, service models and systems built around narrow ideologies and discourses, and to employ a professional curiosity comfortable with the reality that homelessness arises from a complex interplay between social inequality (system), individual choices (sin) and accidents of fate (sick).

Despite the large body of work exploring homelessness, there is limited inquiry into the role of familial and peer relationships as coping mechanisms or recovery strategies. One study (Neale and Brown 2016) explored the role of friendship in interviews with people affected by homelessness and drug dependency. The study identified a common desire for normative friendships with routine contact and communication, enabled by improved access to digital-communication technologies. Scholars have also highlighted the positive role of supportive social networks (Tunåker 2015) and the mutual benefits of recognising the role of *chosen family* (Nobel 2019; Levin *et al.* 2020). However, chapter participants highlighted the ambiguous role of familial relationships, noting that they can be both a crucial support and a trigger for relapse and re-traumatisation. Chapter participants strongly emphasised the role and value of friendship and camaraderie in their everyday coping strategies, suggesting that effective safeguarding interventions should draw on an individual's peer, familial and social networks to improve self-esteem and enable self-advocacy, and as a means to strengthen positive coping mechanisms.

Conclusion

Centring lived experience has generated a chapter rich with examples of imbalance and disconnection between professionals and service users that result in increased or unchanged risk of harm. Homelessness and safeguarding practitioners across the operational and strategic spectrum are invited to examine these imbalances in their own practice, local service pathways and strategic decision-making, to consider how embedding curiosity, power-sharing and resisting prejudice could propagate positive change. The chapter authors and participants jointly conclude that building honest, mutually respectful relationships of all types is not only key to responding to risk, but also to the healing and recovery that many people facing homelessness are seeking.

Acknowledgements

Heartfelt thanks to the 15 people whose words and experiences shaped this chapter; I think they're listening now.

This chapter is dedicated to Raimundus Cinis (1960–2020). His knowing smile, patience and willingness to trust us just one more time taught us more than we can repay with words, and changed homelessness practice in Haringey forever.

Chapter 4

Using Curiosity: A Psychologically Informed Approach to Adult Safeguarding and Rough Sleeping

Sione Marshall, Tim Robson, Nathan Servini and Barney Wells

Introduction

In this chapter we consider the different elements that contribute to effective practice in how individual workers and systems respond to people who are sleeping rough, appear to be self-neglecting, and for whom there may be concerns about mental capacity. In particular, we consider the role of safeguarding (both in a broad sense and how it is defined in the Care Act 2014) and how the use of curiosity, driven by a psychologically informed approach (Ritchie 2015; Levy 2017; Cockersell 2018a), can be used to support reflective and person-centred approaches that also recognise risks and duties.

Despite the established literature demonstrating the effectiveness of psychologically informed approaches internationally (Levy 2017), unconscious processes often prevent practitioners and organisations from translating this evidenced theory into practice.

We define curiosity as the desire to know and learn within the context of not consciously making assumptions. The Department of Health (2018, p.8) describes this as 'exploring and taking into account a wide range of contexts including individual, carer and professional stories, the chronology of critical events, social and economic circumstances and their own practice experiences'.

What does active curiosity look and sound like in effective practice?

To explore this, we consider how using curiosity manifests within the continuous cycle of assessment, intervention and evaluation. Anonymised vignettes from actual case examples are used to demonstrate theory-practice links. The ability to hold a curious stance whilst assessing, intervening or evaluating within the context of safeguarding and homelessness enables work to be informed by both curiosity and professional judgement. The vignettes focus on how we work with people who are rough sleeping. However, implications for practice can be applied more widely to those experiencing homelessness in circumstances other than sleeping rough. We also believe that adopting a curious stance enables us as practitioners to better attend to other differences, whether these relate to culture, race, religion, age, sex and gender, sexual orientation or disability.

This work can be extremely complex and often involves multiple agencies. This chapter is therefore designed to provide an introduction to thinking about how practitioners might use curiosity to inform effective practice.

The Importance of Remaining Curious

The response to an individual sleeping rough is only partly driven by that person's direct communications about their situation, their actual appearance and their behaviour. The response, by professionals as well as other people in a community, is also inevitably impacted by culturally and politically driven preconceptions and biases.

These might include negative ideas associating rough sleeping with anti-social behaviour, substance use, or encroaching on resources or services that are 'meant for residents'. For example, the dishevelled person, smelling of alcohol, sleeping in a hospital waiting area with a large bag, who health staff ask security to 'remove' without any questions being asked about their circumstances. It can also include ideas and stereotypes that are not inherently negative but can still prevent what is actually going on for an individual being properly considered by someone whose role should encompass this. For example, a person who is seen as 'a local character and a free spirit' who is actually placing themselves at significant risk, and where a more than cursory examination of their decision-making should raise concerns that this is being impacted by significant mental health issues.

Effective safeguarding relies on professionals using self-awareness that informs a curious stance, which enables a movement away from pre-conceived ideas and biases. It is important that this extends to considering other aspects of someone's identity, such as their ethnicity, gender or any disability, and experiences beyond their housing situation, and also considers how these identities intersect and the consequences of this. For example, recent research (Stonewall Housing 2018) relating to the experiences of lesbian, gay, bisexual and trans people who slept rough found that they were more likely to end up street homeless, and when in that situation they were more likely to experience mental health issues and face violence than the broader population of people experiencing homelessness.

Sitting at the very heart of any psychologically informed approach is benign enquiry (Stokoe 2020) or the process of developing cooperative relationships with others in order to collect information that will give us the whole story of the individual, team, service or organisation with whom we are working. In essence, to use curiosity to inform our assessment of the past and present situation. Sitting underneath and informing this approach at any stage of work (assessment, intervention or evaluation) is the process of creating the often new, or renewed, experience of a positive relationship. This relationship can then be internalised as a positive experience of self (Cockersell 2018b), and in turn enable positive change for a person.

Alongside a psychologically informed approach, professionals must hold different frameworks, perspectives and goals in mind. Crucial in this context are legal frameworks and duties as well as the knowledge base that underpins assessment of risk, such as epidemiological research around mortality rates and morbidity rates for the homeless population. It is therefore essential that we can retain an ongoing curiosity with which to consider how these frameworks interact and self-awareness in examining how we weigh up decisions.

Assessment

What does this curiosity look and sound like when assessing within a safeguarding context an individual who is rough sleeping? Will curiosity about the person on the street be enabled by policies that dictate 'we don't offer assessment on the street'? Which of these options might provide us with the most accurate picture of this person's past and present life, enabling us as practitioners to hold a curious stance whilst making informed decisions within the context of safeguarding and rough sleeping?

Vignette A: Marek

Marek was a 60-year-old, Eastern European man rough sleeping outside a busy city train station. He drank alcohol heavily. He rarely ventured from his exposed sleeping site. He had been placed in a B&B by the homelessness outreach team but abandoned this accommodation.

Appointments made with his GP were not attended. Following a seizure, he was admitted to A&E but discharged himself against medical advice. A&E staff, respecting Marek's individual rights and lifestyle choices, and accepting that people are experts in their own lives, acquiesced to his discharge. Alarmed by Marek's state of health and choices they passed on their concerns to social services. Winter was approaching and the homelessness team were concerned about the possible consequences of Marek's exposure to the cold weather, with the additional cold weather risks for someone abusing alcohol.

A social worker, accompanied by an interpreter, met with Marek at his sleep site. Normally an assessment would be conducted in a private setting; however, the social worker ascertained that Marek became anxious when away from his position and deemed it less stressful if he remained on site. He therefore sat down with Marek on the street.

Marek struggled to provide critical chronological life events and disclosed that he had memory deficits. He divulged that he was too embarrassed to admit that he was unable to remember the route to and from his B&B accommodation. He revealed that he had a son and gave consent for services to contact him. This aroused the social worker's curiosity. With no contact details and only a name, he decided to attempt to contact Marek's son via Facebook. As he had Marek's permission to do so, the social worker decided that this would not be considered as intrusive surveillance.

The search was successful and email communication with Marek's son revealed Marek's personal story. Two years earlier, Marek had sustained a severe head injury, which resulted in personality changes leading to a breakdown in relationships, employment and loss of accommodation. The initial perception of professionals that Marek's primary problem arose from alcohol abuse and his 'lifestyle choice' of rough sleeping was incorrect.

Crisis depict the high levels of abuse and violence experienced by rough sleepers and suggest that 'rough sleeping can be prevented if services work together to identify people at risk and move people off the streets as quickly as possible'.[1] The homelessness team therefore decided, on the grounds that he appeared to not be making a capacious decision to rough sleep and self-neglect, to refer Marek to safeguarding services. Crisis (2011) has warned that homeless people are three times more likely to die of pneumonia or hypothermia than the general population.

There are many known negative effects on a rough sleeper's mental and physical health; these increase with prolonged rough sleeping, especially if the individual has complex needs. Social workers are occasionally asked to assess the signs and indicators of these risks to rough sleepers. They have a duty to act in the best interests of service users and consider a person's right to respect, privacy and confidentiality whilst also managing and assessing risk within a legal framework (BASW 2018, p.9).

To aid rapport and build relations, the social worker decided to sit on the cardboard next to Marek at his sleep site. Marek seemed comfortable with this arrangement and became more communicative, which enhanced the quality of the assessment.

Active curiosity is fundamental to effective assessment. Demonstrating that he was genuinely interested in Marek and signifying that he was actively listening to his account, the social worker was able to learn more about Marek's experience as he became more relaxed and forthcoming.

Practitioners have a responsibility to consider the use of social media as part of safeguarding investigations but need to be mindful of the ethical implications. It is important to work with those professionals who are best-placed to undertake the task of scrutinising social media and to ensure it is in the service user's best interest. Boddy and Dominelli (2017) advise social workers when working with social media to retain their commitment to ethical values and critical reflective practice, and to link their knowledge of the complex interplay between discourses that underpin daily practice like those related to power, permanency,

---

[1] www.crisis.org.uk/ending-homelessness/rough-sleeping/rough-sleepers-and-complex-needs

authorship, audience, embodiment and professionalism to social media created spaces.

The social worker's curiosity led to the initiative of reaching out to Marek's family. This enabled the social worker to reframe Marek's presentation and reappraise the complexity of Marek's life experiences. It also reinforced the social worker's ability to recognise conflicting interpretations when making judgments of mental capacity and considering appropriate interventions.

The importance of valuing, recognising and prioritising the building of personal relationships as vehicles for personal change is a core tenet of any psychologically informed approach (Ritchie 2015). The ability to engage sits at the core of developing relationships, and this is in turn dependent on the effective use of open questions, affirming, reflecting and summarising (Miller and Rollnick 2013). With this in place, a safe and containing space is created (Winnicott 1965) in which change can be more readily entertained. In summary, the social worker and interpreter through their behaviour and language were able to engage with Marek in a way that enabled him to feel safe enough to engage with an assessment.

Vignette A also illustrates how assessment itself can be a really effective intervention in nurturing the development of a relationship that may later enable positive change, however small. The priority here is to develop the relationship so that assessment can then be completed. Looking at the work through this relational lens, policies and protocols dictating that adult safeguarding services do not assess on the streets no longer seem to make sense. Or do they? What unconscious function might they serve in organisations dealing with the safeguarding of homeless people?

These systems are often put in place to promote detachment from the emotional response experienced when working with people who are sleeping rough. It's easier to have a policy that says 'We don't assess on the streets' than to attend to the discomfort and anxiety of sitting down next to someone who may not have washed for days. These systems are often anti-supportive to staff (Menzies Lyth 1979) and leave both practitioners and those they are tasked to help disabled (Scanlon and Adlam 2019). The reality of scarce resources may be offered to justify these systems. However, the effective use of curiosity can increase our understanding of these unconscious processes. It can also help us understand how, despite an established literature relating to psychologically informed approaches in rough sleeper and homelessness services, some organisations struggle to apply this in practice.

Vignette B: Florence

Florence was a 40-year-old woman with an established diagnosis of psychosis. She believed that a neighbour was poisoning her by piping gas through her letterbox. She therefore decided to abandon her property. Her mother expressed concerns for her daughter's safety, saying she lacked mental capacity and required urgent psychiatric admission.

The social worker established that Florence was sleeping inside an airport terminal. She used the washing and bathing facilities and engaged with security guards who monitored her and offered emotional support. She did not present as distressed.

Florence engaged with the homeless outreach team but was reluctant to return to her property for fear of being poisoned. She had access to her bank account, and during the day she would catch the bus to town and use the library before returning to the terminal at night.

Without a curious stance, Florence's decision to abandon her home might be framed in one of two oversimplified and opposing ways. Firstly, it could be seen as driven by beliefs, whilst experiencing a psychotic episode. Given the general pattern of risks faced by people who sleep rough, assessment under the Mental Health Act (1983) could be indicated. The other oversimplified way of framing the situation would be to focus only on her decision to sleep inside the relative security of an airport environment and take the view that she was taking appropriate steps to preserve her safety and mitigating the risk of harm from others.

Sitting with Florence and developing a relationship that enabled active curiosity about her experience of the world, the social worker was able to help Florence consider how her actions, given her belief that she would be poisoned at home, made sense and were indeed in reality keeping her safe, clean, warm, well-fed, and fairly secure at her chosen site. She posed no risk to herself or others. There was, however, the risk that she could be evicted from the airport. This might mean that she would then be sleeping rough in a situation where she faced greater risks of sexual abuse, violence and stigmatisation (Bretherton and Pleace 2018).

The use of active curiosity enabled the development of a positive working relationship with Florence. This in turn created a space in which Florence could think about her mental health and what changes she might want to make in the future. Within the context of a trusting relationship, she could begin to make sense of her experiences and entertain alternative accommodation to the airport.

Mental Capacity

Whilst the Mental Capacity Act (2005) provides a framework in which decisions can be made on someone else's behalf, the vignette above illustrates how it also provides protection for people to make positive choices about their situation. For this reason, its principles and safeguards have been described as enabling an approach that is person-centred and empowering (Manthorpe *et al.* 2008).

Considering whether someone is unable to make a particular decision due to impairment (by mental health issues, brain injury or substance use) is a key issue in deciding whether someone who is at risk may require a statutory intervention such as a safeguarding adults enquiry or assessment under the Mental Health Act (1983). It is also particularly important when considering chronic and fluctuating risks, for instance when working with someone who is self-neglecting and declining shelter through different seasons and weather conditions. Can the person make the decision being discussed with them at the time that the decision needs to be made?

Some ability to consider mental capacity in line with the functional test of capacity contained within the Act, its principles and the concept of 'Best Interest' should be incorporated into the skillset of anyone working in this area. Consideration of someone's ability to carry through a decision, including incorporating evidence from the person's behaviour as well as what they might say in the course of a discussion, is also important (Cameron and Codling 2020). Resources have been developed specifically to support frontline homelessness workers (Pathway 2017; Homeless Link 2018a).

The first three principles of the Mental Capacity Act (2005) support the process of determining if someone lacks capacity. The final two principles support the decision-making process once it has been established that someone lacks capacity. All five principles are integral to the Act and should be reflected in every stage of working in a psychologically informed way with someone whose decision-making might be impaired.

For example, the second principle of the Mental Capacity Act

(2005) is that all steps should be taken to support an individual to make their own decision. Fulfilling this in a considered and psychologically informed way entails engagement with both the practical and psychological barriers that might be present. Therefore the information necessary to be able to decide should be provided in a form that is accessible to a person who is on the streets, for example assumptions should not be made about whether they can access the internet. It also means taking into account a person's potential life experiences, including trauma and negative experiences of services in the past, and ensuring that this is considered in how options and choices are presented and explored. Research has demonstrated the high levels of complex trauma amongst people experiencing homelessness (Maguire *et al.* 2009, 2010); control is often taken away in traumatic situations and homelessness itself is disempowering (EASL and Homeless Link 2018). This needs to be taken into account; for example, unreasonably short time frames to make a decision should be challenged.

If it is concluded that someone lacks capacity to make a particular decision, the intervention then indicated may be one that prioritises physical safety and welfare over psychological goals, but this may not be correct. The 'Best Interest Checklist' contained within the Act, and the subsequent case law, are clear that regard has to be given to what that individual would have wanted when they had capacity. When someone lacks capacity the substitute decision-maker should take into account, 'so far as practicable, his individual characteristics, likes and dislikes, values and approach to life and not simply what the professional considers to be appropriate' (N v ACCG & Ors [2017]).

Maintaining a position of benign enquiry (Stokoe 2020) should be as central to considerations around mental capacity as it is around any other aspect of assessment. Given the potential implications for the person and the challenges to practitioners whose own valence (Bion 1961) may be to step in and 'rescue', using curiosity to enable self-awareness is, by definition, fundamental in assessing capacity.

Vignette C: Gregory

Gregory, a man in his 60s, slept rough in an area for many years. He declined offers of shelter or assistance even when temperatures were below freezing. He happily spoke to outreach workers, but they couldn't understand his decision-making.

Local mental health services met with him on the street several times. The mental health team, in discussion with the outreach worker, considered his mental capacity concerning his decision to remain street homeless. They did not establish evidence of significant mental disorder, so he could not be considered to lack capacity, nor to meet the criteria for an admission under the Mental Health Act (1983). He said that he would consider accepting accommodation if he felt that his physical health declined. He was discharged by the mental health team, but with advice that street services could re-refer.

Some months later Gregory referenced some unusual ideas about foreign powers influencing the unseasonable weather. Outreach workers re-referred him to mental health services and a psychiatric nurse visited Gregory on the street again. Gregory repeated the idea, but it was not felt to be a belief that was held with delusional intensity and it was not clear that it was linked to the particular decision to decline accommodation. Given this, he was again considered not to be lacking capacity.

The following winter Gregory seemed less robust physically. Outreach workers increased their contact with him and were able to arrange a visit from primary care workers. Gregory continued to decline shelter there and then, but the following week he attended the local housing office and made a homelessness application. He told the housing officer that he was happy for them to get further details from the outreach team and the health professionals he had seen on the street. He was offered and accepted sheltered housing.

Vignette C demonstrates how the outreach team and local mental health services were able to work well together over time to consider their responsibilities towards Gregory. The unusualness of Gregory's decision and the risks he was facing through continuing to sleep rough made it appropriate for the issue of mental capacity to be actively considered and for this to be reviewed when things changed. To achieve and maintain this level of collaboration is both necessary in order to uphold the principles of the Mental Capacity Act (2005), and also extremely challenging.

The outreach team were looking to mental health services to provide 'a solution' that would maintain Gregory's safety, and this, quite appropriately, was not forthcoming, as evidence of mental impairment was not there to justify interfering with his rights to self-determination, whatever the risks. In such a situation it would be common for services to retreat into the safety of defence mechanisms such as splitting, to denigrate the other as not understanding the person at the centre as well as they do, and to retreat from maintaining healthy levels of communication. In this instance both services were able to avoid this; they were able to reflect on the other's perspective, incorporate this into their own understanding, and retain a position of ongoing and benign curiosity. Structures such as reflective practice supported them to do this.

Vignette D: Leonard

Leonard, a man in his late 40s, began sleeping rough in a very public place, drinking alcohol very heavily with no discernible pattern apparent seemingly from waking. He walked with a distinct limp and was seen to wince with pain. He was offered a hostel place but declined; his reasons were unclear. Outreach services also had concerns about his physical health and noted that some statements he made indicated that he might be experiencing 'paranoid' thoughts.

Following a referral to mental health services, a social worker attended with an outreach worker early in the morning. Leonard was not visibly intoxicated. He had no sleeping bag and no socks, although the outreach worker advised that he had been given both in previous days. He was willing to engage in chat and observed social niceties but was guarded when asked about his reasons for declining accommodation. He appeared distracted at times and some of his answers were non sequiturs. He left the assessment and began drinking again.

The mental health social worker discussed Leonard with his team and an appointment with a senior psychiatrist in three weeks' time was made.

One week later, a period of severe weather started and was forecast to continue. Leonard continued to decline any shelter. When the outreach team contacted the mental health team, the original social worker was on leave and they were unwilling to explore bringing the appointment forward. The outreach team made a safeguarding referral to the local authority stressing the immediacy of the risks because of the weather, the lack of information about Leonard's health and the possible concern that his decision-making was impaired. They also completed their own mental capacity assessment using a screening tool (Pathway 2017) which helped them evidence their concerns.

> Multi-agency discussion including primary care and mental health workers followed, and information was gathered from the local hospital about his physical health. It was also established that he was known to homelessness services in a neighbouring area.
>
> It was concluded that an assessment under the Mental Health Act 1983 was indicated. When this took place, his presentation was similar to when seen by the social worker the previous week, but the doctors and AMHP (approved mental health professionals) involved agreed that the criteria for an admission under section 2 were met. In hospital it transpired that Leonard had significant symptoms of psychosis, including intrusive and distressing auditory hallucinations, and that his drinking was in part an attempt to block these out. Ultimately treatment and ongoing support was welcomed by Leonard who was able to go on to regain much more control over his life, for example re-establishing contact with his family and former social circle and taking pride and pleasure in cooking and decorating at the accommodation he moved into.

At the stage where the mental health team declined to bring forward Leonard's appointment, the outreach worker had to trust their own knowledge and judgement in the face of this being dismissed by professionals who likely had more status and qualifications. This included knowledge of Leonard's apparent difficulties in making key decisions and the importance of a decision being needed now; the risks, which had increased very significantly with the change in the weather; and the Care Act 2014, in relation to safeguarding risks of self-neglect.

The outreach worker's ability to appropriately escalate through multi-agency discussion led to Leonard's safety being secured and in due course him gaining more control over his life.

Structures and support in a service, as well as appropriate training and recruitment, can enable individual workers to hold a situation where no dramatic intervention is justified, as with Gregory, and to make a judgement as to when action is needed because of the nature of the risk, as with Leonard.

Intervention
Working Effectively with Individuals
People who are homeless are at greater risk of tri-morbidity leading to a high level of hospital admissions (Stringfellow *et al.* 2015; Lewer *et al.* 2021). Consequently, work often takes place within the context of a hospital admission and involves working with the many different services and teams that operate within this system.

Vignette E: Alice – Part 1
Alice was in her early 50s. She came to the UK as a child refugee, and was sleeping on buses, frequently attending emergency departments with chest and leg infections. She often became agitated with screaming and shouting that attracted the attention of both hospital security and police.

On one such episode she was referred to the hospital homeless health care team because she was refusing to return to existing accommodation citing harassment there. The homeless team made enquiries and found this had been going on for some years.

The team listened to specific requests such as help with contacting other services and offered some simple practical support such as food and drink, help with transport costs, advice about community support services, and help to make contact with them. This developed a long-term relationship with Alice and made her feel as though some of her requests at least were being listened to, although not immediately solving her lack of appropriate accommodation.

In time, she would come and specifically ask to see the team. This often involved taking time to listen to vividly told complaints about how she had been treated. She would then ask for a phone call to be made on her behalf, or a new referral to be made, express thanks and leave the hospital.

The team made routine Duty to Refer referrals on her behalf to housing and helped collect the supporting data she needed for such applications, as well as ensuring continuity of benefits.

The team also liaised with all the other community teams involved – such as street teams, community mental health teams, GPs and district nursing teams – so that everyone was aware of the situation and could work together to support the patient.

By being available to talk to Alice when she presented at hospital, a trusting relationship was built and a fuller picture of her story emerged, which was crucially not just the presenting complaint recorded at reception in the emergency department. She was considered to have capacity around her decisions and not be experiencing safeguarding risks. Gradually rapport was built with her and the network of other community agencies supporting her, which took time and was useful, even though it did not result in an immediate solution, such as being satisfactorily housed. The development of a trusting relationship was itself enabling even though it did not result in a more tangible change that might have more satisfied the staff.

Members of the team encouraged Alice to engage with services, but without an expectation that she would suddenly do so, and meanwhile provided what it was she felt she needed, such as an oyster card or a phone call on her behalf. By listening without immediately offering solutions, staff could find out what Alice wanted, and what was going to enable her to make changes, even if a small step was all that could be realistically expected.

The vignette above highlights the importance of setting realistic goals for both parties. In listening rather than acting, staff were able to develop a relationship with Alice that she trusted enough to then begin to make some positive changes for herself. In using interactions with Alice to be actively curious about her experience of feeling not listened to, staff were able to help Alice enact change for herself.

Working Effectively with Other Professionals

Work with people who are sleeping rough and who are experiencing homelessness is almost always reliant on our ability to work with multiple teams, services and agencies across different disciplines. The open, curious stance needed to develop the positive relationships in our work with individuals is needed in equal measure when working with other professionals.

Vignette E: Alice – Part 2

In the emergency department or hospital wards Alice could switch quickly from apparently everyday conversation to suddenly shouting, being verbally very abusive and threatening to staff. On some occasions staff felt they could not contain the situation and felt intimidated. Whilst temporarily withdrawing calmed the situation on some occasions, on others they would call security staff, which then escalated the situation further, leading to scuffles and sometimes forcible removal from the hospital.

The homeless team included care navigators with a lived experience of homelessness, along with clinical staff, enabling liaison with community services as well as the medical teams in the hospital. The team was there to support Alice rather than being in charge of her care, and took time to focus on the issues concerning her and listen to her at length. However, team members could also feel ambivalent about initiating conversation with Alice if they saw her in passing, knowing that an interaction was likely to take a long time.

A safeguarding alert was raised because of concerns about Alice's safety while sleeping on buses. Despite securing repeated offers of accommodation from a succession of Duty to Refer referrals to different housing authorities, Alice consistently declined every offer, whilst complaining she was being left on the street.

The safeguarding team subsequently reported that the primary concern was the suitability of the housing being offered and advised that Alice should liaise with the housing authority. They were unable to contact her when they tried to see if she needed social care support, concluded that there was no role for safeguarding and closed her case.

From a staff perspective it is not always easy to remain patient and calm in the face of verbal abuse and non-engagement with treatment, due to the anxiety that these behaviours so often provoke in us. However, these behaviours communicate something of a person's experience. People who experience homelessness may feel that they do not fit in with hospital staff or fellow patient culture. This experience can feel stigmatising and can lead to easily interpreting reactions and comments between staff as rejection and disrespect.

It is natural for staff to want to withdraw in response to anxiety felt, and the challenge for them is therefore to hold a curious stance about why a patient may struggle to regulate their emotion. A curiosity about a person's whole story may eventually lead to disclosure of adverse childhood experiences, complex trauma in adulthood as well as ongoing trauma which may not have previously been disclosed.

Once a patient is well enough to not need ongoing expert medical or nursing support they are deemed 'medically optimised', and pressure to discharge them from staff and management grows. If they decide to self-discharge there can be a sigh of relief, tempered by a sigh of despair when the patient needs urgent readmission shortly afterwards.

Although Alice's health improved whilst in hospital, the risk of further deterioration on discharge back to being homeless and sleeping on buses was ever present, and at times the team would need to explain to the medical team that although she was now medically fit for discharge, she could not be safely discharged until accommodation was found for her.

In all these situations 'listening' to a patient's experience as well as our own reaction to this can be key in understanding the situation and possibly help de-escalation.

Alice featured in the list of 'high intensity users' of the emergency departments at various hospitals over a period of five years. At multi-disciplinary meetings, input from the ambulance service and community teams could be added to the records generated in the hospital. A written care plan was devised summarising her needs and which agencies she was in touch with. In practice however there was no evidence that emergency duty staff looked at this care plan in the midst of assessing her current complaints in the course of a busy day.

The safeguarding concern raised about Alice did not result in further insight into her situation, or a proactive solution to her sleeping on buses, which put her at risk. In this sense, a safeguarding process can become a tick box exercise that does not necessarily address the practical needs of the patient.

The vignette above illustrates the process of developing positive relationships as sitting underneath and informing change that enables collaborative and open dialogue between professionals. This in turn enables positive change for those individuals with whom we work. It also highlights the importance of attending to how we as practitioners may respond to the anxieties caused by our experience of working with this population with often limited resources. It is often uncomfortable and anxiety-provoking for us as practitioners when a solution is not readily available that might enable change. When we are prevented from working within our optimum emotional window of tolerance (Siegel 1999) we begin to develop systems or responses, such as tick boxing, to defend against the anxiety created by this (Menzies Lyth 1960, 1979).

Evaluation

The ability to evaluate the effectiveness of any assessment or intervention is essential to developing effective adult safeguarding in homelessness services. The process of evaluation is often seen as the last part in the process of any piece of work. However, effective evaluation is ongoing and present even at the beginnings of assessment. Discerning whether any part of an assessment or intervention is enabling or disabling requires the capacity to reflect (Knott and Scragg 2013).

Reflective Practice

Reflective practice can be divided into two key processes (Schon 1983). Firstly, reflection in action occurs when practitioners apply their knowledge in the moment. For example, in Vignette A, the interpreter and social worker who sat with Marek used the process of reflecting in action to evaluate the effectiveness of their assessment. Secondly, reflection on practice relates to practitioners' evaluation and review of their experience together. This may comprise a facilitated reflective practice group where the team reflected on what might influence Alice's behaviours (Vignette E) but also how their emotional reaction to these behaviours either enabled or disabled effective change for Alice. Using curiosity, the team were able to attend to the emotional response they had when working with Alice. For example, how exchanges with Alice often left them feeling helpless and in turn avoiding interactions with her. With this learning they were then able to consider how sitting with this helplessness rather than avoiding it could enable them to engage with Alice.

The ability to reflect requires curiosity about the self and others. This curiosity depends on the development of self-awareness (Bassot 2016): the noticing of thoughts, feelings and what these engender physically in the here and now. In essence, this is a process of bringing what is often unconscious (but drives behaviour) to the conscious in ourselves as individuals but also within the relevant involved agencies.

Within the framework of a reflective practice model (Gibbs 1988), this encourages a noticing rather than problem-solving stance and facilitates a 'sitting with' rather than 'moving away' from uncomfortable emotions. The team's curiosity in reflective practice when considering their work with Alice shows how the facilitated reflective practice group provided a safe and containing enough space (Winnicott 1965) for the team to sit with and notice uncomfortable and difficult processes and thereby entertain change. This mirrors the process in Vignette A. To enable change the interpreter and social worker held a curious and open stance and were therefore able to create a safe and containing space from which Marek could then entertain making some changes. A reflective practice group provides practitioners with a safe and containing space in an organisation that is otherwise unable to offer these types of spaces, as most of its systems will be busy defending against sitting with and getting up close to the anxieties caused by this work.

Reflecting on Interactions with Individuals

Alice's story (Vignette E) was explored by the hospital homeless team who saw her. Staff were encouraged by the clinical psychologist facilitating the session to exercise proactive curiosity, for example asking the team what they thought might lie behind the behaviours which felt so dysfunctional – what was the behaviour achieving, and what inner emotions or reactions did it express as well as how this behaviour made staff think and feel.

On many occasions Alice found it difficult to regulate her emotion, quickly moving in and out of agitation informed by her belief that people were not listening to her. Exactly what had triggered a 'fight or flight' type response was not necessarily clear, but it certainly indicated she was uncomfortable and did not feel safe in the situation. For emergency department and ward staff not accustomed to such reactions it created similar 'fight or flight' reactions – usually withdrawal and sometimes a call for security.

Discussion in the reflective practice session involved trying to understand exactly what might feel so unsafe for Alice. The team hypothesised that her lack of trust may relate to a history of having suffered chronic childhood trauma. This hypothesis was later confirmed by Alice. The team concluded that reflecting back to Alice an acceptance that she felt frustrated and unsafe could help contain her emotion – but in practice staff still found this difficult to do. Learning to listen to how interactions make us feel both physically and emotionally is key to using curiosity effectively in our work as practitioners. In working with Alice, it was clear that the homeless team staff would often catch sight of her in casual encounters and try to avoid interacting with her, feeling helpless to offer solutions and wanting to avoid the discomfort of hearing the same complaints again.

Reflecting on Interactions with Colleagues and Partner Organisations

Working as a multi-disciplinary team depends on everyone pooling their efforts together, but in conflict situations teams can pull back and decide that they have fulfilled their responsibilities and that the problem now belongs entirely to another team – for example the team that has 'homeless' in its title. Once it was realised that Alice was homeless, other teams tended to immediately suggest she saw the homeless team – as if the homeless team should solve both the housing issue and all other issues. New ways of working encouraging very rapid discharge from hospital that evolved during the Covid-19 pandemic may also reflect discomfort with facing the difficulties patients may have and emphasise passing the perceived problems on to community services to solve.

The reflective practice session considered why other partners might wish to withdraw from what appeared to be a difficult issue, and how to encourage joint working solutions rather than feeling the homeless team should accept the impossible challenge of trying to solve all problems by itself. In this situation open curiosity can enable exploration of how colleagues, partner organisations or management might feel uncomfortable or anxious in response to exchanges with Alice.

Developing a curiosity through reflection supported practitioners in exploring their emotional responses to working with Alice. This in turn enabled them to develop strategies that would help Alice enable positive change.

Conclusion

Using curiosity driven by a psychologically informed approach supports reflective and person-centred approaches in adult safeguarding and homelessness. We have illustrated how holding frameworks of reference that enable a curious stance together with professional judgement can inform our work throughout the cycle of assessment, intervention and evaluation that characterises effective practice with both individuals and other professionals. The insight and related self-reflection that such benign enquiry affords supports the development of explorative questioning (DOH 2018, p.7). This approach can achieve most where it supports the individual through a consistent and containing relationship. As such, effective use of psychologically informed approaches within health and social care contexts, including adult safeguarding and homelessness, has the potential to inform both policy and practice. It can also crucially help us think about the unconscious processes that often prevent practitioners, services and organisations from applying established principles to practice.

The response to an individual sleeping rough is only partly driven by that person's direct communications about their situation, their actual appearance and their behaviour. The response, by professionals as well as other people in a community, is also inevitably impacted by culturally and politically driven preconceptions and biases. Enabling best practice therefore needs to include approaches and systems that support a psychologically informed, reflective and curious approach. Such an approach depends upon a wider universal understanding of human needs, including relationships, containment and attachment (Reid 2018), that can permeate the systemic preconceptions and biases our society has about those who experience rough sleeping and homelessness.

Chapter 5

Health, Homelessness and Housing Supply

Susan Harrison

Introduction

Homelessness means not having a home. Although rough sleeping is the most visible type of homelessness, you can also be described as homeless if your housing is unsuitable or you do not have the right to stay where you are. Government data released in November 2020 revealed 268,385 long-term empty homes in England, a rise of 42,000 on the previous year, and the biggest rise since records began (MHCLG 2020g). There are many different ways of defining homelessness and of determining what is an empty or underoccupied home, but it's a fact that there are many houses that are empty and not accessible to those in housing need (Dorling 2014).

Every week in England and Wales some 15 people who are homeless, or who were previously homeless, die, and many die early, not in old age but in their middle years (ONS 2020). In the same period Scotland had a higher homeless death rate when compared to England and Wales, with a rate of 52.2 per million population aged 15–74 compared to 18.0 in England and 14.3 in Wales (National Records of Scotland 2021). How this happens in one of the richest countries in the world, with a surfeit of housing and accessible and free health services, is not a mystery. It is because of the values, policies and practices of successive governments. Regional and national housing, welfare and immigration strategies have created a context in which access to housing is often limited and unaffordable.

At the same time as access to housing has become more difficult, successive governments have also developed policies and practices to protect people's right to live in safety, free from abuse and neglect. Approaches to safeguarding adults seek to prevent harm and reduce risk. This chapter examines how scarce and unaffordable housing, the health consequences of homelessness, and safeguarding adult policies and practice interact.

Is Safeguarding Personal or Systemic in the Context of Homelessness?

People and agencies who lobby housing policy-makers often talk about us all being one, two or three pay cheques away from homelessness. It is a way of describing how we may all be at risk of homelessness. But the reality is more complicated. In a blog for the London School of Economics, Susan Fitzpatrick asks, 'do such "inclusive" narratives distract from deeper structural and other causes that may be identifiable, and possibly also preventable, should the political will be found?' (Fitzpatrick 2017). In a paper with Glen Bramley (Bramley and Fitzpatrick 2018), she analyses three large-scale UK surveys. Using a critical realist perspective, the authors ask questions about the distribution of homelessness and the interplay between individual, social support and structural factors. In their analysis, they develop a series of vignettes of individuals at higher than average risk of homelessness and simulate the effect of various key changes in life and societal variables. While this approach cannot be used to infer absolute causality, the authors assert that it does suggest that:

> in the UK at least, homelessness is not randomly distributed across the population, but rather the odds of experiencing it are systematically structured around a set of identifiable individual, social and structural factors, most of which, it should be emphasized, are outside the control of those directly affected. (Bramley and Fitzpatrick 2018, p.97)

Intersectionality is writ large as the research suggests that different experiences of exclusion come together to increase the likelihood of homelessness. Poverty, and childhood poverty in particular, is the major predictor of homelessness (Bramley and Fitzpatrick 2018).

For some of us the probability of homelessness is very high. Others of us have the privilege of protective factors that make it less likely that we would ever experience homelessness. We often witness a wilful disregard for the impact of the 'differentials between those of us who have the "capacity" to choose and those of us who, as a result of complex psycho-social process of traumatisation, have less capacity to choose [our lifestyle]' (Scanlon and Adlam 2019, p.40).

People who find themselves homeless or at risk of homelessness are individuals with life histories, skills, experiences and connections to families, friends and communities. They are citizens with human rights. Like everyone else, they want to choose how they live their lives as individuals and with others. But their experience is different to those who have had different life histories and find themselves safe and secure in their accommodation. If your housing is precarious or non-existent, this chapter will describe some of the ways in which your health is at risk in the UK today. When we are wilfully blind (Heffernan 2011) to the consequences of societal inequality that lead to some of us dying young, those who have experienced homelessness suffer most.

Listening to the Voices and Stories of People with Lived Experience

Prioritising your health needs is almost impossible when you lose your home, or your housing becomes precarious. Dealing with losing employment, losing your income and then finding yourself without benefits may already have placed overwhelming demand on your resilience. Navigating the complexity of how health services are organised and delivered is daunting at the best of times. You try to hold things together as best you can, but looking after your health may take a back seat.

People who experience homelessness are able and willing to give voice to their experience. So too are the many charities and enterprises that campaign for transformation in our nation's housing policies. Social media has helped to amplify these voices.

The Bureau of Investigative Journalism describe themselves as holding power to account through collaborative, investigative reporting. They partner with 'reporters, technologists and members of the public in order to tell important stories across the UK' (Bureau of Investigative Journalism 2019). Since 2018 they have been collecting and publishing accounts of the experiences of people who have lived and died on the UK's streets, focusing on the stories of people who died while homeless. Their 'Dying Homeless Project' won several awards, and the archive of the records of individual stories of people who died homeless is now held by the Museum of Homelessness (Museum of Homelessness 2020). The Museum of Homelessness webpages remember and honour people who died homeless, and the very personal memorial accounts serve to support the campaign so that further deaths may be prevented (Museum of Homelessness 2020). The brief accounts on these webpages often report the chronic health conditions that people lived with and which may have contributed to an untimely death.

In 2018 and 2019 *The Guardian* newspaper through its Guardian Cities features ran a series called 'The Empty Doorway' (Hattenstone and Lavelle 2019). Journalists Simon Hattenstone and Daniel Lavelle told the stories of many individuals who had been homeless and died. Other commentators, novelists and politicians published articles in this series calling for policy and practice change. Maeve McClenaghan, closely associated with the Bureau of Investigative Journalism, has recently published a detailed and vivid account of many personal stories of individuals who, isolated and alienated by government policies, became homeless (McClenaghan 2020).

McClenaghan recalls the work of the US statistician Abraham Wald in the Second World War. He and his colleagues were tasked to examine the bullet holes on fighter jets returning safely from combat. The hope was that bolstering the planes' armour differently would reduce casualties. Having set about the task, Wald rapidly realised that the data that was not available was the pattern of bullet holes on the planes that had not returned. McClenaghan (2020) uses this analogy to illustrate the importance of understanding the stories of those who sadly didn't survive homelessness. Reviewing the stories of the many lives cut short, she concludes that it is poverty and inequality that drives homelessness. She makes a passionate call for a reversal of the 'decimating austerity cuts of the past decade' (McClenaghan 2020, p.331).

Health, Housing and Inequalities – Globally and Nationally

The World Health Organization and its member states are committed to a set of key principles, including these statements:

> Health is a state of complete physical, mental, and social well-being and not merely the absence of disease or infirmity.

> The enjoyment of the highest attainable standard of health is one of the fundamental rights of every human being without distinction of race, religion, political belief, economic or social condition.

> *(World Health Organization 2021)*

Sir Michael Marmot over several decades has drawn our attention to the social determinants of health and wellbeing (Marmot 2020). In 2008 the World Health Organization Commission on the Social Determinants of Health (CSDH) published their final report (World Health Organization 2021). They 'affirmed that social injustice was killing on a grand scale', with a toxic combination of 'poor social policies and programmes, unfair economic arrangements, and bad politics being responsible for producing and reinforcing health inequalities' (Marmot and Bell 2012, p.S4).

When we review what happens to people who experience homelessness in the UK, we too must affirm that the social injustice that restricts access to housing contributes to death on a grand scale. The Office for National Statistics carried out a review of the deaths of homeless people registered between 2013 and 2019 (ONS 2019a). These statements are a selection from their 2019 statistical bulletin (ONS 2019a):

- There were an estimated 778 deaths of homeless people in England and Wales registered in 2019. This is the highest number of estimated deaths since the time series began in 2013.

- Almost two in five deaths of homeless people were related to drug poisoning in 2019.

- Suicides among homeless people increased by 30.2% in one year, from 86 estimated deaths in 2018 (11.8% of the total number), to 112 estimated deaths in 2019 (14.4% of the total number).

- Most of the deaths in 2019 were among men (687 estimated deaths among men; 91 among women).

- Among homeless people, the mean age at death was 45.9 years for males and 43.4 years for females in 2019; in the general population of England and Wales, the mean age at death was 76.1 years for men and 80.9 years for women. This represents 30 years of life lost by men, 37 years lost by women compared to the general population.

- London and the North West had the highest numbers of deaths in 2019, with 144 (18.5% of the total number) and 126 (16.2% of the total number) estimated deaths of homeless people respectively.

The ONS acknowledges that records of death are often incomplete and that there are methodological challenges and technical difficulties in gathering, analysing and presenting the complicated reality of the lives and deaths of people who were variably defined as homeless. They conclude that 'the method used provides a robust but conservative estimate, so the real numbers may still be higher' (ONS 2019a, p.3). Other studies, for example the 2012 Crisis study *Homelessness Kills* (Thomas 2012) and the Scottish Government's *Health and Homelessness in Scotland* (2018), confirm the key finding that if you have experienced homelessness, your life chances are compromised, and you are likely to die early.

Common misperceptions about people who are homeless might lead us to imagine that people who are homeless die because of substance misuse, including overdoses. Drug- and alcohol-related poisoning are a significant cause of death among people who are homeless. However, analysis of records reveals a more nuanced picture. In one study the top three underlying causes of death in the homeless group were cardiovascular (including strokes and heart disease), cancer and respiratory disease (Aldridge *et al.* 2019).

The researchers analysed hospital admission records and mortality data for people attending 17 specialist integrated homeless health and care (SIHHC) schemes between November 2013 and November 2016. They compared their results to a sample of people living in areas of high social deprivation. They collected data on 3882 hospital admissions of homeless people that were linked to 600 deaths. They identified that 'nearly one in three homeless deaths were due to causes amenable to timely and effective health care' and concluded that 'the high burden of amenable deaths highlights the extreme health harms of homelessness and the need for greater emphasis on prevention of homelessness and early healthcare interventions' (Aldridge *et al.* 2019, p.3).

Protocols and Guidance

Public Health England (PHE) has produced guidance and e-learning on the health needs of people who are homeless, in their 'All Our Health' documents (Public Health England 2019). The National Institute for Health and Care Excellence (NICE) brings together evidence on health, drugs and technologies, public health, social care, and health care management and commissioning. During 2020 the Department of Health and Social Care in England asked NICE to develop guidance on integrated health and care for people who are homeless through being roofless. PHE worked with NICE to scope the development of the guidelines. The proposed guidelines will also be used to develop NICE quality standards for integrated health and care for people who are homeless. This work is due to be completed in March 2022 (NICE 2021). This approach has been welcomed by homeless health practitioners and advocates and will build on the work of others such as the *Homeless and Inclusion Health Standards for Commissioners and Service Providers* published by Pathway and the Faculty for Homelessness and Inclusion Health (Pathway 2018).

Our Vision for London (2019), a joint statement from the Mayor of London, the NHS, PHE and London Councils, has a chapter on improving the health of homeless people. It highlights the reality that homeless people in London have some of the worst health and shortest lives of all adults. Its ambition is that 'no rough sleepers die on the street, no one is discharged from hospital to the street and there is equal and fair access to healthcare for those who are homeless' (Mayor of London *et al.* 2019, p.46). It commits to action. NHS England has a programme of work that promotes improving access and outcomes to health services for Inclusion Health groups, including people who are homeless (NHS England n.d.). Their webpages gather a range of evidence of services and approaches that promote access to health care for people who are homeless, such as approaches to encouraging GP registration and attendance.

In March 2020, the King's Fund published *Delivering Health and Care for People Who Sleep Rough: Going Above and Beyond* (Cream *et al.* 2020). The researchers looked in detail at four case studies, exploring how they delivered effective health and care services to people sleeping rough. The report describes many of the barriers that people who are homeless might experience when needing to access services. They then identify key principles that support localities to develop better approaches. They set out their challenge as follows:

> We think that any area can make progress if it
> takes steps to find and engage people sleeping rough;
> builds and supports its workforce to go above and beyond existing service limitations;
> prioritises relationships;
> tailors the local response to people sleeping rough; and
> uses the full power of commissioning.
>
> *(Cream et al. 2020, p.13)*

Mr A

In 2011 I was commissioned by the Lambeth Safeguarding Adults Board (LSAB) to review the circumstances that led to the death of a man who was living on the street, a man known by the pseudonym of Mr A (Lambeth Safeguarding Adults Partnership Board (LSAPB) 2012). The task of reviewing involves pulling together an amalgamated chronology of events. Integration of paper records revealed much about the fragmentation in Mr A's life. This is his story. It bears retelling as a poignant example of the injustices that arise when an individual's health needs and housing needs are ignored and neglected.

Mr A was born in Pakistan, lived in Afghanistan, and moved to the United Kingdom in the 1970s. He was employed as a bricklayer for several years. A month before his 64th birthday, Mr A was found dead at his rough sleeping site in a small, sheltered alleyway in South London. He had been sleeping there for some months. When he died, there had been severe cold weather for some days. Mr A was found to have died from pulmonary oedema, pneumonia and hypertensive heart and kidney disease. Untreated hypertension contributed to his untimely death. As heart and kidney damage was identified in the post-mortem examination, he had probably suffered from hypertension for some time.

Mr A also had a serious mental illness, schizophrenia. He was known to consume high levels of alcohol and to neglect his own wellbeing and safety. For extended periods of time Mr A's case was open to statutory mental health services, both health and social care. Yet at the time of his death, they were no longer involved, having discharged him from their care.

Whilst the circumstances of Mr A's death are shocking, it is also important to acknowledge that he had lived many years with an untreated mental illness that would have caused him constant and intrusive psychological distress. Failure to address this meant that amongst many other lost opportunities for wellbeing and a fuller life, he lost the opportunity to have his hypertension diagnosed. Averting the sad outcome of heart and kidney disease would have depended on treating his mental illness sufficiently for him to be able to engage with hypertension treatment (LSAPB 2012).

Safeguarding Adults Reviews

The circumstances that led Mr A to live and die on the street are sadly not uncommon. In 2019 Martineau *et al.* published an analysis of 14 Safeguarding Adults Reviews (SARs) where homelessness was a factor. These investigated the circumstances of 16 adults, seven of whom had experienced rough sleeping. The report identifies the following health needs in the SARs reviewed:

> Incidence of ill health, learning disability, and substance misuse across the 16 cases was as follows:
>
> Long-term mental health problem: 10
> Chronic physical ill health: 10
> Substance (including alcohol) misuse: 9
> Suspected or diagnosed learning disability: 5.
>
> *(Martineau et al. 2019, p.11)*

In reviewing the health and housing needs of the individuals who were the subject of the SARs, the authors adopted the term 'multiple exclusion homelessness' to reflect that homelessness includes health and welfare concerns. The report explores the themes addressed in the individual SARs, including how the individual's health needs were assessed and recorded and then how agencies collaborated or failed to collaborate to recognise and address physical, mental health and substance use needs (Martineau *et al.* 2019).

A common theme in many of these SARs, and in the case of Mr A, were the challenges that arise when someone who is homeless appears to be self-neglecting. People who neglect their hygiene, who don't eat and drink regularly, whose health is deteriorating, who surround themselves with items and possessions they can't discard regardless of material value, whose bodies or living areas may be infested, may be experiencing mental health distress that leads to self-neglect. Individuals in these circumstances may refuse services – either assertively and directly, or by withdrawing so that their needs are less visible to others. How people who self-neglect come to that experience often has a long history reaching back to adverse childhood experiences and other experiences of trauma over the course of their lives (Brown 2019).

The Local Government Association's publication *Adult Safeguarding and Homelessness: A Briefing on Positive Practice* combines the findings and recommendations from individual reviews into a model of and for effective practice. The model has four domains:

>Direct practice with individuals
>
>The multi-agency, multidisciplinary team around the person
>
>The organisational network that surrounds the team that is working with the person
>
>Governance issues.
>
> (Preston-Shoot 2020a)

Individual practice alone is unlikely to be sufficient to support people who are homeless and at risk of neglect and abuse. Practitioners must remain mindful of the context which supports their work.

Covid-19 Response: Authorities, Advocates and Academics

As the Covid-19 pandemic started to take hold in England, campaigners took urgent action to highlight the immediate risks to people sleeping rough or in night shelters, those sleeping in communal settings such as hostels, and people at risk of moving to the street. A third sector homeless health charity, Pathway, and their Faculty for Homeless and Inclusion Health, held their annual conference in March 2020. The conference was attended by people with lived experience of homelessness, frontline practitioners, managers and policy-makers. Dr Al Story, Founder and Clinical Lead of the pan-London Find & Treat Service based out of University College London Hospitals, and Professor Andrew Hayward, Professor of Infectious Disease Epidemiology and Inclusion Health Research, led a plenary session focusing on the likely impact of the pandemic on people who live on the street. They proposed a model of assessing and triaging need and vulnerability to Covid-19 of people living on the street, and then cohorting according to need and vulnerability (The City View 2020). This approach was adopted widely across England.

Reviewing the outcomes from this approach, Lewer *et al.* (2020) have described the population, the risks they faced and the actions national and regional government took. They describe the different types of homelessness including the most precarious arrangements

– 35,000 people living in hostels and another 10,000 sleeping outside or in night shelters in England. They reference the well-known statistics that reveal high mortality rates – around 3–6 times that of the general population – and the consequent increased risk to severe Covid-19.

The English government established a £3.2m funding programme to provide temporary self-contained accommodation for some 15,000 people – the *Everyone In* programme. It was announced in a ministerial letter on 27 March 2020 (MHCLG and Hall 2020). Dormitory night shelters usually run by faith and community groups were closed. NHS England reconfigured their leadership arrangements for homeless health with additional senior capacity. The English regions followed suit with a new focus on the needs of homeless people, working closely with key partners in PHE and local authorities.

An outcome of this work is that almost immediately some 15,000 people who had formerly been living on the street moved into accommodation. Over the course of the pandemic this number has risen to 33,000 (National Audit Office 2021). People were housed in hotels and other temporary accommodation with food and support.

Health and care partners responded by offering primary care and substance misuse services, in-reaching to the hotels. Public health practitioners offered bespoke guidance on infection prevention and control procedures in hotels and hostels. In London, a team at University College London Hospital offered detailed health needs assessments as a way of assessing and responding to individual need, but also to evidence the population level needs. Local authorities responded by supporting people to move on into more settled accommodation in social housing and in the private rented sector. The incidence of Covid-19 amongst people who slept rough and those who were in hostels and hotels was low during the first wave of the pandemic. Some 4% of this population contracted the virus and the number of deaths was low (Lewer *et al.* 2020). By comparison, when Doctors without Borders tested 818 homeless people in France in late June and early July 2020, they found that 40% had been infected with the virus (Medicins Sans Frontiers 2020).

Groundswell are a third sector agency who exist 'to enable people who have experience of homelessness to create solutions and move themselves out of homelessness – to the benefit of our whole society'. During the pandemic they were commissioned by NHS England to undertake research to understand the impacts of Covid-19 on the lives of people experiencing homelessness. They have published a rich archive of accounts, stories and experiences (Groundswell 2021). This process has supported health and homelessness commissioners and providers to better shape services to the lived experience of people who are experiencing homelessness. It provides a repository of important insights that has the potential to support further service development. People talk openly about their fear and worry about the pandemic, but also their concerns and scepticism about the offer of hotel accommodation; many years of mistrust and disappointment present in the moment of facing new decisions. Some people were separated from friends and acquaintances who ended up in different hotels; loneliness during the first lockdown was felt keenly as it was by all. Regular food, a safe en-suite room with clean linen, housing support and health outreach were immediately life enhancing. Preparing to think about the future and move on to more settled accommodation presented new concerns and challenges.

As this work developed in Spring 2020, there was much optimism and a great deal of commentary in the professional press and social media about how homelessness was being addressed very effectively, when the political will and resources were available. At a stroke rough sleeping was virtually wiped out. Through the *Everyone In* programme, England had come close to implementing a comprehensive Housing First approach – housing and wrap-around care for all who slept rough (see Chapters 8 and 13).

The detail of how the *Everyone In* programme worked has been reviewed by the National Audit Office. Their report supports parliamentary scrutiny of the government's response to the pandemic. It is a 'facts only' account focused on the period March 2020 to November 2020 (National Audit Office 2021). A further value for money report will follow later.

London's Response

The Healthy London Partnership (HLP) – part of the NHS in London, supporting partnership work across the capital – was tasked to establish a Coronavirus Response Cell to coordinate London's NHS response to *Everyone In*. HLP established the Homeless Health Operations Centre, a cross-system approach to support the London Covid-19 Homeless Health Response Cell. Implementing the approach set out by Dr Story and Professor Hayward, and working in partnership with the Greater London Authority and the Rough Sleepers' Strategy Group convened by London Councils, they supported housing partners to offer a triage and cohorting process to move people into one of three types of managed accommodation:

- COVID CARE: Providing higher level of medical support for those presenting with symptoms.
- COVID PROTECT: Providing support and care for people who are most at risk.
- COVID PREVENT: Providing support and care for those who are less vulnerable.

HLP supported the NHS in London to organise and deliver clinical services directly into accommodation, including outreach Covid-19 testing. London's Clinical Advisory Group agreed standards of care. Homeless people who had been admitted to hospital were able to be discharged directly to hotels set up through the *Everyone In* initiative. Throughout the pandemic, homeless individuals who were found to be positive were supported to self-isolate in dedicated provision with nursing and medical support. The wide range of homeless health work that London has delivered during 2020 can be reviewed on the HLP website (HLP 2021).

One of the important health interventions delivered during the pandemic was the offer of individual comprehensive health needs assessments. Clinicians at the Find & Treat service at University College London Hospital developed an assessment tool – the Mini Covid-19 Homeless Rapid Integrated Screening Protocol (CHRISP) (HLP 2020). CHRISP assessments were offered to residents in the hotels set up by the Greater London Authority, and then more broadly. This has enabled individuals with health needs to have those needs identified and referrals to other health services to take place. The assessments have also served to identify the kinds of housing support and tenancy sustainment options that people might need as they moved on into more settled accommodation. Aggregated data from just under 1500 assessments have also served to provide a picture of the needs in the population. Unsurprisingly, given what is already known about the health needs of homeless people, that aggregated picture confirms high levels of health needs among people who were living on the street at the time the pandemic took hold in London.[1] The range and combinations of need also strongly suggest care and support needs that would require social services support.

Building Back Better? Or Not?

Over time some of the initial optimism waned. While many people were supported to move from hotels and other temporary accommodation to more settled living arrangements, this was not possible for all. A particular challenge are the needs of non-UK citizens. Before the pandemic, at any given time close to half of the people living on London's streets were not UK-born (GLA 2020). Those without rights to reside in the UK have very restricted rights to work or housing. Indeed, often their rights to remain living in the UK are also limited (see Chapter 9).

The resourcing that came with the *Everyone In* programme was fixed, and as the months went by, new people facing economic hardship became homeless and moved onto the street. In anticipation of winter 2020/2021, the government again funded a range of temporary accommodation to enable people to come in off the street. However, there were significant concerns that this would not be sufficient. The optimism that street homelessness could be eradicated, and individual and population health could be protected, faded.

The third sector charity St Mungo's published *Housing and Health: Working Together to Respond to Rough Sleeping during Covid-19* (St Mungo's 2021). Their recommendations include a call to secure the successes of the *Everyone In* programme by ensuring that sufficient, safe accommodation is available for all who need it. Their recommendations include a special focus on people who have no recourse to public funds (see Chapter 9). Their report includes strong recommendations for continuing to build and maintain health, care and housing partnerships at the local and national level, supporting the delivery of integrated services at a population level, and to individuals.

Homelessness is a consequence of poverty and housing policy that makes affordable accessible housing very scarce. If we are homeless, we are not safe. The impact of the *Everyone In* programme was that many people were offered some safety through the provision of self-contained accommodation and three meals a day. It was a systemic safeguarding

---

1   Correspondence in 2020 between University College London Centre for Inclusion Health and the Healthy London Partnership.

intervention that has enabled many people to find a different path forwards for their lives.

This begs a question then about the role of safeguarding in relation to people who live on the street or are in very precarious accommodation. In 2017 when working in the HLP I was involved in listening to the views of people who were homeless about whether and how safeguarding approaches were helpful to them. I spoke directly to people who had formerly been homeless and commissioned two focus groups with people who were very close to street living. Again and again people told us that the most helpful interventions would be safe and secure housing and steady income preferably through work, but also through welfare benefits. These listening exercises were carried out to support the development of London-wide protocols, but regrettably they were not published. While there are many first-person accounts of individual experiences of homelessness, it has not proved possible to find any published accounts of the views of people who are homeless about safeguarding policy and practice. This could be an area for important further work.

Can We Make a Difference through What We've Learned?

As the Covid-19 pandemic took hold in early 2020, a powerful coalition of people and agencies pulled together. They were supported by emergency planning governance arrangements but also included a high degree of self-organising in response to the emerging Covid disaster. The government funded hotel accommodation and food for all people sleeping rough – a systemic safeguarding intervention that has enabled many people to be immediately safer. The former barriers that required people to evidence their immigration status, their local connection to a housing authority and their ordinary residence that establishes who funds their social care were all suspended. In the London context this enabled a smooth pathway into accommodation, regardless of which of London's 33 local authorities you slept rough in. The integrated humanitarian response swept away protocols which often serve to exclude homeless people.

Third sector charities in partnership with academic institutions have described and quantified the costs of homelessness. This includes the cost of homelessness services as well as the cost of opportunities and health forgone in the lives of people who experience homelessness

(GLA 2020).[2] In the early stages of the pandemic much of that resource was harnessed to offer temporary accommodation and then move-on accommodation for people who had slept rough. Justice was not withheld by many stakeholders who were eager to offer more than just charity.

Conclusion

In the words of Augustine of Hippo, 'Charity is no substitute for justice withheld.' The just, humanitarian endeavour that enabled everyone to come in from the street was a powerful systemic intervention that helped many people to be safer. Making this policy approach sustainable is the challenge we face. Citing the World Health Organization: 'social injustice [is] killing on a grand scale, with a toxic combination of "poor social policies and programmes, unfair economic arrangements, and bad politics"… [This is] responsible for producing and reinforcing health inequalities' (Marmot and Bell 2012, p.S4). People without homes are diminished, they have poorer health, they die young. Our focus on health and homelessness is not to help homeless people to be healthier. It is to call out the injustices of our housing, welfare and immigration policies and to demand fundamental reform. Reformed policies will lead to better outcomes for people in housing need, and so for us all.

---

2 See for example www.crisis.org.uk/ending-homelessness/homelessness-knowledge-hub/cost-of-homelessness.

Chapter 6

Understanding Assessments and Protection Planning Duties for Adults Experiencing Homelessness

Fiona Bateman and Bruno Ornelas

Introduction

Much is already known about what works in safeguarding and homelessness. The challenge now is for system leaders and practitioners to effect changes in practice so assessments are coordinated across sector disciplines and geographical boundaries. This chapter considers how housing, health and social care legislation supports practitioners to exercise their professional judgement in ways which incorporate relevant laws, ethics and rights-based thinking. Practitioners often report how narrow interpretations of the legal framework provide only short-term relief to caseloads, resulting instead in escalation of individual needs, increased harm and reliance on reactive services with practitioners often operating in crisis mode (Preston-Shoot *et al.* 2020).

This chapter, therefore, focuses on legal literacy by exploring the six key safeguarding principles (Department of Health and Social Care (DHSC) 2020) as a foundation to assist practitioners to understand and apply fundamental legal principles of equality and human rights when working alongside people experiencing homelessness. It explains how the choice of wording within legislation is deliberate, demonstrating how the law is designed to facilitate good multi-disciplinary practice. For example, regarding eligibility for statutory needs assessment and safeguarding duties, the former is triggered by the 'appearance of care and support needs' (s.9 Care Act 2014) and the latter criteria of 'reasonable cause to suspect' which, as Mr Justice Scott Baker confirmed in R (S) v Swindon BC and Wiltshire CC [2001], 'is quite low. This is hardly surprising as their obligation is to investigate.' We explore how practical application of a wider understanding of the legal duties to assess can support effective preventative safeguarding practice. Finally, we underscore the importance of fact-finding and analysing key information to help make sense of the person's unique circumstances and demonstrate, through case studies, how awareness of all relevant statutory duties supports effective protection planning.

The six key safeguarding principles in practice

Empowerment: This requires an understanding of how the person's care and support needs impact on their ability to make a decision, stay involved in safeguarding or associated assessment processes and ultimately protect themselves. The person's views and desired outcomes should be understood in context and remain central to any assessment or safeguarding process.

There is a legal duty, under ss.67–68 Care Act 2014, to consider whether a person requires an independent advocate to actively be involved in an assessment or a safeguarding enquiry. Practitioners must also consider whether it is necessary to make reasonable adjustments to ensure that those with protected characteristics[1] are not discriminated against as a result of organisational barriers (e.g. rigid operational service criteria, appointment times) which could prevent them securing support. This legal duty is reinforced within the definition of organisational abuse, namely mistreatment, neglect or poor professional practice as a result of the structure, policies, processes and practices within an organisation that violate the person's dignity, resulting in lack of respect for their human rights (DHSC 2020, para.14.17).

Practitioners may also have a duty (under s.149 Equality Act 2010) to actively consider vulnerability. The Supreme Court in Hotak v LB Southwark [2015] confirmed the test for vulnerability is a practical and contextual one taking into account all relevant features, including a person's ability to find accommodation or, if they cannot find it, to deal with the lack of it.

---

1 'Protected characteristics' are defined within s.4 Equality Act 2010 as age, disability, gender reassignment, marriage and partnership, pregnancy and maternity, race, religion or belief, sex and sexual orientation.

Prevention: Anyone carrying out public functions, including assessment and safeguarding roles, owes a positive duty under the Human Rights Act 1998, Article 2 (the right to life) and Article 3 (the prohibition on torture, inhuman or degrading treatment), to respond appropriately where there is a real and imminent risk. Likewise, there is a duty to prevent social care needs escalating (under s.2 Care Act 2014) and to prevent homelessness (s.195 Housing Act 1996). This requires local authorities proactively to provide advice and support before eligibility thresholds for services are crossed. This means all practitioners should consider the risks of abuse and neglect faced by anyone at risk of rough sleeping and factor this into their decisions regarding any powers they may have to prevent harm. Practitioners must take into account everything they can reasonably be expected to know and record why they believed any action or inaction was within legal powers, necessary in the circumstances and proportionate to the risk.

Proportionality: Statutory assessments are not expected to be undertaken in isolation, or only to tackle the presenting crisis. Instead, statutory guidance encourages inquisitive enquiry, including reviewing the case history so any presenting safeguarding issues are understood in context. The s.42 safeguarding enquiry duty can provide an effective mechanism to enable multi-agency risk management,[2] but there may be other models locally, including those which make use of assertive outreach or trusted assessors. Local safeguarding information-sharing protocols set out expectations regarding inter-agency communication, providing practitioners with a road map for how and when to share necessary information to proportionately manage risk.

Protection: Assessment and safeguarding duties are triggered on a deliberately low threshold of the appearance of need. There is a clear expectation that safeguarding concerns should not be triaged on the basis of the setting where care is provided, the person's mental capacity or the availability of services to meet likely need. The 'Making Safeguarding Personal' approach does not mean partner agencies are absolved of statutory or professional responsibilities if an adult says they do not

---

2   There are a range of resources for those working with risk to support implementation of the Making Safeguarding Personal principles available at: www.local.gov.uk/our-support/our-improvement-offer/care-and-health-improvement/making-safeguarding-personal/working-risk; and section 42 enquiries at: www.local.gov.uk/making-decisions-duty-carry-out-safeguarding-adults-enquiries.

want an enquiry to be undertaken under s.42 Care Act (Cooper 2019). Rather, careful consideration is needed of the circumstances and any inability or external pressure that impacts on the person's ability to understand the risk or freely decide to refuse support. Practitioners should remain mindful of relevant enduring duties to assess (s.11(2) Care Act 2014) if there is a risk of abuse and neglect, irrespective of the person's capacity to refuse support.

Partnership: There are explicit legal duties for 'relevant partners', defined by s.6(7) Care Act 2014, to co-operate to fulfil assessment and safeguarding functions. Refusal is only permitted if the partner can evidence in writing that the request is incompatible with their own duties or would have adverse effects on their own functions. Statutory bodies may also owe reciprocal legislative duties to refer for assessments, for example where a person may require social care support on discharge from hospital, is threatened with homelessness, the person is young (16–17) or a care leaver (18–24), or would leave custody without accommodation.[3]

Accountability: The public law nature of assessment and safeguarding decisions means practitioners, especially those working within 'relevant partner' agencies, must ensure they have met their professional duties in a lawful, reasonable and fair way. For example, deciding someone is medically fit for hospital discharge is a clinical decision, but deciding whether a hospital discharge is safe is a separate public law decision. As such, practitioners (and ultimately hospital managers) should ensure they have complied with their statutory duties to consider if the adult has an appearance of need on discharge and make necessary referrals in line with duties set out within the Care and Support (Discharge of Hospital Patients) Regulations 2014 to ensure essential care is available. Cornes *et al.* (2019) argue that failure to do so could constitute neglect, requiring an organisational safeguarding response. Public law principles of fairness are reinforced by specific legal duties for statutory bodies to provide assessment findings and reasons for their decisions in writing, for example under s.203(4) Housing Act 1996 and s.12(3) Care Act 2014.

---

3   More information about reciprocal duties to refer in respect of Housing Act duties is set out within s.213B Housing Act 1996 and Chapter 4 of the Homelessness Code of Guidance available at: www.gov.uk/guidance/homelessness-code-of-guidance-for-local-authorities/chapter-4-the-duty-to-refer-cases-in-england-to-housing-authorities.

The Importance of Fact-Finding in Assessments and Safeguarding

Negotiating statutory initial screening processes to access adult social care assessments and safeguarding processes can be difficult for people experiencing homelessness. Past trauma or negative experiences can impact on a person's ability to identify risk or access support. Repeating one's personal history for numerous assessment processes can be frustrating, intimidating or traumatic, particularly for those who have already experienced exclusion from statutory support. It can be difficult for social care practitioners to conceptualise how the causes and effects of homelessness may prevent a person from achieving activities of daily living or to keep themselves safe (Martineau *et al.* 2019). In addition, variations in judging what is dangerous and what is safe are in practice often difficult to reconcile. Such divergences can result in high-conflict situations across the workforce. Cornes *et al.* (2018, p.7) identified that high-conflict situations could lead to 'poor interim outcomes for service users with increased expenditure upstream, including repeat admissions to hospital and the need for potentially more costly care and rehabilitation packages'. Bridging this gap, by finding a common language across sectors, reduces conflict and brings about more collegiate ways of working. This includes understanding and interpreting key information for the purposes of making sense of the person's unique circumstances and situation.

The Safeguarding Toolkit was developed to assist practitioners to objectively set out the person's needs and ability to protect themselves from harm; a collaboration between academic researchers, legal experts and statutory and non-statutory practitioners (Ornelas *et al.* 2019). It is framed by three key questions, which act as sub-headings, designed to aid fact-finding and decision-making with the adult experiencing multiple exclusion homelessness. No solitary practitioner is expected to have all the required expertise; instead what is needed is sufficient knowledge to trigger active assessment in line with the relevant statutory eligibility criteria for those at risk of homelessness appearing to need social care or necessary care/treatment for physical or mental health concerns. To do this successfully requires legal acumen, not least to navigate the numerous statutory guidelines that govern practice across these areas. This also requires investigative skills as people experiencing homelessness may unfortunately feel stigmatised by their circumstances, may be reluctant to acknowledge the full extent of their needs or may have become reliant on informal support and relationships which remain important to them, even if their carer is unable to safely provide necessary care or is abusive (Preston-Shoot 2020a).

To protect against normalisation of risk or, conversely, a lack of professional curiosity, it is important to objectively document the person's relevant past history (or 'chronology') and their current ability to manage daily living and health needs. Succinctly detailing previous interventions (including hospital admissions, periods of homelessness and causes/triggers for each period of rough sleeping and any neglect/abuse suffered during those periods) can help to identify previously unmet needs or, conversely, the person's own strengths and abilities which will help form a protection plan. Likewise, ascertaining previous addresses and involvement with statutory services may be key to identifying which agencies should be involved. This can also help to identify if organisations' 'usual practice' could impede effective engagement so that access to advocacy and 'reasonable adjustments' form part of the protection plan.

Have You Somewhere Safe to Sleep Tonight, Can You Get the Help You Need to Stay Safe?

Interventions should concentrate on getting the right response at the earliest opportunity. Key to this is that practitioners, particularly housing and social care professionals, GPs, district nurses and carers, know how to:

- Identify signs of abuse, detailed at para.14.16 Care and Support guidance (DHSC 2020).

- Understand how to conduct a safe enquiry.

- Report and secure preventative support for an adult at risk.

All practitioners therefore require time and support to navigate the various assessment and treatment pathways and identify suitable provision.

'Safeguarding is everyone's business', meaning that practitioners must act on concerns whenever there is reasonable cause to suspect the person has care and support needs, is at risk of abuse or neglect and is unable to protect themselves.[4] This begins by actively gathering infor-

---

4   Section 42(1) Care Act established that a duty to carry out a safeguarding enquiry arises whenever there is reasonable cause for concern that the three criteria are met, namely that the person:
    is an adult with care and support needs
    is at risk of or experiencing abuse or neglect (including self-neglect)
    as a result of their needs, is unable to protect themselves.

mation, including considering long-term risk to people experiencing homelessness. This is often overlooked whilst practitioners focus on the most pressing problem or crisis.

The s.42 duty requires wider consideration to promote the person's 'wellbeing'. This is defined within s.1 Care Act 2014, obliging any practitioner carrying out assessment, care planning, review or safeguarding to promote the person's personal dignity and the control they have over day-to-day life, and consider the suitability of their living conditions, emotional, social and economic wellbeing and their contribution to society. Similarly, any action required to remove or reduce risk should apply the statutory guidance which is designed to protect a person's human rights. Such personalisation of safeguarding, care or treatment plans was one of the most frequently mentioned aspects of good practice identified by Preston-Shoot *et al.* (2020). Conversely, failure to adhere to these obligations can result in poor outcomes, as it did in the Mr Yi case study below, triggering the duty to conduct a Safeguarding Adult Review (SAR).

Case Study: Mr Yi

Proper consideration of Mr Yi's personal dignity, living conditions and control over his life should have resulted in effective, cost-neutral interventions preventing harm. In 2015 Mr Yi lived in sheltered accommodation following approximately four years' rough sleeping. He had been assessed as unable to manage the activities of daily living, but his capacity to manage financial affairs and adhere to service expectations of 'engagement' with house rules wasn't considered.

He was evicted due to rent arrears. Staff responsible for initiating those proceedings should have been aware, because of findings in previous Court proceedings, that Mr Yi lacked capacity to defend possession proceedings and so should have ensured he was represented at the hearing. Failure to do so likely breached his human rights protected by article 6 (right to a fair hearing) and article 8 (right to respect of private, family life, home and correspondence). Had proper consideration occurred, Council staff or the Court would have identified a need to appoint a deputy (under s.16 of the Mental Capacity Act 2005) to assist Mr Yi in managing his financial affairs, ensuring his rent was paid and preventing further periods of homelessness. Similarly, between 2016 and 2017 he was assessed by health, housing and social care departments across three London boroughs. Again a decision was made to evict him from emergency homeless accommodation because, having suffered a subdural haemorrhage which further limited his cognitive abilities, he was deemed 'not independent' and hostel staff believed his behaviour could place him or others at risk of harm in that environment. Throughout this period staff assessing Mr Yi did so without regard to the duty to promote his wellbeing or the requirement they 'consider carefully the suitability of accommodation by reference to the applicant's particular medical and or physical needs and to any social considerations relating to the applicant and his or her household' (Homelessness Code of Guidance 2018b, paras.17.4–17.6).

(Adapted from Bateman 2019)

Do You Understand Why I Am Concerned about the Level of Risk to Your Wellbeing?

This question should assist practitioners to explore with the person their understanding of the risks they face, how these impact on their immediate and longer-term wellbeing and their plan/wishes to address these. Prior to asking the question, practitioners should clearly set out what they believe the risks are, how likely those risks are to impact on the person's wellbeing and safety, and whether any statutory assessment duties are relevant. Supporting a person prepare for a conversation will enable their better involvement in an assessment or safeguarding process. Practitioners must make necessary adjustments to help people think through their needs and the outcomes they want to achieve, so that any follow-on conversations are not treated as routine.

Section 1(3) Mental Capacity Act 2005 requires we consider how to maximise the person's involvement, because this is proven to result in the best outcome and because 'the freedom to choose for oneself is a part of what it means to be a human being' (Heart of England v JB [2014], p.1). Our legal system has built-in checks to protect against arbitrary use by public bodies of their powers against individuals. So, ask – what is the right time and place to hold that conversation, and who else should be involved to help the person understand and weigh up the information?

Where there are concerns that the person may have substantial difficulty being involved then advocacy should be explored. Advocacy is still underused in safeguarding enquiries.[5] This absence not only undermines the legality of any subsequent decision (R (SG) v Haringey LBC [2015]), it is a contributory factor in numerous SAR reports.

It will also be crucial to understand whether the person can execute any decision. Analyses of SARs frequently note that:

> faced with unwise decisions practitioners sometimes relied on an assumption the individual was making a 'lifestyle choice' rather than exploring whether the adult had difficulties carrying out decisions even when they had stated the intention to do so. It was easy to overestimate comprehension and overall cognitive ability, particularly in the presence of verbal skills. (Preston-Shoot *et al.* 2020a, p.116)

The case study of 'Steve' provides a practical example of this and how thorough evaluation of the risks associated with homelessness and exclusion enables effective interventions that uphold 'Making Safeguarding Personal' principles.

Understanding Needs and Risk in Context

Case Study: Steve

Steve had significant physical disabilities (requiring a wheelchair to mobilise), substance misuse and mental health concerns. Whilst rough sleeping he was unable to meet his basic care needs or get around without informal support from peers. Steve recognised this was often exploitative, reporting their behaviour had triggered his most recent eviction and that he had been compelled to provide his bank card to them in payment for their support. Large withdrawals of cash without his consent had followed.

Even within a hostel setting, staff reported that he couldn't safely access facilities to meet his personal care or nutritional needs. They raised concerns that Steve was often tearful and withdrawn, 'refusing to come out of his room, stating he can't go on any longer'. Social care staff were initially reluctant to assess Steve, concerned that they did not have legal powers to require residential or nursing

---

5   In 2019–2020 NHS Digital (2020) reported that only 87% of individuals assessed as lacking capacity received support from friends, family or an advocate despite this being a statutory duty.

care providers to accommodate someone with 'his type of need', and were not aware of any that would admit someone with a chronic substance misuse issue. They reported that Steve refused support, as he stated that he wouldn't move into a care home.

Hostel staff, aware they did not have suitable facilities to provide the level of care Steve required, but unwilling to withdraw support and make him homeless, referred him for advocacy support. His advocate subsequently secured agreement from local authority staff that he was in urgent need of accommodation where care and support services could be provided by reminding practitioners of the flexibility afforded services to provide ordinary accommodation through social care legislation if it is necessary to meet the person's need for care and support (s.8 Care Act 2014), and that this was not dependent on Steve first successfully completing a detox or rehabilitation programme.

For Steve, his housing and social care needs were interdependent. His substance misuse raised additional areas of risk and capacity that needed careful, multi-agency exploration. That investigation was led, with advice from the multi-agency team which now included mental health practitioners, by the advocate. This explored with Steve the risks posed, including his refusal to participate in statutory assessments. Agreement was reached with Steve that assessments could be conducted away from statutory offices, at a time best for him. During the discussions Steve raised concerns that when he moved into his own home, his peers would likely expect to use the home and his income and this wasn't what he wanted but didn't know how to prevent it.

The multi-agency team identified a wheelchair-accessible property and provided re-ablement support to assist Steve in relearning skills and regaining his independence for personal care, cooking, etc. This also ensured staff could monitor and respond if concerns regarding 'cuckooing' emerged. A nearby pharmacy was identified which could provide medication to manage his substance misuse. He was also provided with an alarm which he could trigger discreetly if peers did put him under further pressure.

Two years on, he has a home and manages his health and substance misuse issues with very limited ongoing social care involvement. Health, housing and social care services jointly commissioned 'legal literacy' training and now routinely conduct assessments for people experiencing homelessness with assertive outreach and advocacy staff outside the office.

Given the nature of homelessness and increased risk that those exhibiting institutionalised behaviours are targeted by others looking to exploit their vulnerabilities, including to pursue organised criminal activity, practitioners should set out any indicators that give rise to suspicions that the adult's decision-making may be impaired by external coercion. As Steve's example shows, it is not lawful or even practical to ignore relationships or informal care arrangements that are important to the person simply because these give rise to safeguarding concerns.

If an adult experiencing homelessness has become dependent on informal support, practitioners should consider if the carer themselves poses a risk and the carer's capacity to understand caring obligations, as this will impact on any protection plan. 'Trudy's' experience below demonstrates how taking into account those risks early within the assessment and care planning processes facilitates good risk mitigation practice without having to employ paternalistic, overly risk averse practices often denounced by the Courts as the 'protection imperative'.

Case Study: Trudy

Trudy had, for many years, provided care for her adult disabled son. Workplace stress triggered a mental health crisis, aggravating trauma she experienced in early childhood. As a result she became unable to care for her son, her home or herself. She lost her property following debt proceedings initiated by the local authority, and her son moved into residential care under the guardianship of the local authority. Despite an initial finding of 'intentional homeless', she was provided with temporary accommodation in recognition of her vulnerability. Trudy, still angry at the local authority, refused to pay service charges and became street homeless, often sleeping nearby her son's placement. Staff involved in her son's care reported concerns that her behaviours undermined his placement. For many years Trudy had sporadic interactions with both statutory and non-statutory services, which were often managed in crisis mode.

Despite involvement from housing, adult social care, safeguarding, mental health and the police, there wasn't common agreement about Trudy's ability to make decisions. Many practitioners felt she was making 'unwise decisions' and that this limited their ability to offer support. An advocacy charity became involved when risks posed by Covid-19 meant she would need to be accommodated urgently. The advocate, working with statutory assessors, quickly established that, whilst she had no formal psychiatric diagnosis, she presented with symptoms of anxiety, depressed mood and emotional instability. A multi-agency capacity assessment found Trudy's intellectual function was high, but ability to retain and process information was limited by the loss of complex brain function inherent in complex trauma. Mental health practitioners offered advice to colleagues, aware that the impact of trauma can make it difficult to distinguish between unwise but capacitated choices and incapacitated beliefs, or what weight should be attached to the deeply held incapacitated beliefs, to ensure that any protection plan didn't unintentionally cause additional trauma by imposing support, even when this was deemed necessary to reduce risk.

The team around Trudy concluded that an application to the Court of Protection should be sought on the grounds that she lacked capacity to manage her finances, care and support needs and understanding where to live. She also lacked capacity to understand the restrictions and criminal sanctions imposed on public health grounds during the Covid-19 outbreak. Her failure to understand and comply with these placed her at risk, in terms of physical and verbal abuse from those fearful of her behaviours, and caused her increased anxiety as she had lost face-to-face contact with her son. Whilst the application was prepared, staff worked closely with Trudy to explain risks and offer opportunities for appropriate accommodation within an Extra Care facility, with additional behaviour management support for her care staff.

It is recognised that as time goes on, because of the potential for Trudy to recover capacity function in the long term if complex trauma treatments are successful, her care and support plan may decrease. Equally, the multi-agency team recognise this would not be possible without suitable accommodation and substantial support in the short to medium term. Now this is in place Trudy has commenced treatments and is regaining contact with her son.

What Help Do You Need Now to Protect You and How Should Partner Agencies Work Together?

This question should help the adult and practitioners agree on effective interventions to safeguard against abuse and neglect. Essentially practitioners should ask themselves not 'what does the law permit?' but rather, 'what do we want the outcome to be and how do we use our collective legal powers to get there?' To do this, practitioners will need to be receptive to constructive challenge across specialisms and sectors.

Practitioners regulated by professional bodies will be aware of their duties to raise safeguarding concerns, including duties to 'whistle blow'. Local escalation policies provide mechanisms to ensure that disputes are resolved quickly, so practitioners need to be confident to use these when necessary and have regard to explicit instructions within statutory guidance that it is dangerous and unproductive for disputes about funding responsibility to prevent or delay the provision of social care (DHSC 2020, para.19.11), health care (DHSC 2019, p.213) or homelessness support (MHCLG 2018b, paras.10.6, 10.14, 15.16).[6]

Protection Planning for People Experiencing Homelessness

Where a protection plan is required under s.42(2) Care Act 2014, it must meet relevant partners' statutory duties either by reducing risk of harm or by demonstrating further action would be unnecessary or a disproportionate interference with the person's human rights. The Care Act 2014 does not provide powers to compel an adult at risk to accept support, but powers under other social care legislation (e.g. Mental Health Act 1983) or partner agencies' legal powers should be explored, particularly if imminent or significant risk remains. We saw this applied at a macro level in 2020 in response to the risk from Covid-19, where public health legal powers backed up by criminal sanctions (and, for those who lacked capacity, authorisation by the Court of Protection) were mobilised to accommodate all rough sleepers.

For people experiencing homelessness most protection plans will have to consider the provision of accommodation to protect the

---

6   Most inter-agency safeguarding policies and the ADASS guidance on cross boundaries safeguarding arrangements (available at www.adass.org.uk/media/5414/adass-guidance-inter-authority-safeguarding-arrangements-june-2016.pdf, p.18) reiterate it is dangerous and unproductive to delay support because of funding disputes.

adult at risk. Utilising s.42 duties can reduce professional conflict on responsibility, because the duty to make enquiries does not depend on concepts of 'ordinary residence', but arise if the adult is physically present in the area. Indeed a person's 'ordinary residence' or 'local connection' is only relevant after the person has been assessed as eligible for accommodation and/or social care support. It does not prevent a local authority from carrying out an assessment of need, providing advice and information, or providing services to prevent homelessness or an escalation of needs. Nor does it prevent urgent provision as there are powers to provide this under s.19(3) Care Act 2014 and s.188 Housing Act 1996. If, during the course of an assessment or safeguarding enquiry, it transpires the person has a stronger local connection or is ordinarily resident elsewhere, that local authority can then be required, under s.42(2) Care Act 2014, to set out the action they will take to meet their relevant duties.

Practitioners must also focus on what type of accommodation is 'suitable' (see Chapter 8). From a safeguarding perspective this should provide case-specific analysis of whether the support can obviate the vulnerability. Likewise, the needs of carers should form part of any assessment in line with s.10 Care Act 2014. In R (Daly and others, formerly MA) v DWP [2016] the Supreme Court confirmed there are legal powers to provide discretionary payments for extra bedrooms if this is necessary. Practicalities as to how the person will access other necessary support or medical treatment are crucial, so the location of accommodation is part of the care planning and housing duty. This was confirmed by the Supreme Court in Nzolameso v City of Westminster [2015]. SAR reports demonstrate how crucial it is to share information about known safeguarding risks (especially of fire or suicidal ideation) with accommodation providers so that they can work with the person and commissioners of care to reduce this risk. Again, the law does not just permit this sharing of information; s.25(3) Care Act 2014 requires it.

In many cases the local authority may have a continued duty to provide relief and advice and assistance under the Housing Act 1996. Anyone leading on the development of a protection plan should ask housing practitioners to consider whether they can assist with information, advice or practical support to help secure suitable accommodation. In the Mr Yi SAR practitioners understood that conducting assessments without relevant information, advocacy support for Mr Yi and proper consideration of his ability to manage essential tasks resulted in two evictions onto the streets. Many concluded this was organisational abuse and a breach of Mr Yi's human rights, but equally many practitioners feared this could leave hostel staff (or indeed hospital staff) providing accommodation-based care beyond their capabilities (Bateman 2019).

Those ineligible for provision under the Housing Act 1996, either because they lack capacity to apply or because they are subject to immigration control – for example, a condition of their entry into the UK is they have 'no recourse to public funds' – could still be entitled to accommodation-based support. A local authority or clinical commissioning group[7] should provide accommodation when the person has a need to be 'looked after':

> Looking after means doing something for the person being cared for which he cannot or should not be expected to do for himself: it might be household tasks which an old person can no longer perform or can only perform with great difficulty; it might be protection from risks which a mentally disabled person cannot perceive; it might be personal care, such as feeding, washing or toileting. This is not an exhaustive list. The provision of medical care is expressly excluded... [I]f there is a present need for some sort of care, then obviously the authorities must be empowered to intervene before it becomes a great deal worse. (Lady Hale in R (M) v Slough [2008] UKHL 52, p.33)

The act of 'looking after' should be of such a nature that the individual would still require this intervention even if they were wealthy. In R (SG) v Haringey LBC [2015] the Court confirmed:

> in most cases the matter is best left to the good judgment and common sense of the local authority... [A]ccommodation-related care and attention means care and attention of a sort which is normally provided in the home or will be 'effectively useless' if the claimant has no home.

It is a well-established principle that the duty to assess under the Care Act 2014 is not targeted at any specific individual or sets of needs and configurations. Since the case of R v Bristol City Council ex parte Penfold [1998] the duty to assess is recognised as triggered at a low threshold, namely the 'appearance of' care and support needs. This means the

---

7   A clinical commissioning group is responsible for commissioning care (sometimes jointly with the local authority) if someone is eligible for aftercare under s.117 Mental Health Act 1983 or for NHS Continuing Health Care.

focus of a social care assessment is not to determine if the adult will require services, but whether the adult is unable to achieve daily living tasks and what impact that inability has on the person's wellbeing. Once this is understood the local authority is expected to work with the adult to carefully consider how best to meet those needs.

Corner *et al.* (2021) identified the importance of, but also inherent challenges in, identifying care and support needs in the context of adults experiencing multiple disadvantage, including a lack of understanding of severe substance misuse and complex trauma, and their impact on the adult's ability to achieve in the ten domains of the Care and Support (Eligibility Criteria) Regulations 2015. Supplementary guidance such as the 'Multiple Needs Care Act Toolkit' (Ornelas *et al.* 2018) provides ways in which practitioners can best describe care and support needs for adults experiencing a range of issues as a result of homelessness.

If an adult is eligible for social care, there is wide scope (s.8 Care Act 2014) to enable innovative commissioning, even on a spot purchase basis, as seen in the response to the risks posed to rough sleepers by Covid-19.

The Courts have warned, for example in R (Barrett) v Westminster City Council [2015], that particular care should be given before seeking to discharge any duties by signposting to alternative support (e.g. universal services or charitable provision) to ensure that they actually exist and have resources to meet the adult's needs, including any risk of abuse and neglect. Practitioners will be required to evidence that decision-making was reasonable and considered wider legal obligations or statutory powers. The request for each area to audit homeless health services[8] could act as a catalyst enabling practitioners across the statutory, charity and third sectors to develop professional networks so that a culture develops of 'no wrong front door'.

Conclusion

Professionals who work with people who are experiencing homelessness need to be prepared to exercise their professional judgement in ways which incorporate the relevant laws, ethics and rights-based

---

8   The request for local audits of homeless health provision was supported by the Department of Health and Public Health England and should be undertaken with reference to a toolkit devised by Homeless Link available at: www.homeless.org.uk/sites/default/files/site-attachments/Homeless%20Health%20Needs%20Audit%20toolkit_0.pdf.

thinking. A good starting point is knowing what the legal rules are, so that practitioners feel well equipped to apply the scope of different (sometimes overlapping) legal frameworks relevant to the people they are working with. Preston-Shoot (2020a) reminds us that opportunities for joint working become missed opportunities when professional boundaries become barriers, or when interpretations of policy and the legal rules are narrowed or misunderstood. Practitioners should also be mindful that reliance on the more bureaucratic aspects of operational legal responsibility alone may not be enough, and should endeavour to interpret and apply the legal rules in ways that are underpinned by human rights principles and professional ethics, a significant aspect of safeguarding decisions given their public law nature.

Part 2

BEST EVIDENCE FOR MULTI-AGENCY AND MULTI-DISCIPLINARY TEAMS AROUND THE PERSON

Chapter 7

Working Together to Safeguard Individuals at Risk: Bristol Creative Solutions Board – A Case Study

Kate Spreadbury and Paul England

Introduction

An estimated 58,000 people per year in the UK experience multiple disadvantages, a combination of homelessness, substance misuse, mental health issues, abuse and offending. The estimated cost of public spending on this group is between £1.1bn and £2.1bn a year, largely because people are not able to access services to meet needs and prevent crises, becoming frequent users of emergency services or detainees in the criminal justice system (Making Every Adult Matter (MEAM) 2020). People who experience multiple disadvantage may neglect their own health and wellbeing and be subject to abuse and exploitation, but are often 'invisible' to services, not considered either in multi-agency forums or as meeting the criteria for the Care Act 2014 section 42 duty (Martineau *et al.* 2019). Using adult safeguarding to prevent and respond to risk in this group 'is a complex area of safeguarding adults' practice, that requires an integrated whole system response but, perhaps, has been consigned to the "too difficult" box for a long time' (Preston-Shoot 2020a, p.4).

There are challenges to creating an integrated whole system response for people who are multiply disadvantaged. Spending cuts to public sector budgets have challenged the post Care Act 2014 aspirations of a more person-centred and flexible system (Cornes *et al.* 2018; Dobson

2019a), and increased siloed and defensive working practices (Clark *et al.* 2015), leaving people with multiple needs either continuously passed between or excluded from mainstream services (Simcock and Machin 2019). Commissioning practices which focus on one problem and reward defined outcomes lead to fragmented uncoordinated services which expect to work with only one aspect of the person's life within rigid criteria (Miller and Appleton 2015; Dobson 2019a). Commissioned services are required, for example, to have a strong emphasis on 'recovery' within a certain timescale. What recovery means, and who is perceived to be able to achieve this, can influence whether a person with complex needs is able to access supported housing, mental health services and/or addiction services.

> The individual is on the fringes and has usually not engaged with services for a while or may not have any experience of engaging with services. They are often afraid of professionals… They may need help from a wide range of services, mental health, physical health, addiction, police, probation. It is a real slog to try to engage with all those agencies. It feels like groundhog day telling the same story again and again. (Expert by experience)

Initiatives to address multiple disadvantage, including the national charity coalition 'Making Every Adult Matter' (see MEAM 2019, 2020) and the National Lottery Community Funded 'Fulfilling Lives',[1] support local areas in England to develop new ways of working, promoting better collaboration and coordination between services, co-production of solutions with frontline workers and service users, and shared learning, and ultimately changing the way that the systems around people experiencing multiple disadvantage work. Outside of these initiatives commissioning organisations have also created local multi-agency partnerships to support individuals and change cultures, most notably the Plymouth Creative Solutions Forum (Plymouth City Council 2019a), established in 2016. The people referred to these partnerships are often at risk of abuse and/or (self-)neglect and have met the criteria for the s.42 (Care Act 2014) safeguarding enquiry duty. A range of approaches will have already been tried and failed, and a creative multi-agency response which can consider 'flexing' the systems around the person must now be considered. Each partnership arrangement reflects the

---

1 See www.fulfillinglivesevaluation.org.

local context in which it operates but also has common features which promote successful outcomes in terms of individual and system change.

This chapter explores some of these common features via a case study, the Bristol Creative Solutions Board (BCSB), established in August 2019. We include the voices of people with lived experience and others who contribute to the BCSB. Good practice points on promoting successful outcomes in terms of individual and system change are included throughout.

Bristol Creative Solutions Board

The BCSB was initiated by Golden Key in partnership with the local authority, Bristol City Council.

> We had already identified the need for a different way of working, the need for a different response to people who 'fall through the cracks' and become the subjects of Safeguarding Adults Reviews. We wanted to do something but had little in the way of time resource to create this. (Local authority senior representative)

Golden Key is a partnership between statutory services, commissioners, the voluntary sector and people with lived experience across Bristol. It focuses on people who experience a mixture of homelessness, long-term mental health problems, dependency on drugs or alcohol and offending behaviour, and is in year six of an eight-year project funded by the National Lottery Community Fund as part of the 'Fulfilling Lives' programme.[2] Ten BCSB stakeholders engaged in reflective discussions about their experiences of the Board with one of the authors who also attended a BCSB meeting. The second author is the independent facilitator of the Board.

The purpose of the BCSB is to:

- meet to discuss individuals at risk where current responses are not working and to creatively plan and action a different solution, with the person at the centre
- use this learning to inform how the whole system might need to change and flex to deliver better outcomes for all.

Core members of the BCSB are senior managers from the local

---

2   See www.fulfillinglivesevaluation.org.

authority (including housing, social care and adult safeguarding), the police and clinical commissioning group, together with representatives from mental health (including drug and alcohol services) and acute trusts, primary care, probation and third sector organisations. Board members need to be able to direct staff and resources, and honour the commitments made at the Board. Experts by experience are also core members of the Board as the vision is that lived experience informs system change.

The Board meets for two hours. Practitioners working with the individual briefly present the solutions that they have identified through the referral process that may 'unstick' or change the way in which organisations are working with the person. The meeting then divides into small groups to reflect on these proposals: what changes need to happen? How can the system 'flex' or change to interrupt the identified cycle that the individual and workers are trapped within? How can (further) abuse and neglect be prevented? The meeting reconvenes and plans the actions to be taken. These actions are sometimes initiated during the meeting with a break to allow emails to be sent or for discussion between colleagues. The second part of the meeting reflects on the learning about the system. What are we learning about ourselves, our organisations, and the way we work together? What small changes can we make? What could the likely long-term impact be? (See O'Connor and McDermott 1997.)

How People Are Referred to the Board

The referral process ensures that only those for whom no other solution can be found are presented to the Board. Those most at risk, complex and 'stuck' can produce learning that generates other avenues for those in a similar situation. The people referred usually experience a cyclical pattern of agencies engaging and withdrawing, compounding the person's risk of abuse, exploitation and self-neglect. Figure 7.1 illustrates that the system around Peter (see case study later in the chapter) repeats, failing to engage or support Peter in a cycle of self-neglect, potential exploitation and deteriorating mental and physical health.

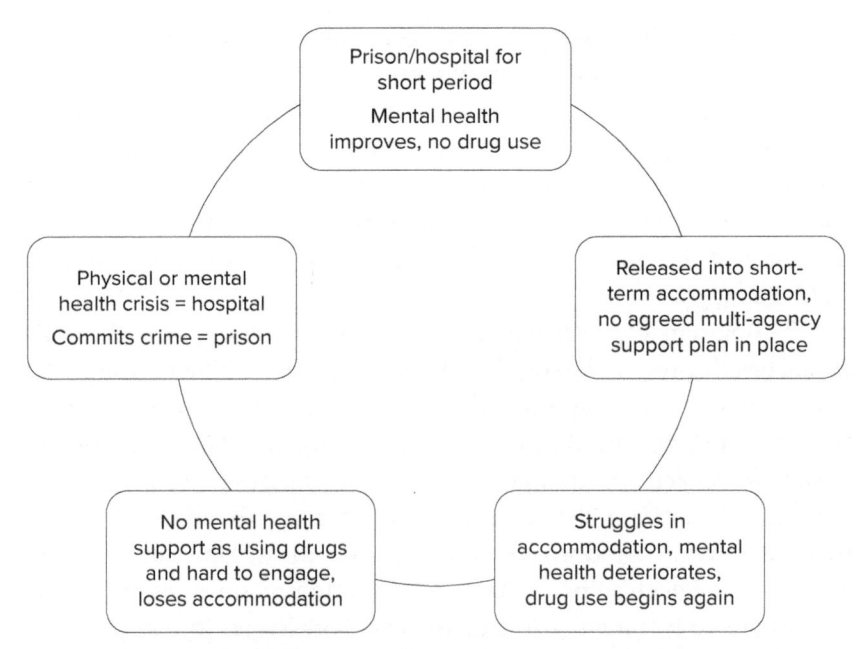

```
                    ┌─────────────────┐
                    │ Prison/hospital │
                    │  for short      │
                    │   period        │
                    │ Mental health   │
                    │ improves, no    │
                    │ drug use        │
                    └─────────────────┘
   ┌──────────────┐                      ┌──────────────────┐
   │ Physical or  │                      │ Released into    │
   │ mental health│                      │ short-term       │
   │ crisis =     │                      │ accommodation,   │
   │ hospital     │                      │ no agreed multi- │
   │ Commits crime│                      │ agency support   │
   │ = prison     │                      │ plan in place    │
   └──────────────┘                      └──────────────────┘
   ┌──────────────┐                      ┌──────────────────┐
   │ No mental    │                      │ Struggles in     │
   │ health       │                      │ accommodation,   │
   │ support as   │                      │ mental health    │
   │ using drugs  │                      │ deteriorates,    │
   │ and hard to  │                      │ drug use begins  │
   │ engage, loses│                      │ again            │
   │ accommodation│                      │                  │
   └──────────────┘                      └──────────────────┘
```

Figure 7.1 How the system around Peter repeats the same cycle

The BCSB referral process is *person-centred*, *strengths-based* and *multi-agency*, which encourages respectful and empathetic consideration, bespoke solutions and the engagement of all organisations. Before individuals are referred to the BCSB, consent is sought from the person, and they are invited and supported to contribute as much as they wish to the process.

Gaining consent can take time; people may be mistrustful of agencies or feel there is no point in the process. The referrer must have a relationship with the person which will enable them to consider their reservations and the degree to which they want to participate. Participation, at whatever level the person chooses, emphasises the BCSB's respectful and empowering approach. But for some, participation can feel disempowering and has the potential to awaken previous trauma; participation cannot be insisted upon. The six principles of adult safeguarding and Making Safeguarding Personal (DHSC 2020) are reflected in the referral process. The multi-agency-informed referral is coordinated by a Golden Key project worker and includes three key elements, as follows.

The first is *person-centred*. The perspective of the person begins the written referral information:

Who am I? What am I like when things are going well? Preferred name (nicknames), age, gender, ethnicity, spirituality, interests, characteristics, skills, strengths, resources, things I am proud of. What would other people say about me? Preferences, phrases or language that are helpful when you talk about me. Where and how do I spend most of my time? How do I prefer to be contacted? People/agencies that are currently supporting me or who I have contact with. What is going well at the moment? Other things that it is important for people to know about me.

Each referral is accompanied by a psychological formulation, ideally undertaken with the person themselves, or, whilst they might consent to the work being undertaken, they may not wish to be involved. Formulations can also involve everyone who knows the person from different organisations, which provides multiple perspectives. The formulation draws on a systems perspective, identifying the cycles, barriers and blocks in the person's system, and takes account of the socio-political context of their experiences. It enables the 'team' to understand how a person's history might be triggering or driving behaviours or motivation – allowing a whole team shared perspective. The BCSB expert by experience supports the focus on the person's perspective in the meeting.

The approach is *strengths-based* (Colomina and Pereira 2019). Practitioners and the organisations they work for can be 'burnt out' and downhearted about people who have spent years 'in the system' and about the system itself (Raman 2019; Watson *et al.* 2019). Focusing on strengths does not mean ignoring challenges, but builds a stronger basis for change, and a different perspective for discussion. Language such as 'will not engage' or 'makes unwise choices' is replaced with constructive considerations about how to engage and how to make sense of the life circumstances the person is in, and how systemic factors that create barriers to change can be 'flexed' in order to support that change.

All agencies contribute to the *multi-agency* referral. Contrasting perspectives from all agencies who work with the person create a fuller picture and support the involvement of all Board members to understand the role their organisation can play, and improve interaction at the Board. If agencies identify a risk of, or actual, abuse or (self-)neglect, a referral is made to the local authority for consideration of the s.42 Care Act 2014 safeguarding enquiry duty.

The referral process is part of getting people to think differently about the situation and can also be an intervention in itself. During the referral process there may be an indication that there is another approach to try before coming to the BCSB; for example, multi-agency discussion identified that a person met the criteria for higher support, which opened the door to the possibility of detox; for another, the services involved were working well together and decided to offer more flexible drug and alcohol service appointments to build their engagement with the person. These proportionate responses pay attention to the person's self-determination, support them in making choices and can address or prevent further abuse and/or self-neglect. Connections with other organisations and learning from the referral process can be translated into day-to-day multi-agency working. The Board focuses on people subject to cyclical patterns, lack of collaborative working, blocks to progression and cumulative risks.

Good Practice Point
Making a referral into a 'creative solutions' process is the beginning of generating a different way of understanding a person and their situation. Make sure the referral gives people permission to think differently; the information sought, language used and multi-agency discussion prior to the Board will all start to create 'solutions', even before the case has reached the Board.

The Centrality of Systems Thinking to the BCSB

We also began to create a common understanding about 'system flex' – and thinking systemically. It would be hard for someone to join who is not able to engage in systemic thinking now. The Board needs people who are willing to flex and do not block, a cultural behaviour that austerity has forced us into; we attempt to preserve limited resources by building walls reinforced by rigid ideas about eligibility. (BCSB member)

The BCSB gives organisations a place to work collaboratively on system change, using complex adaptive systems theory and methodology to inform the design and delivery of its work. A complex adaptive system can be defined as a system that has multiple parts (agents) that are able to change and alter as a result of learning from the system itself and its experiences (Zimmerman *et al.* 2001). As a system the BCSB can, by embracing these various agents, open itself to change as it attempts to learn from itself and its context (Antonacopoulou and Chiva 2007).

The rationale for this approach was both to inform the way in which the Board works and to facilitate an approach that might impact the wider organisational systems and embed a way of working that would be sustainable in the long term. Non-linear or 'systemic thinking' is essential to this approach; linear or cause-and-effect thinking may meet short-term aims but have negative consequences in the future, for both individuals and/or the systems around them. As Senge (1993, p.57) reminds us, 'today's problems come from yesterday's solutions'.

System change focuses on creating change at a structural level by seeking to influence the ways in which organisations work together. Complex system change draws attention to what needs to happen at a micro-level to create 'ripples' of change in a system (Wheatley 1999). These changes can be far more responsive to the environment and allow more iterative and emergent change to happen, creating opportunities for organisations to truly work together to address the needs and risks experienced by multiply disadvantaged people. Using this approach, some key features were built into how the Board developed their work:

- Making sure the people who can facilitate system change are connected directly or indirectly to the Board.

- Developing relationships and partnerships as foundations for building a robust system that was able to challenge itself and its work in order to learn and adapt (Wheatley 1999).

- Making time to allow the Board to reflect, understand and learn from its work in real time that will translate into positive change both within the Board and across wider local systems that the Board influences or is connected to (Senge 1993; Sinek 2017).

These three key features are explored below.

Getting the Right People to Facilitate System Flex and Change into the Room

Golden Key undertook considerable preparatory work with organisations, talking with partners across statutory and non-statutory services.

Co-ownership and the goodwill of the local authority were important in terms of the influence and impact of the Board. Organisations generally welcomed the approach, and, after exploring good practice elsewhere, met with the support of an independent facilitator to consider what arrangements would work locally for a Bristol 'Creative Solutions' Board. Partners wanted an independent Chair, supporting the BCSB to function as a partnership, with an emphasis on the role of the Chair in promoting challenge to organisational thinking, flexibility and reflection. In addition to the Chair, an independent facilitator was considered useful in supporting the learning and reflective elements of the BCSB using a systemic thinking approach.

Getting agreement from all organisations about how sensitive information should be shared was initially difficult. Some BCSB members came to the meeting early in order to read the information as it could not be transmitted to them securely. These issues have now been resolved, but getting agreements about data-sharing can present hurdles to successful partnership working (Richardson and Asthana 2006).

At first the senior leaders invited to the Board were seen as the creators of solutions as well as the enablers to unblocking the systems that would allow change to take place. However, the Board quickly realised that frontline workers and people with 'lived experience' were usually best-placed to understand and construct the solutions to the complex problems that the Board were faced with solving. Consequently, the Board members in senior positions began to understand their role as the facilitators of making the system adapt in order to let frontline workers get on with what they needed to do (Marquet 2015).

Good Practice Points

Relying solely on the input of senior managers or of practitioners misses the importance of embracing the whole system (Stacey 2011), not only across organisational boundaries but up and down organisational hierarchies. A key learning for the Board was the importance of representation from all parts of the system to contribute to individual and systemic change, and including people with lived experience.

The Board reflects on its own process at every meeting and retains the flexibility to change how it works; this models the

> process of change for individuals and systems. The Board has developed through collaborative thinking between partners and is not 'owned' by one organisation, although Golden Key workers play a crucial role in supporting the Board.

Experts by experience are core members of the BCSB; they are members of Independent Futures, which acts as an advisory group to Golden Key and other organisations. An expert by experience offers a perspective that professionals cannot achieve, increasing understanding and empathy toward the person and their circumstances.

> We are still learning how we can make the process truly person-centred. People get set up to fail with unrealistic expectations on them. But in reality, professionals do not have all this time to know the person. We need to get people around the person, with the time, in the room. (Expert by experience)

Practitioners from all the organisations working with the person also attend the Board to present potential solutions and the identified blocks to moving forward. Presenting to senior managers can be intimidating; staff may have had negative experiences of doing so in the past. There are considerable power differences between the representatives of different parts of the system: senior managers on the Board are likely to be qualified 'professionals' with statutory roles and use professional jargon. Preparation before the BCSB is key for practitioners:

> We make sure they know they are leading on what the solutions will be. It is about listening to them and being confident they will not be asked why what they tried did not work in the past, we are where we are and they are the experts in the room. (Golden Key project coordinator)

Prior to the meeting experts by experience meet with the practitioner presenting the case to talk about the person, to get their perspective and identify the issues that may need to be highlighted.

> People with lived experiences sit in a room with professionals; this takes confidence. To have a purpose and make a difference the person needs to have training that promotes confidence, professionalism, communication skills, public speaking, presenting an idea. To be a contributor

builds up confidence; if you are present but cannot contribute you are left feeling humiliated, less confident, demoralised, you can be damaged. Without communication skills you cannot contribute those valuable perspectives. (Expert by experience)

> **Good Practice Point**
> It is important to be aware of power differentials within the room, and to consider how all individuals and organisations can be prepared to give their essential contributions with confidence.

Developing Relationships and Partnerships

People around the table did not initially know each other and you cannot switch that on, you need to build trust. (BCSB Chair)

The importance of developing good working relationships within organisations has been long acknowledged as important (Mullins 2002; Gallos 2006). In complex systems, relationships need to go beyond the superficial level of 'knowing about' others to understanding how others think, what makes them engage positively with their role in the organisation and what their aspirations are. As these relational bonds form and strengthen they create robust links in teams that work for the common good of the systems they reside in (Wheatley 1996; Sinek 2017).

When working across organisational boundaries, these relationships become even more important (Clark *et al.* 2015). Conscious effort and time has been given in the meetings to building and nurturing relationships, and members were encouraged to continue to develop these outside the meetings. Building workplace relationships often focuses on professional identity in the system, which excludes those who do not have a professional identity such as experts by experience. The BCSB used various approaches to build relationships between all stakeholders; for example, members were asked to introduce themselves without divulging their professional title. This allowed the forming of relationships that moved away from hierarchical positions within the system. At subsequent meetings time has been given to the simple act of asking people 'how they are' rather than 'what they have been doing'. These simple, micro-level changes in approach begin to create a caring system that models an approach to how the Board works internally that extends to how it works externally.

A dynamic partnership willing to be flexible, to break organisational norms, is supported through the creation of genuine and trusting relationships:

> Creating partnerships can be hard; it's about influence without managerial authority. When the partnership is strong you can do things under the auspices of partnership that you cannot do as an organisation. (BCSB Chair)

What can be done as a partnership transcends organisational policies and procedures; an individual organisation may not have the manoeuvrability to make a decision, but a partnership can. For example, one organisation had strong nationally agreed policies on not supporting people to sleep rough but to use the options on offer. These policies were one of the barriers to engaging with Sally, a woman sleeping in a tent who tried to avoid any interaction with the public or agencies. Sally appeared to be severely self-neglecting but it seemed impossible to speak with her or gain her trust. The Board discussed offering her equipment to ensure her physical wellbeing whilst living in the tent and potentially to make a connection with her. As the organisation trying to engage her could not do this, the Board as a partnership made the decision to do so, overriding one organisation's policies.

As the BCSB partnership has developed, the meetings have become a place where assumptions and preconceptions about organisations, individuals and possibilities can be challenged. Professional curiosity (Thacker *et al.* 2019) is promoted via challenge from members; ideas about 'lifestyle choice' or the normalisation of the risks people face are examined through the fresh eyes of partners on the Board. This 'cuts through' unhelpful thinking. The support of experts by experience is invaluable:

> [T]hey bring a realism to discussions and also challenge assumptions and stop the Board making paternalist decisions. Their presence was an inhibitor at first, say we offend or show our ignorance? But we have now formed trusting relationships with our experts too. (BCSB member)

Partnership creativity is also applied to the environment in which meetings are held. People were too comfortable sitting around a large table; this arrangement did not encourage thinking outside the usual boxes. The meeting now takes place in a room with tiered seating and no tables. Working in a virtual 'space' during the 2020/2021 Covid-19 pandemic opened up a different way of encouraging non-hierarchical creative thinking. Small rather than large groups are used to action plan so that everyone has time to consider potential creative solutions.

BSCB members agreed to attend meetings without deputising, to invest time in the development of different ways of working together. There are always competing priorities of equal importance and urgency; prioritising work that could have long-term benefits over immediate demands is challenging. However, Board members have found that prioritising the support for colleagues' BCSB work is rewarding: well-functioning systems understand the importance of interdependence which sometimes requires resourcing a system even when there is not an obvious direct benefit for that part of the system.

> **Good Practice Points**
> Planned time spent in developing trusting relationships is not wasted but valuable and can lead to effective partnerships based on trust which are able to be reflective, flexible and decisive.
>
> Stable membership is essential in developing trusting relationships, new ways of thinking and commitment to a genuine partnership.

Learning and Reflecting

Time is spent at each BCSB meeting focusing on learning about the systems they are working in, for example regarding the management of risk. The simple act of surfacing this, combined with the relationships that people have with other members of the Board, has begun to manifest itself in a greater appetite for risk that is managed in the system rather than being handed to any one individual or organisation (see below).

Board members apply the learning gained from reflecting on the systemic blocks and circumstances of the individuals presented at the Board. For example, adult social care would end their involvement if people had not engaged or had moved into a hospital or prison. Learning about the need for long-term involvement led the local authority social care Board member to change how cases were managed; people with long-term complex needs no longer go into a 'pool' or have their involvement shut down. It is now understood how much this practice can block the possibility of other organisations being supported to work with the person or the person experiencing consistency in the approach taken.

Above all the learning has been about what can be achieved through genuine collaboration:

> ...but the Board is relaxed, this is where we are. Board members are so signed up to the values and a lot comes down to the chairing, keeping everyone challenged and moving forward. I expected meetings to be bleak and they are not... Creativity can come from working at an optimistic level, not from being sad or depressed. A feeling of hopefulness can move you forward together with good heads. We have permission to be hopeful, which is not part of our working life. (Board members)

Good Practice Point
Make time to reflect on what has been learned from the individual case: what has been learned about the system, about how each organisation works and how we work together? Sharing these observations will spark reflections in others, and the resultant micro changes begin to effect wider changes in our partnerships.

Managing Risk

For any system to work effectively it needs to create a culture that reflects the aspirations of that system; the various parts of the system may have to make themselves vulnerable in order to achieve this end. In terms of safeguarding, the BCSB has had an impact regarding their approach to risk. The Board has begun to understand how, if individual organisations manage risk alone, it can often be passed around the system:

> For agencies there is a fear of opening the doors and getting swamped. It is easier to say yes if the support is coming from somewhere else. Managing this level of risk is scary – there is much fear. (Board member)

This tendency to 'hand off' risk can often be experienced by people as 'being passed from pillar to post'. When a complex system is working effectively, risk is held by the system, regardless of whether this system flows across organisational boundaries. Consequently, the person will experience service delivery as something that is consistent and committed to delivering a positive outcome. No matter how much emphasis is placed on a systemic approach to working across organisations, when under pressure most organisations migrate back to cultures that are predicated on hierarchical, linear, cause-and-effect structures (Zimmerman *et al.* 2001; Rumlet 2017). However, when personal relationships underpin the system, there is the opportunity for colleagues to genuinely support each other. Whilst a single organisation or individual may hold risk in a hierarchical structure or as a consequence of legal duty, the support that comes from the relationships formed in a complex system will assist in sharing this risk. Accountability can be held within the system and partners become accountable to each other as well as the service, and the person we are working for. Additionally, because accountability is shared by the system, holding others to account begins to shift to a desire to support those who are not fulfilling their role.

The Board uses various strategies to promote common understanding about the risks people face; creating a common language with which to discuss risk is essential (Local Government Association 2020b):

> [O]ften we have parallel conversations about risk but see risk in a different way; our concepts of risk and what is risky will be different. We think we have a shared language but we don't. (Board member)

The meeting uses a numbered risk matrix to enable more nuanced conversations about risk – 'why did you rate this risk as a five?' – and to expose different perspectives on the risk, promoting a shared understanding.

Case Study: Peter

Over time Peter's mental and physical health had declined. He experienced head injuries whilst incapacitated, has frequent infections and is vulnerable to assault or assaulting others in shared accommodation or on the street as he feels convinced others intend to harm him. Self-neglect is having a severe impact on his health and he is at high risk of physical abuse. Transitions into the community are unplanned or quickly fall apart as he struggles to keep appointments and fit in with the expectations of health, social care or housing agencies. Agencies tend to disengage when he refuses support.

Adult social care think he is not eligible for support under either s.9 or s.42 of the Care Act. He is viewed as intentionally homeless. Shortly before Peter's case was presented at the Board he was admitted to an acute hospital.

He wanted to be 'settled' but was very fearful of living in shared spaces, and this contributed to drug use and poor mental health. His perspective was shared along with other referral information and the blocks and repetitive cyclical patterns he was caught in (see Figure 7.1 earlier).

Solutions developed and agreed included:

- Assessment of care and support needs whilst Peter was in hospital with a preparatory session for assessing staff beforehand with the BCSB member.

- Identification of a housing solution — long-term individual accommodation with support, bypassing hostel or other group living situations. Flexibility in timescales to apply and agree accommodation as Peter was unable to meet the usual time parameters.

- Creation of a team around Peter whilst he was still in the hospital to support his transition into accommodation and begin the work to prevent and mitigate further self-neglect and the deterioration in his mental health that has led to abuse. The team was supported by a social worker, head injury practitioner and drug and alcohol worker. The mental health provider was willing to act as mentor to the team.

- Flexible appointments for Peter with the local drug and alcohol agency — he could attend during a 'morning' or 'afternoon' slot rather than at a set time which he was not able to manage.

Good Practice Point

Collaborative working underpinned by collective responsibility is supported by genuine relationships of respect and understanding between and within organisations. Creating a common language and understanding about risk supports collective management of risk.

The Future

Learning from the BCSB is being used to inform changes in how organisations work with each other and with people who experience multiple exclusion. This informs initiatives in Bristol, including the 'Change for Good' project (Golden Key 2020). This project will initially focus on those who have been housed in hotels during the Covid-19 pandemic but aims to extend its remit to redefine how organisations work with all those facing multiple complex needs. The Covid-19 pandemic has shed light on people who have previously been deemed 'hard to reach' or 'hard to engage', but are now being seen. The learning from the BCSB has particularly emphasised the need for consistency of relationship with the person and for agencies to commit to each other, 'sticking with each other' through the entirety of the person's journey.

Changing cultures takes time, is hard work and needs committed investment from all involved.

> [P]eople have brought back examples and actions from the BCSB and said to teams 'why don't we?' This is challenging and invigorating. Micro pockets of cultural change from micro events, driven by case studies which create the human stories. We get the energy to think – what can we do better? The leadership in the room says yes, and this supports practitioners to work together to find solutions. It's a different way to lead – let's look at this, what is within the realms of possibility, not sticking to criteria. (Board member)

Embedding new ways of working that span organisational boundaries and established ways of working means challenging current cultures, and the values and beliefs that underpin them (Yukl 2002; Rumlet 2017). 'System flex' and the different mindsets created by the BCSB can pave the way toward the desire for further sustainable change, such as through integrated commissioning to create solutions.

Acknowledgements

Many thanks to Aileen Edwards, Alison Comley, Alex Collins and everyone in the Golden Key partnership for their generous contributions to this chapter.

Chapter 8

Sustainable Housing

Imogen Blood

Introduction

The Care Act 2014 recognises that the suitability of a person's living accommodation is a core component of their wellbeing (DHSC 2020). Homelessness impacts significantly on mortality and morbidity, particularly in relation to infections, mental health, and cardiovascular and respiratory conditions (Aldridge *et al.* 2018). People who are sleeping on the streets are especially vulnerable to abuse and attack, which can result in physical injury, anxiety and trauma (Sanders and Albanese 2016). The stress and uncertainty of housing instability, including frequent moves and stays in temporary, insecure or unsafe accommodation, can also cause or exacerbate mental health conditions and trauma (Pattison and McCarthy 2020).

Decent housing is a fundamental need for everyone; but it is particularly important for those with histories of abuse or trauma, mental health and/or substance use issues, and physical or cognitive impairments. Without a safe and secure base, it can be very challenging, both practically and psychologically, for people to engage with treatment for addictions and physical and mental health conditions, especially where this might trigger, or actually necessitate, an individual to revisit past trauma. Housing alone may not be *sufficient* to initiate recovery and a sustainable exit from homelessness for those with multiple and complex needs, but it is certainly necessary.

Yet, as learning from Safeguarding Adults Reviews (SARs) highlights (Martineau *et al.* 2019; Preston-Shoot 2020b), people experiencing multiple needs in relation to their mental health, substance use and/or past offending often experience significant barriers to finding suitable accommodation. Examples of these barriers include: a lack of suitable supported accommodation (especially for those still drinking or using drugs, for those with impairments or high physical care needs, and for serious offenders), and evictions, abandonments or exclusions by housing providers.

The national context to these failings includes the acute shortage of decent, affordable housing (Robertson 2017) and substantial cuts to local authority funding over the past decade (Oakley and Bovill Rose 2020). The way in which housing-related support is funded (with an increasing reliance on housing benefit, following the demise of the Supporting People programme (Blood *et al.* 2016)) means that local authorities tend to commission housing and support as a package. This has often been delivered in congregate settings, such as hostels. However, these environments often do not work well for people with the highest and most complex needs. Congregate living can be extremely stressful for people with mental health challenges (Pattison and McCarthy 2020); rules relating to drug and alcohol use are problematic for current users, whilst the presence of other users is challenging for anyone trying to abstain (Blood *et al.* 2017). Research with long-term rough sleepers has found that many prefer the privacy and sense of control they have managed to create for themselves on the streets to hostel environments, which they perceive to be stressful (Groundswell 2018; Garratt and Flaherty 2020).

This chapter considers local authorities' duties to provide assistance or accommodation to those at risk of or experiencing homelessness, reflecting on the implications for people experiencing multiple exclusion, as highlighted by the thematic SARs (e.g. Martineau *et al.* 2019; Preston-Shoot 2020b; Preston-Shoot and Cooper 2020). It reviews the different types of accommodation and associated support which may be available, the relevant legal frameworks, and considers the barriers and risks faced by multiply excluded single homeless people. The chapter concludes with a summary of the evidence for best practice in providing housing and support for multiply excluded homeless people.

Local Authority Homelessness Duties

The Homelessness Reduction Act 2017 introduced two new universal duties: a 'prevention duty' and a 'relief duty'. Under the prevention duty, local authorities must 'take reasonable steps' to prevent homelessness for anyone who is at risk of becoming homeless within the next 56 days.

Under the relief duty, local authorities again must 'take reasonable steps' to help secure accommodation for those who are currently homeless and eligible (i.e. on the basis of their nationality/immigration status). Note, however, that local authorities only have a duty to actually provide accommodation to those who are assessed as being in 'priority need'. This includes both 'interim accommodation' (often termed Temporary Accommodation (TA)) while the authority makes inquiries into the person's circumstances (e.g. whether or not they have made themselves 'intentionally homeless'), and ongoing accommodation, if it concludes that a 'main' duty is owed.

Research conducted by Crisis (Boobis *et al.* 2020) has found that, in most areas, the Act has significantly widened access to advice and support for homeless people without dependent children, many of whom would have been previously turned away from local authority Housing Options services (Dobie *et al.* 2014). Single people owed a relief duty are typically offered advice and support on finding a private rented sector property (Boobis *et al.* 2020), as discussed below.

Evidence from Homelessness Reviews and wider research highlights some of the potential pinch-points within this statutory decision-making process for those experiencing multiple exclusion homelessness. For example:

- Decisions about whether or not a person is sufficiently 'vulnerable' on account of their physical or mental health condition for them to be deemed in 'priority need'. This is inevitably a contested 'grey area', compounded by the fact that 'vulnerability' is still used in homelessness legislation as a criterion for 'priority need', but adult social care and safeguarding teams have moved away from this concept since the Care Act 2014 (Mason *et al.* 2018). A theme from safeguarding reviews (e.g. Isle of Wight Safeguarding Adults Board and Preston-Shoot 2018; Preston-Shoot 2020b) is that these decisions are sometimes made by housing departments without proper health and mental health input. A recent Court of Appeal decision (Guiste v Lambeth LBC [2019]) emphasised the importance of obtaining and properly weighing up expert medical advice; a point also raised in research (Bretherton *et al.* 2013).

- Decisions about whether a person is judged to have made themselves 'intentionally homeless' by leaving their last temporary or settled accommodation, which a person with complex needs may be more likely to do, for example in response to real or perceived threats, anxiety or depression. The Code of Guidance in s.9.17 (MHCLG 2018b, p.73) states that an act or omission should not be viewed as 'deliberate' if it was 'the result of limited mental capacity; or a temporary aberration or aberrations caused by mental illness, frailty, or an assessed substance misuse problem'. Again safeguarding reviews (e.g. Preston-Shoot 2020b) have criticised the lack of medical input in these decisions.

- Whether people with complex needs who have experienced domestic violence and abuse (especially where this has occurred *since* becoming homeless) have these needs recognised and are therefore deemed to be in 'priority need' and offered appropriate and safe services. This is highlighted as an issue in safeguarding reviews (e.g. Preston-Shoot and Cooper 2020), by government reviews (e.g. MHCLG 2019), in a survey of homelessness agencies (Homeless Link 2020) and by a current sector-wide campaign (APPG n.d.). Many specialist refuges are unable to support women with complex needs, whilst 78% of homelessness accommodation projects are mixed (Homeless Link 2020), which makes it almost impossible for them to create a safe space for female survivors (Reeve *et al.* 2006).

- The distinction between 'family' and 'single' homelessness in policy fails to recognise the complex family circumstances of, particularly, homeless mothers with multiple needs (Bimpson *et al.* 2020).

- People experiencing multiple exclusion homelessness may decide not to 'present' to the council as homeless or may find services inaccessible when they try to. Common themes emerging from research with this cohort (Blood *et al.* 2017, 2020a) include: lack of trust of authority, past experiences of being refused help or of there being 'too many hoops to jump through', or the service offer not being suitable or effective.

Supported Accommodation

Homeless Link (2020) estimates that, in 2019, there were a total of 33,898 bedspaces in 991 accommodation projects for single people experiencing homelessness in England. This includes hostels, supported accommodation projects and foyers, but does not include night shelters, emergency accommodation hubs or specialist projects for people with mental health, substance use or offending issues. These services typically provide an alternative source of accommodation for those deemed not to be in 'priority need' by the local authority. Almost all projects responding to the Homeless Link survey receive local authority funding for housing-related support; they are effectively 'commissioned' services (though the authority has no statutory duty to provide them).

Accommodation providers responding to the Homeless Link survey estimated that 31% of those they accommodate have complex needs (defined as 'two or more of the following support needs: mental health, alcohol or drug abuse, learning difficulties, or offending behaviour'), and 34% have a 'dual diagnosis' of mental health and substance use issues.

Since housing benefit is also a key source of funding for these projects (Homeless Link 2020), those without recourse to public funds (e.g. due to their nationality/immigration status) are typically excluded, though some projects will make exceptions (Homeless Link 2018b). Over the past decade, many local authorities have also introduced local connection rules to restrict access to hostels and other supported accommodation projects where they fund the support (Homeless Link 2018b), often by establishing a 'pathway' model to which they control referrals. The intention is to ration limited resources and also to reduce the likelihood of 'importing' homeless people from other areas. However, these rules can impact disproportionately on people with multiple or high support needs, because they are at higher risk of long-term homelessness, and may have moved across areas, and/or lost their belongings (European Observatory on Homelessness 2015).

Research commissioned by St Mungo's (Oakley and Bovill Rose 2020) found that, in 2018/2019, English local authorities spent nearly £1bn *less* in total on support services, including supported accommodation for single homeless people, than they had spent in 2008/2009, as a result of cuts to their funding from central government. This has resulted in the loss of accommodation units, with Homeless Link reporting a 30% decline in the number of bedspaces from 2010 to 2019

(Homeless Link 2019). It has also led to a reduction in the value and length of support contracts commissioned by local authorities (Blood *et al.* 2020b). Where accommodation projects are operating on tighter budgets, often with reduced numbers of staff and fewer specialist posts, they are less able to accommodate those with the highest levels of need safely.

The Homeless Link annual survey (Homeless Link 2020) found that accommodation projects frequently refuse referrals because the person's needs are too high or too complex, or because they are assessed as presenting too high a risk to staff or other residents. A fifth of projects that had seen their funding reduced in the past year felt that this had further reduced their capacity to support people with complex needs. Accessing mental health services for residents was reported by accommodation providers to be a significant challenge; this can be particularly problematic where people are also using substances (Homeless Link 2018b; MHCLG 2020b).

Where commissioned services feel unable to manage the risks associated with those who have the highest levels of need, or where they are excluded from services for other reasons, these individuals are likely to end up in situations that can present much higher risks to themselves, including safeguarding risks such as self-neglect and abuse from others. This may include rough sleeping, staying at other people's homes or finding accommodation in the 'non-commissioned' exempt accommodation sector.

Non-Commissioned Exempt Accommodation

Where accommodation is provided by a not-for-profit landlord who also provides the claimant with care, support or supervision (directly or via a third party), the individual can claim 'exempt' housing benefit which is paid directly to the landlord at a higher rate than 'general needs' rents in both the social and private sector (Boath *et al.* 2010). There is no regulation of the support element of this package and local housing benefit teams vary in their approach and capacity to monitor these claims (Blood *et al.* 2016). Where the local authority commissions the support element, there should be some contractual monitoring of quality and safety, but as local authority funding has reduced, an unregulated sector about which there is limited data has grown to meet increasing demand. There is no reliable national data on the size of this sector; even at a local authority level, there are often significant gaps in the data.

Raisbeck's (2018) research into the non-commissioned exempt sector in Birmingham has identified:

> A complex network of providers and arrangements, the nature of which often impacts upon the level of control, regulation and monitoring local authorities and governing bodies are able to exercise, and thus what assurances around adult safeguarding and resident safety are available. (p.18)

Raisbeck's later report estimates that around 11,000 people in Birmingham 'are living in potentially unsafe and unsuitable "exempt" accommodation' (2019, p.4). Typically, this is in smaller shared house settings (with up to six individuals sharing), through a wide range of referral routes, including 'on the day' crisis placements with minimal assessment, often offering accommodation on a licence basis, and with little publicly available information about the provider and their offer. Those living in this accommodation share: an urgent need for accommodation; the perception by housing providers that they are 'high risk' or 'complex' in their needs; and exclusion from mainstream homelessness and housing systems.

Research for Riverside (Blood *et al.* 2020b) highlighted the huge range of providers' motivations within this sector, which includes veterans' charities, faith groups, and other larger but reputable providers who have either adapted to loss of local authority funding or actively chosen to avoid the restrictions of local authority contracts. However, there is also emerging evidence of commercially driven operators in this sector. The Supported Housing (Regulation) Bill (2020/2021) was put forward in December 2020 by a Bristol MP in response to seven deaths at a large supported housing project in the city. The Charity Commission's report into the charity running the project identified a number of concerns, including the failure to report serious safeguarding incidents appropriately (Charity Commission for England and Wales 2019).

Raisbeck's (2018) qualitative research identified a number of issues relating to adult safeguarding in the Birmingham exempt sector. These included:

- The accommodation of sex offenders and women vulnerable to domestic abuse or sexual exploitation in these schemes, sometimes together and alongside people with a range of other complex needs, due to a lack of appropriate provision for these cohorts.

- 'Enforced sharing' with a lack of choice, control or even information about house shares; (fear of) harassment, theft and violence from other residents and their visitors.

- Lack of security and privacy (e.g. no lock on a shared bathroom in mixed provision).

- Variable safeguarding training for and practice by providers.

- Frustrations expressed by some providers about a lack of response from statutory agencies when they had reported incidents and concerns. A perception by social workers that the individual does, at least, 'have a roof over their head', that there is nothing that can be done because they 'have capacity', or an assumption that the level of care and support provided is much higher than it is (p.59).

- A feeling reported by many residents that there is no safe or effective way to complain and that they have very limited choices.

In many areas, local authorities and their partners depend on this non-commissioned sector to provide both temporary and longer-term accommodation; yet their power and capacity to control quality is currently limited by a lack of regulation in the sector. As a result, risks both from and to the most vulnerable are effectively outsourced to the least regulated services in the health and social care system. MHCLG funded pilots in five areas from October 2020 to October 2021 to test different approaches to improving quality, enforcement, oversight and value-for-money in short-term supported accommodation and to understand whether and which regulatory changes are needed, or whether a better resourced partnership approach could make improvements within the current frameworks (MHCLG 2020e). These activities included: raising awareness about tenants' rights and improving complaints processes; offering training to providers and seeking to engage them in partnerships and forums; partnership work between housing benefit teams, adult social care, police and housing enforcement to tackle poor performance.

Access to Private Rented Sector Housing

Local authorities direct the majority of single people presenting as homeless to the private rented sector. Since the Localism Act 2011, authorities also have the power to end the main housing duty by arranging an offer of suitable accommodation in the private rented sector. Most local authorities provide a range of services to assist those experiencing homelessness into the private sector, though these tend to focus on families and others in 'priority need'. Assistance may include:

- Cash to help with a deposit and rent in advance (this may be funded through a Discretionary Housing Payment).

- A written guarantee (or 'bond') to the landlord that any unpaid rent or damage to the property will be covered up to a certain amount.

- Assistance with benefit claims or interest-free loans from the Department for Work and Pensions.

- Tenancy sustainment – though typically very light touch, usually in response to problems within the early stages of the tenancy.

- A landlord/tenant finding and matching service, though this tends to be focused on those owed a main duty; single people often need to find a property themselves, unless they are assessed to be in 'priority need'.

In most areas, people who are dependent on state benefits face significant challenges finding and securing decent private rented accommodation; these barriers tend to be even greater for people experiencing multiple exclusion homelessness. Key issues include: affordability, Universal Credit, quality and security of tenure.

Affordability

'Local Housing Allowance' (LHA) rates set by central government determine the maximum amount of financial support people claiming Universal Credit can receive to assist with paying rent (i.e. as part of the 'Housing Component') in the private rented sector. The LHA rate varies according to:

- The geographical area in which the property is located. England is divided into 152 Broad Rental Market Areas (Cambridgeshire Insight 2020), and there can be significant variations in the rental market within each area.

- The size of property to which a household is entitled: couples and singles aged 35 and over can claim the one-bed rate; those under 35 are eligible only for the 'shared room' rate, unless they can demonstrate one of a number of exemptions. These include: care leavers aged under 22; people receiving a Severe Disability Premium; those aged over 25 who have either spent at least three months in a specialist homelessness hostel and received resettlement support or are ex-offenders subject to MAPPA arrangements (DWP 2014). This may include some of those experiencing multiple exclusion homelessness.

Affordability is most challenging in London, the South East and around some larger, especially historic, university cities. However, following a freeze in LHA rates in 2016, research carried out by Crisis and the Chartered Institute of Housing in 2018 (Basran 2019) found that the rates failed to cover at least 20% of the private rented sector in *most* regions of England. Affordability was a particular challenge for the under 35s: in 8% of 182 English areas analysed, there was no shared accommodation which could be afforded within the LHA shared accommodation rate; and in 27% of areas, less than 5% of rents were affordable within the rate.

The situation was improved – at least temporarily – by the Social Security (Coronavirus) (Further Measures) Regulations 2020, which increased the LHA rates applicable from April 2020 to March 2021 (Valuation Office Agency 2020). The intention is that the increased rates cover 'rent at the 30th percentile' (i.e. would pay the rent of 30% of homes on the rental market in an area). However, even where properties can be found with rents which are affordable within LHA rates, many landlords require a deposit and rent in advance.

Universal Credit

In a national survey (Simcock 2018), 62% of landlords reported being unwilling to let to tenants who are claiming Universal Credit; this rose to 82% of landlords asked in a separate survey (Gousy 2016) if they would consider letting to a homeless person. Although stigma undoubtedly contributes to this, the primary concerns are financial: 61% of landlords who had let to claimants reported rent arrears averaging £2400 due to delays in payments from DWP, tenants being responsible for paying rent, and delays in setting up Alternative Payment Arrangements so the landlord could be paid directly (Simcock 2018). Many mortgage lenders and insurers include conditions preventing lettings to Universal Credit claimants; and high street lettings agencies typically require affordability and credit checks.

Quality

Out of all properties in the private rented sector, 27% do not meet the Decent Homes Standard (ONS 2018) and it follows that most of these will be concentrated in the cheaper end of the market. Problems relating to fire or carbon monoxide risk, ventilation and damp, thermal efficiency, disrepair or infestations can pose direct threats to safety and wellbeing. Where demand is high and tenants face multiple barriers, few feel able to complain, especially to what have been termed 'rogue' landlords (Shelter 2014). Homelessness Thematic Reviews cite allegations of abuse and sexual assault by landlords in the cases of individuals who have later died (Preston-Shoot 2020a; Preston-Shoot and Cooper 2020). A recent peer-led research study with homeless people on the streets of Oxford (Blood *et al.* 2020a) encountered individuals with multiple support needs who felt trapped in poor quality rented accommodation because they felt unable to challenge their landlord and did not want to risk making themselves 'intentionally homeless' by abandoning the tenancy. One person even reported preferring to sleep rough than return to an infested property.

Insecurity of Tenure

Most private sector tenancies are Assured Shorthold Tenancies (ASTs), which became the default tenancy under the Housing Act 1996, and are usually fixed at six months. After that period, and under section 21 of the 1988 Housing Act, the tenant can be evicted for no reason, provided the landlord follows the proper procedure. The government has temporarily extended notice periods in response to the pandemic (Shelter 2021), and, before that, had consulted on the abolition of section 21 (Wilson 2019) in recognition of the growing number of homelessness presentations caused by eviction from the private rented sector (Fransham and Dorling 2018).

Access to Social Housing

For people on the lowest incomes, social housing still typically offers greater security of tenure, more affordable rents, higher property standards and more opportunity to challenge the landlord's service than the private rented sector. This is despite the introduction of shorter, fixed-term social tenancies by the Localism Act 2011, the stigma of social housing and its concentration in areas with high rates of crime and anti-social behaviour (Mattinson *et al.* 2019).

However, there has been a steady reduction in the supply of social housing in recent decades (MHCLG 2020c): new development has not kept pace with properties sold under 'right to buy' policies (Cole *et al.* 2015). Moreover, where new properties are being built by councils and housing associations, they are more likely to be for 'affordable' rent (up to 80% of the local market rent level) than 'social' rent (ONS 2019c).

Demand for social housing now far outstrips supply in most parts of the country. In 2019/2020, there were a total of 1.1 million households on housing waiting lists held by English local authorities, 46% of whom were waiting for a one-bedroom property (MHCLG 2020b). Given the Spare Room Subsidy (commonly known as the 'Bedroom Tax'), a single person or couple without dependent children would usually not be offered a property with more than one bedroom. Local authorities and housing associations are therefore faced with the challenge of how best to ration increasingly scarce social lettings to those who need or 'deserve' them the most. Social landlords also have to balance the objective to meet housing needs with that of managing the risk of anti-social behaviour, rent arrears and tenancy failure, which can be expensive for them and damaging to communities (Greaves 2019).

Under s.167(1) of the Housing Act 1996, every local authority is required to have an allocation scheme for determining priorities between applicants and the procedure to be followed in allocating housing. The 'Housing Register' is effectively a waiting list held or outsourced by one or more local authority and the housing associations operating in that area. Although housing associations may allocate some of their properties outside of the register (depending on the 'nominations agreements' they have with the local authority), the register is the primary route to accessing social housing, often allowing applicants to then bid on available properties through a Choice Based Lettings system. The Localism Act 2011 allowed local authorities to determine which households should be prioritised and which excluded from the

Housing Register. Subsequently, there have been significant variations in allocation policy, as well as in supply, from area to area.

Not only has the overall size of the social rented sector reduced in recent years, but the *proportion* of those lettings which are made to single homeless people has also decreased (Rowe and Wagstaff 2017). Many of the sanctions and restrictions used to manage risk and ration supply impact disproportionately on single homeless people, especially those with multiple or high support needs. For example:

- Most local authorities restrict access to the Housing Register to those who can demonstrate a 'local connection' to the area, whether through 'normal residence', employment or family connections, as defined in Part VII of the Housing Act 1996. As described in the previous sections, this can be particularly challenging for those with longer histories of homelessness and complex needs to evidence.

- People with former tenant arrears or a history of anti-social behaviour or convictions may be excluded, though there are varying policies about whether and how these exclusions can be overcome (e.g. after a set period of time, once arrears have been repaid to a certain threshold, or if a change in behaviour can be evidenced) (Blood *et al.* 2020a).

- Choice is often 'designed out' for those in the greatest housing need, who may be sanctioned for refusing a 'reasonable' offer or for not actively bidding; yet those with past experiences of trauma, substance use or mental health conditions may have very good reasons for wanting to avoid a certain area.

Recent peer-led research with homeless people on the streets of Oxford (Blood *et al.* 2020a) found that many interviewees with long-term histories of homelessness, even where they were local to the area, did not appear to even be on the waiting list for social housing. Some had given up or been put off by staff warning them how long they would have to wait; some had not been able to demonstrate a local connection; others were barred from the register and not clear on what they needed to do in order to overcome these sanctions.

Supporting individuals to access the register (whilst managing expectations about the wait) and monitoring exclusions at local authority and landlord level can support better understanding of demand, and the removal of individual and systemic barriers. This alone though will not address the fundamental issue of lack of supply.

Equality and Diversity Considerations

There is limited research evidence in relation to race and ethnicity and multiple exclusion homelessness; however, the following key points emerge from the wider literature and provide important context.

- Overall, people from Black and minority ethnic (BAME) backgrounds are at greater risk of homelessness: during 2019/2020, a quarter (24%) of people making homelessness applications to local councils were from BAME groups, even though they make up just over a tenth (11%) of all households in England (Shelter 2020).

- People from BAME backgrounds are over-represented in institutional settings, which means they are at greater risk of losing their housing and being homeless on discharge or release. For example, 27% of the prison population is from BAME backgrounds (Ministry of Justice 2020b), and people from BAME backgrounds are significantly more likely to be compulsorily detained under the mental health legislation than people from white backgrounds (Barnett *et al.* 2019).

- Intersectionality between protected characteristics is likely to be significant; for example, single BAME women experiencing homelessness are more likely to have left their last settled accommodation as a result of domestic violence and abuse than single white women (Kowalewska 2018).

- Women, LGBTQ+ people, some BAME groups and disabled people can be deterred from using homelessness day centres and night shelters (Pattison and McCarthy 2020). Despite this, Homeless Link's most recent annual survey of providers suggests that people from BAME backgrounds still make up 16% of those using day centres and 18% of those using accommodation-based services (Homeless Link 2020).

- In the analysis informing Lankelly Chase's *Hard Edges* report, less than 10% of those identified as experiencing multiple exclusion homelessness had migrated to the UK as adults; however, there were significant variations by area, with much higher proportions in central London boroughs, such as Westminster (Bramley *et al.* 2015).

- EU migrants who are experiencing homelessness, and especially those who are sleeping rough, are at particular risk of barriers around application for the EU Settlement Scheme post-Brexit. For example, they may experience difficulties in providing identity and residence evidence (Sumption and Fernández-Reino 2020).

- Although women and UK-born people from BAME backgrounds were under-represented in the Lankelly Chase multiple exclusion homelessness cohort (Bramley *et al.* 2015), it is recognised that these groups face significant and distinct challenges which need to be met and experience a range of social inequalities which contribute to their experience of multiple disadvantage (MEAM n.d.).

- It is likely, but by definition hard to prove, that multiply excluded women and people from BAME backgrounds are more likely to experience 'hidden' homelessness, sofa-surfing or rough sleeping away from public view. Given the policy focus on rough sleeping, there is a risk that their needs are further overlooked.

People from BAME backgrounds and disabled people may also face a number of barriers when trying to access settled housing. For example:

- There are huge systemic barriers facing those who, due to their immigration status, have no recourse to public funds. Without access to housing benefit, they are dependent on charities for accommodation.

- Several studies have evidenced the discriminatory impact of the 'Right to Rent' policy, in which private sector landlords have a duty to carry out immigration status checks before letting property (Foster and Bellis 2019). The evidence suggests that landlords – especially in high-demand areas – are more likely to reject any prospective tenant from BAME backgrounds in case they should fall foul of the law.

- Fears over racial harassment in certain areas can influence – and hence limit – the housing options of people from BAME backgrounds (Kowalewska 2018).
- There is a national shortage of housing which is both accessible and affordable for disabled people (Equality & Human Rights Commission 2018).

National analysis of SARs has highlighted a lack of systematic consideration of race and ethnicity, and – to a lesser extent – disability and gender (Preston-Shoot *et al.* 2020), in both the reviews themselves and in the practice they describe. In particular, they note:

- A lack of consideration given to the actual or potential risks of harassment, discriminatory abuse or attack facing people from BAME backgrounds, women and LGBTQ+ people experiencing multiple exclusion homelessness, and how previous experiences may influence current behaviours.
- The invisibility of differences resulting from culture, gender and/or disability, which can lead to communication and behaviour being misinterpreted and safeguarding risks missed as a result.
- Unconscious bias in decision-making (e.g. that a 'failed asylum seeker' has acted deceitfully).

Some of the barriers highlighted in this section demand policy or structural change; however, there are steps which can be taken by practitioners and local systems to better address the needs of multiply excluded women, disabled people and people from BAME backgrounds. These include actions to increase awareness, staff development and accountability, such as: unconscious bias training for decision-makers; regular audits of cases through the lens of the Equality Act 2010; reflective supervision or communities of practice with a focus on anti-discriminatory practice.

Good Practice

There is a strong and developing evidence base around what works in supporting people with histories of multiple exclusion homelessness into housing and helping them to sustain a tenancy. This evidence base includes:

- Evaluations of the Housing First model, for which there is substantial, international evidence of effectiveness (Housing First Europe Hub 2021).

- The national evaluation of the Making Every Adult Matter (MEAM) approach (Cordis Bright 2020), which shows the most positive individual outcomes in relation to accommodation.

- The Fulfilling Lives programme (CFE Research 2018), funded by the National Lottery Community Fund to deliver more joined-up services to people experiencing multiple disadvantage.

- Local evaluations – for example of Changing Lives' interventions with victims of domestic abuse who also have multiple and complex needs (Changing Lives 2018) and of Threshold's Housing First project for female offenders with complex needs (Quilgars and Pleace 2018) – provide further insights into effective practice with women.

- Homeless Link's *The Future Hostel* project (Homeless Link 2018b) (funded by MHCLG) to bring together best practice and learning from the hostel sector.

Recurring themes from this evidence base suggest that the core components of successful approaches are:

- The opportunity to build secure, trusting and long-term relationships with a small and consistent team of workers.

- The capacity to provide person-centred 'wrap-around support', e.g. advocating for people; attending appointments and court appearances; supporting people to make homelessness and housing applications; providing emotional, social and practical support.

- Organisational processes and procedures which are sufficiently flexible to allow for a personalised, psychologically informed and situational response to behaviours, rather than the application of sanctions and blanket bans.

- A non-judgemental, psychologically informed and strengths-based approach, which understands the impact of trauma and actively avoids re-traumatising individuals.

- Persistence and 'assertive outreach', where the *service* takes responsibility for maintaining engagement with individuals and adapts practice to ensure this.

- The maximisation of individual choice and control, e.g. about how a person wants to be supported, where and how they want to live (this may include, for example, the use of personal budgets to purchase household items or pursue interests).

- A move away from a one-size-fits-all approach to commissioning congregate supported housing to a more flexible approach in which support can be tailored around the lifestyles, resources, strengths and preferences of the person.

- For this to take root, there is an urgent need to invest in trauma-informed learning and development, and resilience for people working across housing, support, care and health systems. This is essential if we are to move away from the dominant blame- and deficit-based views of people experiencing multiple exclusion homelessness, which too often dismiss those in the greatest need as 'undeserving' or 'hard to engage'.

- System change: providing education and challenge to mainstream services to make their practice and policies more inclusive of people experiencing multiple exclusion homelessness.

- Investment in better training for and advice to staff working in both statutory and non-statutory settings on the relevant legislative frameworks (including the Care Act 2014, the housing and homelessness legislation, and the Mental Capacity Act 2005), so we can better advocate, challenge, debate and reach informed joint decisions.

- The involvement of people with lived experience in service design and delivery, since they alone have a view of the 'whole system'.

So, where does housing fit into this? As the name suggests, an essential component of the 'Housing First' model involves removing the conditionality from the route back into housing for the multiply excluded homeless. The first of the Housing First principles recognises that 'people have a right to a home' (Homeless Link 2017a). The model recognises that the traditional 'staircase' pathway (Johnsen and Teixeira

2010), in which a person is required to stabilise their substance use and mental health within a hostel environment in order to demonstrate their 'readiness' for a tenancy, is not realistic for people with multiple, layered and connected experiences of trauma, addiction and mental ill-health. Instead, the aim is to fast-track the individual into their own tenancy as soon as possible, providing wrap-around support to them in their own home for as long as they need it, thereby avoiding the cliff-edge of support which many experience on resettlement. High rates of tenancy sustainment follow from a person being effectively 'tenancy-supported' in their home, rather than from requiring them to be 'tenancy-ready' before handing over the keys.

Padgett's (2007) qualitative research with previously homeless people with severe mental illness housed through Housing First in New York highlights the 'ontological security' that follows from having a home, in contrast to their preceding experiences of the 'institutional circuit'. Interviewees spoke of freedom and privacy, self-determination, the pleasure of simple routines and the opportunity to reconstruct their identities from the secure base of their new homes. This emphasises the importance of choice and control in the process of homemaking; it is not a question of 'being placed' or of 'being accommodated'.

Providing temporary accommodation in congregate settings is no substitute for the ontological security of a long-term home; however, the Future Hostel report describes best practice by providers which aims to maximise privacy and security within hostels. For example, Look Ahead's Warwick Road hostel in Kensington and Chelsea provides self-contained flats to its residents; whilst Changing Lives' Francis House for women with complex needs in Newcastle does not allow residents to go into each other's bedrooms (Homeless Link 2018b).

Access to affordable and good-quality accommodation is a significant challenge for Housing First schemes operating in England, including the high-profile combined regional authority pilots in Liverpool, Manchester and the West Midlands (MHCLG 2020d). In 2020, 81% of Housing First services reported using social housing instead of the private rented sector, a significant shift from 2017 (Housing First England 2020). However, securing long-term funding in order to guarantee the ongoing provision of wrap-around support remains the biggest challenge for many projects; without this, it can be difficult to convince social landlords to offer long-term tenancies and reassure prospective tenants that they will not be set up to fail.

There is increasing and largely consistent evidence of what works to successfully house people experiencing multiple exclusion homelessness, but it is equally clear that there are no quick fixes for those who have experienced long-term, complex and inter-linking experiences of trauma, abuse, loss, mental and physical illness and substance use.

Conclusion

If hostels and other congregate settings are to accommodate those with multiple and complex needs safely, they need to be well designed and adequately resourced. Project staff need the skills, empathy and time to work in a trauma-informed way, and they must be able to draw in timely support from other professionals, especially where there are safeguarding concerns. Where individuals have experienced trauma and/or are at risk of abuse, privacy and safety from other residents are of paramount importance. Where a number of people with complex and high needs are being supported at the same site, a lot of staff energy tends to be focused on managing the interactions between individuals and enforcing the rules.

The option to move directly into self-contained and ideally permanent housing, thereby avoiding or minimising time spent in the hostel 'pathway', is essential if people are to be supported safely out of multiple exclusion homelessness. For this to happen, there needs to be a focus throughout the system on *ending* homelessness as quickly as possible, by providing stable housing with the support a person needs to successfully maintain a tenancy; essentially a 'housing-led' approach (Blood *et al.* 2020b).

This requires a significant shift in thinking and in practice: towards the idea that housing is a right rather than a privilege to be earned once a person is 'tenancy-ready'. It means starting the 'move on' planning at the earliest opportunity, making sure people are on the Housing Register or that there is a transparent and realistic plan to remove any sanctions, alongside efforts to secure shorter-term accommodation. This planning will only be effective if it is co-produced with the individual, and it can take a considerable amount of time and consistency of relationship to build sufficient trust to do this.

Emerging learning from Community Solutions' work in the US suggests that an assertive casework system, which coordinates local multi-agency effort and is underpinned by effective governance and real-time data collection, can be effective in supporting people out of multiple exclusion homelessness (Maguire 2018). Through the use of a shared *By Name List* and a nominated lead worker, the aim is to stay with the individual until they are securely housed and effectively supported. This approach reduces the risk of cases being closed by individual services because they have completed (or attempted to complete) their specific intervention: a pattern evident in many of the homeless deaths reviewed by Safeguarding Adults Boards.

Commissioners and policy-makers need to accept that some people will require intensive and open-ended support if they are to settle, recover from trauma and reintegrate into mainstream life. This has to be underpinned by longer-term funding commitments for housing-related support from central and local government.

Ultimately, we cannot create sustainable and person-centred housing and support for people with complex needs who are experiencing or at risk of homelessness unless we increase the supply of affordable, secure and good-quality housing, and reduce the barriers which this group regularly encounter when trying to access it. As well as changes to development policy and funding, this requires bold partnership working between local authorities, health, criminal justice and the community and voluntary sector to both challenge and reassure landlords that individuals will receive the wrap-around support they need. It requires a review of allocations policy and practice to ensure there is clarity around what individuals need to do in order to remove exclusions, and a shift away from insisting applicants are 'tenancy-ready' towards a focus on ensuring people are 'tenancy-supported'.

Chapter 9

People with No Recourse to Public Funds Experiencing Homelessness

Catherine Houlcroft and Henry St Clair Miller

Introduction

Restricting access to state support for people who require leave to enter or remain in the UK is a key element of immigration policy. Consequently, constraints are placed on a local authority's ability to prevent or alleviate homelessness when a person has no recourse to public funds and is excluded from basic welfare and housing services, with statutory 'safety-net' support only available to families and adults with care needs.

However, 'Everyone In', the emergency response to accommodate rough sleepers and others who were homeless during the Covid-19 pandemic, has shown what can be done to assist people who are normally restricted from accessing housing assistance when lives are at risk. This also exposed the government's long-term commitment to end rough sleeping by 2027 (MHCLG 2018a) to be largely incompatible with immigration-related sanctions and the use of the 'No Recourse to Public Funds' (NRPF) condition. The former Chair of the Rough Sleeping Taskforce, Baroness Casey, told the Housing, Communities and Local Government (HCLG) Committee (2021, Q248) that 'one of the causes of rough sleeping is an inability to manage immigration properly', and the Local Government Association (2021) called for the NRPF condition to be lifted so 'councils can ensure that everyone who is vulnerable can access help if needed' during the pandemic.

Assisting people with no recourse to public funds who are homeless is a challenging area of practice, which lacks a coherent government policy response. This chapter highlights the opportunities local authorities have to meet accommodation needs and achieve sustainable outcomes for adults who are ineligible for benefits and homelessness assistance.

'Everyone In'

In March 2020, the government announced its strategy to protect the lives of rough sleepers and people at risk of rough sleeping during the Covid-19 pandemic by requiring local authorities to provide self-contained accommodation, regardless of a person's immigration status (MHCLG and Hall 2020). This resulted in local authorities supporting people with no recourse to public funds who were ineligible for homelessness assistance (Part VII Housing Act 1996) and who did not qualify for 'safety-net' support that can be provided by social services to destitute families (section 17 Children Act 1989) and adults with care and support needs (Part 1 Care Act 2014).

In the following months, the government's position on assisting people with no recourse to public funds shifted, with councils advised that they 'need to apply the law and that means making an individual assessment' (Hansard HC Deb. 2021). Unclear guidance in relation to what assistance could be provided and a lack of adequate funding led to the HCLG Committee (2020, p.3) appealing 'on humanitarian grounds for the Government to improve its support to councils for people with no recourse to public funds during this crisis, or hundreds will return to the streets with potentially disastrous consequences'. Changes to government messaging regarding the qualifying criteria and funding deficits were subsequently observed by the National Audit Office (NAO) (2021) to lead to inconsistent local authority responses to accommodating homeless people with no recourse to public funds in later months, despite the pandemic remaining a public health risk. Clarity about the legal powers that local authorities could rely upon to accommodate people during the public health emergency was only obtained following a legal challenge against a council.

Who Has No Recourse to Public Funds and What Does This Mean?

In order to correctly assist people to access the right support services, practitioners will need to understand how a person's immigration status impacts on their entitlements. It is particularly important that those in decision-making roles avoid incorrectly denying a person services to which they are actually entitled.

A person will have no recourse to public funds when they are 'subject to immigration control' (section 115 Immigration and Asylum Act 1999). This includes people who have a form of limited leave to enter or remain that is subject to the NRPF condition and people without valid leave to enter or remain in the UK, who are often described as having 'irregular' status, or being 'unlawfully present' or 'undocumented'.

A person who is subject to immigration control is excluded from claiming most benefits, specifically those that are classed as 'public funds', homelessness assistance and a local authority housing allocation.[1] Being subject to the NRPF condition also has wider consequences, as entitlement to the housing component of Universal Credit will often determine whether a person can access hostel or refuge accommodation.

Social services assistance and NHS treatment are not classed as 'public funds' for immigration purposes and therefore can be accessed by a person who is subject to the NRPF condition. However, immigration status can be a determinative factor when establishing eligibility for certain services, such as the provision of free hospital treatment to overseas visitors.[2]

Accommodation and financial support can be provided by social services to people who are excluded from benefits due to their immigration status when duties are engaged under section 17 of the Children Act 1989 or Part 1 of the Care Act 2014. This 'safety-net' support is costly to councils and is not directly funded by central government, even though accommodation may need to be provided until immigration claims are determined.[3]

References to people with no recourse to public funds also include

---

1   Benefits classed as 'public funds' are defined in s.115 of the Immigration and Asylum Act 1999 and para.6 of the Immigration Rules.
2   For more information about charging for secondary NHS care, see: Public Health England, Migrant Health Guide, available at: www.gov.uk/guidance/nhs-entitlements-migrant-health-guide.
3   The following legislation that applies in Wales, Scotland and Northern Ireland enables accommodation and financial support to be provided to families or adults with care needs, although qualifying criteria may be different to the equivalent English legislation: Social Services and Well-Being Wales Act 2014; Social Work (Scotland) Act 1968; Children (Scotland) Act 1995; Health and Personal Social Services (Northern Ireland) Order 1972; and Children (Northern Ireland) Order 1995.

European Economic Area (EEA) nationals who are ineligible for benefits. This situation could arise when a person with pre-settled status is unable to demonstrate a qualifying right to reside, when a person enters the UK after 1 January 2021 with leave that is subject to the NRPF condition, or when a person is unlawfully present, which applies if a person failed to apply to the EU Settlement Scheme before the deadline of 30 June 2021.[4]

How Many People Have No Recourse to Public Funds and How Many Experience Homelessness?

The Migration Observatory (2020) estimated that 1.4 million people may have leave that is subject to the NRPF condition. The Office of National Statistics (2019b) describes the difficulties of providing an official estimate of the number of people living in the UK without status, but researchers have calculated that, in 2017, there could be between 800,000 and 1.2 million 'unauthorised migrants' living in the UK (Connor and Passel 2019). By the end of September 2020, 1.6 million grants of pre-settled status had been made under the EU Settlement Scheme; a form of status that does not confer automatic entitlement to benefits (Home Office 2020).

The number of people who access support from the local authority is small in comparison. At the end of March 2020, 2450 households in 66 local authority areas were being provided with accommodation and financial support by social services (NRPF Network 2020); 1088 people counted by local authorities in the rough sleeping snapshot in autumn 2019 were non-UK nationals, making up 28% of the total number, with 22% holding European Union nationality (MHCLG 2020f). In London, non-UK nationals made up half of the rough sleeper numbers.

However, 'Everyone In' revealed that the rough sleeping snapshot was not indicative of the numbers requiring support during the

---

[4] EEA nationals and their family members who were living in the UK before 31 December 2020 are required to apply for status under the EU Settlement Scheme by 30 June 2021. They may be granted settled status (indefinite leave to remain) or pre-settled status (five years' limited leave to remain). The Home Office may accept a late application in certain circumstances, but a person who fails to apply by the deadline will become unlawfully present on 1 July 2021. A person who has pre-settled status will need to be exercising a qualifying right to reside in order to access benefits. The exclusion of pre-settled status as a qualifying right to reside for the purposes of claiming Universal Credit is subject to a legal challenge in the Supreme Court. For up-to-date information about this see the Child Poverty Action Group, available at: https://cpag.org.uk/welfare-rights/legal-test-cases/current-test-cases/eu-pre-settled-status.

Covid-19 pandemic, with the government vastly underestimating this need. Furthermore, the NAO (2021) observed that many people accommodated during the pandemic were not able to move on from their temporary accommodation due to having no recourse to public funds, including 2000 people in London who remained in hotel accommodation at the end of September 2020.

Homelessness amongst people with no recourse to public funds is often hidden, as illustrated by the experience of Birmingham, where 62% of people accommodated through the council's 'Everyone In' response had no recourse to public funds, whereas only 10% of individuals identified in the most recent rough sleeper count were subject to that status (Local Partnerships 2020).

With many adults with no recourse to public funds reliant on voluntary and community sector (VCS) provision, the impact of night shelters and shared accommodation facilities closing due to the pandemic may have also contributed to the need for emergency support from local authorities. In 2019/2020, housing and hosting projects that are members of the No Accommodation Network (NACCOM) (2020) accommodated 3373 people, 1636 of whom had no recourse to public funds, with projects turning away 1849 people due to a lack of accommodation. With homelessness a real risk for people with no recourse to public funds, it is essential that local authorities are aware of the legal powers they can rely on to provide accommodation.

When Can a Local Authority Provide Accommodation and Financial Support to a Person with No Recourse to Public Funds?

Destitute families with no recourse to public funds can be provided with accommodation and financial support by social services (section 17 Children Act 1989), but a local authority's statutory responsibilities to accommodate an adult who is ineligible for homelessness assistance may be less clear.[5]

When a homeless adult has no recourse to public funds, the

---

5 Accommodation and financial support must be provided by social services to a family with no recourse to public funds when a parent is unable to meet the child's housing and basic living needs due to their lack of access to benefits and other resources, in order to safeguard and promote the welfare of a child in need (section 17 Children Act 1989).

following legislation must be considered, alongside any government guidance or funding criteria:

- Part 1 of the Care Act 2014, subject to Schedule 3 of the Nationality, Immigration and Asylum Act 2002.
- Section 117 of the Mental Health Act 1983.
- Section 188(1) of the Housing Act 1996.
- Section 138 of the Local Government Act 1972 and section 2B of the National Health Service Act 2006.

Part 1 Care Act 2014

Adults may be provided with accommodation under Part 1 of the Care Act 2014 when they have care and support needs arising from a physical or mental impairment, or illness (the Care and Support (Eligibility Criteria) Regulations 2015). When the eligibility criteria are met, the local authority can meet an adult's needs by providing accommodation of any type (sections 8(1) and 18 Care Act). When deciding how to meet needs, consideration must be given to the suitability of the person's living accommodation (section 1(2) (h)). A failure to provide accommodation, preventing the required care from being delivered, could result in a human rights breach.

When an adult is 'subject to immigration control', however, the duty to meet needs will not be engaged when needs for care and support have arisen solely due to the person being destitute, or because of the physical effects, or anticipated physical effects, of being destitute (section 21).[6]

The local authority may meet urgent needs, pending the outcome of assessments (section 19(3)), and non-eligible care and support needs (section 19(1)). These powers must be carefully considered as they enable the local authority to prevent homelessness whilst assessing need and/or when a person has care needs that do not meet the eligibility threshold.

The local authority will generally only be responsible for providing

---

6 'Subject to immigration control' is defined by section 115 of the Immigration and Asylum Act 1999, i.e. a person who has: leave to enter or remain that is subject to the NRPF condition; leave to enter or remain in the UK that is subject to a maintenance undertaking; or no leave to enter or remain when they are required to have this.

accommodation to a person seeking asylum when residential care is required (Home Office 2004).

The local authority can undertake a safeguarding enquiry (section 42 Care Act) regardless of the adult's immigration status. The enquiry would need to address how accommodation needs can be met should the person lack the means to access housing due to having no recourse to public funds.

Section 117 Mental Health Act 1983

A person who has been compulsorily detained (section 3 Mental Health Act) will qualify for aftercare services when they are discharged from hospital. Aftercare can include the provision of supported accommodation, where this is required to reduce the risk of the person being readmitted to hospital (section 117 Mental Health Act). Aftercare must be provided free of charge and is not subject to any immigration restrictions.

Section 188(1) Housing Act 1996

When a housing authority has reason to believe that an applicant may be homeless, eligible for assistance, and has a priority need as defined in section 189, there will be a duty to secure accommodation (section 188(1) Housing Act). This duty will not be engaged when a person clearly has no recourse to public funds but could apply when further investigations into a person's eligibility are needed.

Section 138 Local Government Act 1972 and Section 2B National Health Service Act 2006

The local authority has powers to provide accommodation to reduce risks to life during a public health emergency (section 138 Local Government Act 1972) and to improve the public health of residents (section 2B National Health Service Act 2006). These powers enable local authorities to accommodate people with no recourse to public funds through initiatives intended to save lives by alleviating the effect of the Covid-19 pandemic, such as 'Everyone In'.[7]

---

7   Ncube v Brighton and Hove City Council [2021] EWHC 578.

In determining whether accommodation can be provided using these powers, the local authority may also take into account the availability of other statutory support, such as Home Office asylum support, but can accommodate to reduce public health risks should such alternative support not be immediately available.[8]

Schedule 3 Nationality, Immigration and Asylum Act 2002

Section 54 and Schedule 3 of the Nationality, Immigration and Asylum Act 2002 place a bar on providing support under Part 1 of the Care Act 2014 to an adult who is 'in breach of immigration laws' and is able to return to their country of origin to avoid a human rights breach (Article 3 European Convention on Human Rights and Fundamental Freedoms) that may arise from their destitution in the UK.[9]

When Schedule 3 applies, in addition to the needs assessment, the local authority must undertake a human rights assessment in order to establish whether the person can reasonably be expected to return to their country of origin. The assessment must identify whether return is prevented because of an outstanding immigration claim, ill-health preventing travel or other exceptional reason. When a person is unable to avoid destitution in the UK by returning to their country of origin, the local authority will be required to provide support when a duty or power to meet care and support needs is engaged (sections 18 and 19(1) Care Act 2014). A general duty to provide support to prevent a breach of human rights does not arise from Schedule 3 however.

When the person can be expected to avoid destitution in the UK by returning to their country of origin, the local authority will be limited to offering travel assistance and support whilst return is arranged, and

---

8   Information about different support options for people with no recourse to public funds is available on the NRPF Network website: www.nrpfnetwork.org.uk/information-and-resources/rights-and-entitlements/support-options-for-people-with-nrpf.

9   A person will be 'in breach of immigration laws' if they are a visa overstayer, illegal entrant, or are an appeal rights exhausted (ARE) asylum seeker who made their asylum claim in-country (rather than at port of entry).

In R (Limbuela) v Secretary of State for the Home Department [2005] UKHL 66, the Court found that a decision that compels a person to sleep rough or without shelter and without funds usually amounts to inhuman treatment and therefore engages Article 3 of the European Convention on Human Rights (the right not to be subject to inhuman or degrading treatment). In R (Kimani) v London Borough of Lambeth [2003] EWCA Civ 1150, the Court of Appeal found that 'a State owes no duty under the Convention to provide support to foreign nationals who are permitted to enter their territory but who are in a position freely to return home' (para.49).

a decision to refuse or withdraw support will not give rise to a human rights breach.[10]

When a person is 'in breach of immigration laws', the local authority must still undertake its duties to safeguard and protect adults with care and support needs, and therefore can assess need and meet urgent needs pending the outcome of assessments or whilst a safeguarding enquiry is undertaken.

Practice Considerations When Assisting People with No Recourse to Public Funds

'Everyone In' enabled local authorities to meet a person's presenting needs without the constraints imposed by immigration-based exclusions or other eligibility criteria; as a consequence, people who were normally ineligible for homelessness assistance could access accommodation. The impact of this is illustrated by the comments of a beneficiary of support during the pandemic:

> I called the council and straightaway they don't lead you to the No Public Fund Department. [Normally] they would send you to different sections and… they would ask you different questions. Then they [would say], 'Oh in that case we can't deal with your case, you have to ask this and that.' [Before] it was quite difficult to get to the No Public Funds Department, but [during the pandemic] once I get in touch with them, it was very, very quick and they were very, very supportive in supporting me. In fact, within just six days, they were able to provide me a placement that I can stay in.[11]

The legacy of 'Everyone In' at a national and local level is not presently known, but the conflict between laws that exist to protect individual rights and those designed to exclude based on a person's immigration status remains. Whilst local authorities need to protect and safeguard people in need when statutory provisions are lacking, or when government direction is purposefully vague, how can a local authority work innovatively to achieve an effective offer of support to people with no recourse to public funds?

Practice points will be considered in turn.

---

10   R (AW) v London Borough of Croydon [2005] EWHC 2950 (Admin), para.35.
11   Telephone interview with interviewee A conducted on 14 December 2020.

Strategic Oversight

Housing authorities are required to consider the needs of people with no recourse to public funds within their wider homelessness strategies (MHCLG 2018b), and to take steps to prevent homelessness by providing signposting information and advice to individuals who are ineligible for homelessness assistance (section 179 Housing Act). When considering what support may be provided to a person with no recourse to public funds, the local authority will need to be mindful of the current strategic direction that is set by the government to address immediate need in an emergency situation or to achieve the longer-term aim of ending rough sleeping.

Providing accommodation and subsistence is expensive, costing between £17,000 and £18,000 per household per annum, so budgets must account for this to ensure legitimate spend is not omitted from financial planning.[12] Oversight of the accommodation and financial support provided to households with no recourse to public funds by social services and/or housing authorities will help establish whether an 'invest to save' approach of resourcing specialist workers can achieve more expedient case-resolution. A strong understanding of caseload pressures may also help inform applications for government grant funding.

As many homeless adults with no recourse to public funds will not qualify for statutory 'safety-net' support, the following could be considered:

- The possibility of making innovative investments, such as capital spend on new bedspaces, to enable a genuine 'housing first' response whilst eligibility or immigration status is being determined.

- Establishing local partnerships with VCS organisations, referring to NACCOM for examples of different housing models.

- And, as noted, resourcing specialist caseworkers to deliver the response.

---

12 NRPF Network data (2020) shows that at the end of March 2020, the average annual cost of accommodation and financial support was £18,592 for an adult with care needs and £15,592 for a family with a child in need; researchers (Scanlon and Whitehead 2020) estimated that the cost of providing accommodation only to rough sleepers with no recourse to public funds during the Covid-19 pandemic was between £13,500 and £19,900 per annum.

Decision-Making Oversight

Local authorities must comply with public law principles to ensure that rational, fair and consistent decisions are reached. Decisions about support provision carry added weight due to safeguarding risks where no assistance is provided to an individual, and financial risks to the local authority, where intervention results in a long-term support commitment. Oversight of human rights assessments will be particularly important to ensure that correct considerations have been made to determine whether accommodation can be provided under the Care Act 2014 to a person who is 'in breach of immigration laws', or whether return to country of origin is offered. Frontline workers will need to be appropriately supported when they are inexperienced in carrying out such assessments, or when the application of the law or government guidance is unclear.

It must be clear who is responsible for providing oversight under existing governing structures, particularly if there are no specialist workers within the local authority. One option could be for the case owner to present the facts of the case to a panel comprising a legal officer, manager and welfare rights adviser, who can guide and authorise any decisions.

Clearly communicating any decisions that are made with a person who is provided with accommodation is necessary to build a positive working relationship. The local authority should:

- be open and honest so that the person is aware of the conditions of any support offered or limitations of the local authority's engagement

- ensure that the person understands from the outset that all relevant options will be explored, such as regularisation of status through immigration advice and return to country of origin, should immigration claims not succeed

- be clear about the grounds for providing support and confirm this in writing.

Timely Referrals and Needs Assessments

It may be challenging in practice to undertake holistic decision-making due to responsibility for support provision falling to different departments (or authorities in two-tier areas). Social workers must be aware of how a person without care needs can access any emergency support the local housing authority is currently offering, whereas housing officers will need to ensure appropriate referrals are made to Adult Social Services when a person appears to have care and support needs.

Adult Social Services will be required to undertake a needs assessment when a person presents with 'an appearance of need' (section 9(1) Care Act), and emergency accommodation may be provided whilst the assessment is carried out (section 19(3)), even where a person is 'in breach of immigration laws' and a human rights assessment is required. Ensuring that such interventions are undertaken early would provide a period of stability in order to establish engagement with an individual, and may even reduce risks to life.

However, the fact that a statutory duty to provide accommodation only arises when Care Act eligibility criteria are met does not readily invite or enable 'accommodation-led' responses, increasing the risk of delaying potentially life-saving intervention when people are initially encountered by outreach services. For example, a rough sleeper outreach worker made the following observations about working with an EEA national, whose health had deteriorated to the point of critical illness leading to several hospital admissions (pre-pandemic):

> [The person] had complex needs that presented challenges regarding engagement, and his lack of documentation prevented him from being able to access services. On reflection, more timely interventions, such as offering accommodation appropriate to his needs, ensuring his needs were assessed prior to hospital discharge, and making a safeguarding referral in order to ensure a plan for accommodation was considered, may have helped to stabilise his situation sooner.[13]

Reaching a reasoned conclusion about a person's level of need, whether the eligibility criteria are satisfied and how eligible needs may be best met takes time. The needs assessment will also be informed by the input of other professionals and may require a full diagnosis of underlying health conditions to be completed. It will be necessary to identify whether the person is a potential victim of trafficking, modern slavery or domestic abuse, and to confirm their current immigration status and entitlements. It is important that these enquiries are undertaken with minimal delay as it may not be possible to establish whether a person has eligible needs and what type of accommodation and support is required to keep them safe

---

13 Email interview with interviewee B conducted on 24 July 2020.

from harm until after such investigations are completed. Whilst assessments are pending, there is a risk that any accommodation provided on an emergency basis may not adequately meet the person's needs, so close monitoring of the situation may be required.

Internal protocols between housing and social services authorities may help to ensure that:

- referrals into social services demonstrate that the assessment threshold is met by setting out the person's health and/or mental health issues, vulnerabilities, and any supporting evidence
- priority is given to needs assessments in order to reach a timely decision on eligibility for support
- expenditure on emergency accommodation is reduced.

Meeting Accommodation and Subsistence Needs

Any support provided must adequately alleviate the person's situation of destitution in order to reduce the risk of exploitation, abuse and reliance on unsuitable income sources, as well as mitigating the impacts of continued financial hardship on the person's health and wellbeing.

When a person qualifies for care and support, there is a broad power to meet needs (section 18 Care Act). Any decision regarding how to meet needs must take into account factors that affect the person's wellbeing and reduce safeguarding risks.

Accommodation must comply with local housing standards, and subsistence support must at the very minimum cover the person's basic living needs. Although a placement in a hotel or B&B may meet need on an emergency basis, when support is likely to be ongoing for many months, or even years, accommodation that is suitable for longer-term habitation may need to be sought, such as a self-contained property.

In setting subsistence amounts, taking feedback from recipients of support will indicate how they are managing and whether any additional assistance could be provided to help with budgeting or accessing other entitlements. The following view expressed by a recipient of subsistence payments resulted in the local authority fully meeting the cost of utilities and assisting the person to obtain free prescriptions:

> In my situation, I'm not well and I think maybe [the local authority should]…at least put out a bit more money, because living [on] £90

for two weeks, it's very little. It's really very little, because when you… budget it, when you take off this, this, this, you really find that you don't have anything… You have to put electricity [on], you have to buy medication. I feel myself sometimes really stressed. That money is really, I don't know, but it's really little, very little.[14]

Although a fair and efficient way of determining subsistence levels is for the local authority to refer to standardised rates that have been set internally, there must be flexibility to ensure that a person's needs are adequately met and any views they have are responded to (NRPF Network 2018). A knowledge of what additional entitlements the person may have is also required, such as how to access free prescriptions through the NHS Low Income Scheme.

Establishing a Sustainable Outcome

A thematic review of ten deaths of individuals sleeping rough in Redbridge between October 2017 and November 2018, undertaken by the Safeguarding Adults Board (SAB), identified that the majority of those who died were non-UK nationals with an undetermined immigration status and no recourse to public funds. The review observed that:

> …they were not recent arrivals in the UK. Only one of the non-UK nationals had been living in the UK for less than a year and five had been here for over ten years… There are a number of obstacles to successfully work to achieve either establishing individuals' right to remain in the UK or, where appropriate, voluntary return to their country of origin. (Redbridge SAB 2019, p.25)

The provision of accommodation and subsistence support will continue whilst the person continues to be in need of care and support or whilst a local decision is made to continue to accommodate rough sleepers who have been supported during the pandemic. For the majority of households supported by social services, a change of immigration status that allows access to public funds is the most likely exit pathway, rather than return to country of origin.[15] For EEA nationals, access to

---

14　Telephone interview with interviewee C conducted on 26 November 2020.
15　NRPF Network data (2020) shows that, in 2019–2020, 82% of family households and 51% of adult households exited support following grants of leave to remain, 19% of adult households exited support after becoming eligible for benefits (EEA nationals), and 7% returned to their country of origin (all non-EEA nationals).

employment is often a route to establishing eligibility for benefits and housing assistance.

Achieving any outcome, whether regularisation of immigration status or a supported return to country of origin, can be a lengthy process, with the average period for an adult supported under the Care Act being 1055 days (NRPF Network 2020), and with many people accommodated through 'Everyone In' still living in temporary accommodation ten months on (MHCLG 2021).

Assisting a person to obtain documentation, proof of identity, or chasing up outstanding immigration claims through legal representatives and/or the Home Office is extremely time-consuming and requires perseverance, as described by a local authority rough sleeper outreach worker:

> I arranged for [the person's] embassy to provide a temporary passport whilst he waited for an appointment to get a new one issued but it was extremely difficult to escort the client to appointments as he is constantly on edge and becomes tired and impatient. He starts experiencing pain in his legs and his stomach… [He is] reluctant to engage with authorities following previous enforced returns, which likely resulted in him deteriorating over the years.[16]

Redbridge SAB (2019) identified challenges working with the High Commission of India to obtain information they may hold about their citizens which could be helpful to the immigration adviser. Subsequently, the High Commissioner agreed to the SAB Chair's request that a specific contact person is nominated with whom the immigration advice agency could liaise and that enquiries would be responded to.

It is therefore essential to work proactively with the individual to determine an appropriate exit strategy, which will usually be dependent on the person's immigration options. The caseworker will need to provide a lot of support and encouragement, particularly where an individual is suspicious or fearful of the immigration authorities. As emphasised, to support a trusted working relationship, it is important to be transparent about the service provided and any limitations from the outset of engagement.

Practitioners will need sufficient understanding of the potential routes to regularisation available in order to help people to access

---

16   Email interview with interviewee B conducted on 24 July 2020.

immigration advice.[17] A competent immigration adviser should be able to provide fair and impartial analysis of the options available to a person, which includes giving an honest opinion where there is no basis for making an application or poor prospects of an application or appeal succeeding.

The following steps may need to be taken to help achieve sustainable outcomes:

- Explain what is expected of the individual, such as accessing immigration advice, in writing, using interpretation and translation services as required.

- Map immigration advice provision in the local area, including only regulated advisers in signposting lists.

- Consider commissioning a third sector organisation to deliver immigration advice where there is insufficient local capacity or to assist with complex matters.

- Employ a dedicated staffing resource or ensure workers are given responsibility to address the individual's immigration needs within their role.

- Engage the advice and assistance of any colleagues with specialist knowledge of working with people with no recourse to public funds in other departments, such as social services.

- Consider whether any government funding streams can be drawn on to resource this work, at least on a short-term basis.

In some cases, there will be no route to regularisation, access to public funds, or return, leaving individuals trapped 'in limbo'. In such cases the local authority may be under a duty to provide 'open ended' support; for example, an EEA national with care and support needs who has obtained pre-settled status but is unable to get into work or meet the 'right to reside test' to qualify for benefits will not qualify for settled status for another four years. The NRPF Network advocates on behalf of local authorities when poorly constructed policy or law creates such

---

17 Immigration advice is regulated by the Office of the Immigration Services Commissioner (OISC) and can only be provided by OISC registered or exempt advisers. The NRPF Network provides information to help find an immigration adviser at: www.nrpfnetwork.org.uk/information-and-resources/rights-and-entitlements/support-options-for-people-with-nrpf/legal-advice.

'cost-shunts' to councils or increases destitution. Local authorities are encouraged to raise such difficulties with the NRPF Network.

Working with the Home Office

Working with the immigration authorities can be a controversial area of practice but it does not need to compromise a duty of care to the individual when engagement is undertaken to identify and achieve sustainable outcomes. For example, working with the Home Office will be necessary in order to achieve more expedient decisions on applications for leave to remain submitted by an immigration adviser, or to establish whether a person qualifies for Home Office asylum support. Equally, without knowledge of a local authority's involvement in supporting an individual, there is a risk that the Home Office could make an incorrect decision, such as applying the NRPF condition to a grant of leave when the person is destitute, or instigating enforcement processes with no regard for interventions undertaken by social services.

Contact with the Home Office does present a risk of possible detention and/or removal action for individuals who are 'appeal rights exhausted' or who are otherwise liable to enforcement action. A person with valid leave to remain may be at risk of having their leave curtailed if their circumstances have subsequently changed. The recent addition of rough sleeping as a ground of refusal or curtailment of leave is not conducive to engaging and building trusting relationships with people who need to make difficult decisions about their future.[18]

Interim support can be provided before a person's immigration status and entitlements have been confirmed, and delays in determining these must never prevent the local authority providing accommodation on an emergency basis pending the outcome of any assessments.

In the first instance, the person would need to be asked about their current immigration status to establish:

- whether any identity documents exist

---

[18] On 1 December 2020, the Home Office added rough sleeping as a discretionary ground for refusal or curtailment of leave under the Immigration Rules. Home Office guidance (2021, p.5) states: 'the rule will be applied to those who refuse to engage with the range of available support mechanisms and who engage in persistent anti-social behaviour'. The rule does not apply to people with: refugee status or other types of leave granted following an asylum claim; leave under the family or private life rules; or leave granted under the EU Settlement Scheme. It may apply to people who have visitor, student or work visas, including EEA nationals who arrived with such leave after 1 January 2021.

- their nationality and own understanding of their immigration status
- their immigration history, including when they entered the UK and what type of claims they may have made (where this is needed to understand their needs or if a human rights assessment is being undertaken)
- the outcome of any legal advice they have received about their options.

The Home Office will only provide an immigration status check when the local authority has a statutory basis for requesting this and a formal mechanism must be used, such as the NRPF Connect database or the Home Office Status, Verification, Enquiries and Checking email service.[19]

If a status check is requested from the Home Office, the person will need to be advised:

- on what information has been shared and why
- to inform their legal representative about this
- to keep the local authority, their legal representative and the Home Office updated about any changes to their circumstances.

When the Home Office does not have information about an individual, this should not lead to an assumption that a person does not have lawful status. For example, people described as the 'Windrush generation' are likely to have indefinite leave to remain or the right of abode in the UK, but this may only be established by accessing immigration advice.[20]

Supporting a Return to Country of Origin

When there is no route available to a person to regularise their immigration status, taking up a voluntary return may be the only way that they can avoid remaining in the UK at risk of destitution, exploitation and detention or enforced removal by the Home Office.

---

19 Local authorities using NRPF Connect are listed at: www.nrpfnetwork.org.uk/nrpf-connect.
20 The Home Office has an application process for people to prove their right to remain if they settled in the UK before 1988. A person will need to be signposted to an immigration adviser to find out if this may apply to them. Details of the Windrush Scheme are available at: www.gov.uk/windrush-prove-your-right-to-be-in-the-uk.

When social services' support is provided, uptake of return remains low, which may be attributed to the significant number of people who are able to regularise their immigration status when they are properly supported to do this (NRPF Network 2020). It is also a challenge for a person to make balanced and informed decisions when they are homeless, as summarised by the reflections of a local authority rough sleeper outreach worker:

> The barriers [the service user] faced in accessing support due to being unable to access benefits...are likely to have resulted in him deteriorating over the years. There is also a question of whether a return may have been more successful if this had been facilitated with additional support and with the agreement of the individual.[21]

A discussion about return will always be a challenging conversation when this is often the least preferable outcome for the individual concerned. The person's ability to make an informed decision will again depend on practitioners engaging with the person about their immigration journey, informing them about their return options, and providing an opportunity to access immigration advice about the implications of return. A person who is assisted by the Home Office to return voluntarily may qualify for additional integration assistance if they have claimed asylum or if they do not have current immigration permission and meet the Home Office vulnerability criteria.[22]

When a local authority concludes that a person who qualifies for support under the Care Act 2014 can return to their country of origin to avoid destitution in the UK, social services may continue to provide accommodation and financial support whilst a return is arranged, either by the Home Office or local authority.

Conclusion

Although this is a challenging area of practice, there are opportunities to enable people with no recourse to public funds to be provided with accommodation, support and assistance to obtain a sustainable solution to resolve their homelessness. To support efficient, effective and lawful service provision, a local authority must also ensure there is managerial

---

21 Email interview with interviewee B conducted on 24 July 2020.
22 More information about the Home Office Voluntary Returns Service is available at: www.gov.uk/return-home-voluntarily.

oversight of decision-making and, where necessary, invest in specialist responses to help keep costs to a minimum. However, improving outcomes for people experiencing homelessness who are excluded from benefits and mainstream housing by their immigration status cannot be sustained at a local level when the statutory framework lacks a standard support offer. Local authorities can engage with the NRPF Network to help evidence and raise these challenges strategically with government.

Part 3
BEST EVIDENCE FOR LEADERSHIP AND STRATEGIC PARTNERSHIPS

Chapter 10

Learning from Safeguarding Adults Reviews and Fatality Reviews

Michael Preston-Shoot and Gill Taylor

Introduction

This chapter serves two purposes. Firstly, it reviews the learning from Safeguarding Adults Reviews (SARs) where multiple exclusion homelessness, defined below, is a feature. This part of the chapter concludes with an evidence base for positive practice that is built from SAR findings and recommendations, and from surrounding research.[1] Secondly, the chapter picks up the interest in learning from reviews conducted in rapid time by focusing on Fatality Reviews concerning people who experienced homelessness. This approach to learning from the outcomes of policy and practice has been developed in the London Borough of Haringey and been strongly supported by Haringey Safeguarding Adults Board.[2]

This chapter challenges the assertion that Safeguarding Adults Boards (SABs) have not engaged with homelessness and have failed to use SARs as a vehicle for sector-led improvement and enhancement. That perspective was forcibly expressed in the government's Rough Sleeping Strategy (MHCLG 2018a), developed in response to rising concerns and the increased visibility of homelessness as an issue across the country, but particularly in big cities. The Strategy commented that:

---

1 Michael Preston-Shoot is the principal author of this part of the chapter, drawing on his involvement with SAR research projects.
2 Gill Taylor has led on this development and she is the principal author of this part of the chapter.

> We agree with the Advisory Panel, who were clear that Safeguarding Adults Reviews are powerful tools, which unfortunately are rarely used in the case of people who sleep rough. We will work with Safeguarding Adults Boards to ensure that Safeguarding Adults Reviews are conducted when a person who sleeps rough dies or is seriously harmed as a result of abuse or neglect, whether known or suspected, and there is concern that partner agencies could have worked more effectively to protect the adult. Lessons learned from these reviews will inform improvements in local systems and services. (MHCLG 2018a, p.31)

Additional evidence to challenge this myth comes from SAB Business Managers. A 38% response was achieved from a survey (n=50/132) (Lloyd-Smith and Bampton 2019). Of those responding, 54% stated that the SAB had received SAR referrals involving homelessness, with 12 reviews commissioned and 7 awaiting a decision; 14 SARs either had been completed or were expected to reach a conclusion between January and October 2019. Of the SAB Business Managers who responded, 76% commented that the SAB had discussed homelessness and engaged in various activities subsequently, including awareness-raising, training and knowledge-dissemination events, collaboration with Community Safety Partnerships and local agencies, and policy development.

The Strategy clearly intends that lessons learned will inform improvements locally. Lessons clearly do emerge from SARs, and from Fatality Reviews. Reviews have enabled the articulation of an evidence base for good practice to guide the development of policies, procedures and practice. However, some of the lessons learned require change at a national level of law and policy. That message has clearly been demonstrated by the Coronavirus Act 2020, the investment and the coordinated action to provide temporary accommodation during the pandemic for people experiencing homelessness, and the subsequent ambition to keep everyone in accommodation through centrally led initiatives not just to house people who had been homeless but also to meet their health and social care needs.

The evidence base within this chapter provides guidance for commissioners and service providers, for managers and practitioners across statutory and third sector agencies, and for SABs locally and nationally. The evidence base presents a set of standards or quality markers against which to evaluate the outcomes in future cases. Fundamentally, both SARs and Fatality Reviews offer findings and recommendations for learning, for practice and service improvement and enhancement.

Definitions

Some key definitions underpin what follows. This chapter employs the term 'multiple exclusion homelessness'. Multiple exclusion homelessness refers to extreme marginalisation that may include childhood trauma, physical and mental ill-health, substance misuse and experiences of institutional care (Mason et al. 2018). For many of those who are rough sleeping, homelessness is a long-term experience and associated with tri-morbidity (impairments arising from a combination of mental ill-health, physical ill-health and drug and/or alcohol misuse) and premature mortality (Mason et al. 2018).

The mandate for commissioning a SAR requires that the adult has needs for care and support. Regulations provide a definition. Care and support needs arise from or are related to physical or mental impairment or illness. This can include conditions as a result of physical, mental, sensory, learning or cognitive disabilities or illnesses, substance misuse or brain injury (Care and Support (Eligibility Criteria) Regulations 2014).

Safeguarding Adults Reviews – The Legal Mandate

SABs are under an absolute duty to conduct a SAR where an adult with care and support needs has died as a result of abuse and/or neglect, including self-neglect, whether known or suspected, and there is concern that partner agencies could have worked more effectively to protect the person. There is a comparable absolute duty where the person has experienced serious abuse and/or neglect but survived. In these circumstances there is no discretion; a review is mandatory. Serious abuse and/or neglect are defined as including where the person would have died but for intervention or where they have experienced permanent harm or reduced capacity or quality of life (DHSC 2020).[3] The impact of abuse and neglect can include fear, shame, trauma, suicidal ideation, self-neglect, mental health and/or acute hospital admission, substance misuse, poverty and homelessness. The duty arises irrespective of whether or not the person has received services as a result of their care and support needs.[4]

SABs may also commission reviews involving adults with care and

---

[3] Section 44(1), section 44(2) and section 44(3), Care Act 2014; Statutory Guidance sections 14.162 and 14.163.
[4] Section 44(1), Care Act 2014; Statutory Guidance section 14.165.

support needs where the mandatory criteria are not met.[5] Such reviews are discretionary and are indicated where a SAB believes that useful learning may be identified, including about good practice.

Not all SABs appear to have grasped the distinction between mandatory and discretionary reviews, between the absolute duties in sections 44(1), (2) and (3) Care Act 2014 and the discretionary duty within section 44(4); there continue to be incorrect references to statutory and non-statutory SARs (Preston-Shoot et al. 2020). All SARs are statutory. Similarly, the Rough Sleeping Strategy had not grasped the inclusion of care and support needs in the statutory mandate applicable to SARs. Many people experiencing homelessness will have care and support needs, but not all. Fatality Reviews are particularly useful when reviewing cases where individuals may not have had care and support needs.

Safeguarding Adults Reviews – Human Stories

Twenty-five reviews in the first national analysis of SARs in England (Preston-Shoot et al. 2020) involved individuals who were or had experienced homelessness. This represents 11% of the sample (n=231). All but five of these SARs were published in some form. Collating SARs that include a focus on homelessness is challenging in the absence of a complete and fully functioning national repository. However, SAB responses for the aforementioned national analysis and for a prior thematic review (Martineau et al. 2019), coupled with searches of SAB websites, has enabled a compilation of published reviews (see Table 10.1).

Table 10.1 Safeguarding Adults Reviews

Torbay	Ms Y	2011	Teeswide	Josh	2019
North Yorkshire	Robert	2012	Camden	UU	2019
Lambeth	Mr A	2012	B, C and Poole[6]	Harry	2019
Lambeth	Mr D	2016	Solihull	Rachel	2019
Solihull	Mr S	2016	Gateshead	Winnie	2019
Southwark	Adult A	2016	Tower Hamlets	Ms C	2019

---

5   Section 44(4), Care Act 2014; Statutory Guidance section 14.163.
6   Bournemouth, Christchurch and Poole.

Nottingham and Nottinghamshire	Adult C	2017	Northamptonshire	Jonathan	2020
Buckinghamshire	Adult T	2017	Leeds	Thematic	2020
Brighton and Hove	X	2017	Worcestershire	Thematic	2020
Merseyside	Lynn and Natalie	2017	North Yorkshire	Ian	2020
Haringey	Robert	2017	Oldham	Thematic	2020
Lincolnshire	Thematic Review	2017	Manchester	Thematic	2020
Wiltshire	Adult D	2018	Bexley	Paul	2020
Essex	Frank	2018	Oxfordshire	Thematic	2020
Waltham Forest	Andrew	2018	Tower Hamlets	Thematic[7]	2020
Doncaster	Adult G	2018	Cornwall	Jack	2020
Bexley	AB	2018	Cambridgeshire and Peterborough	Peter	2020
Manchester	AB	2018	Tower Hamlets	Mr K	n.d.[8]
Devon	Adrian Munday	2018	Solihull	Paul	n.d.
Isle of Wight	Howard	2018	Stockport	Katie	n.d.
Milton Keynes	Adult B	2019	Calderdale	Thematic	2021
Southampton	Adult P	2019	Haringey	Thematic	2021
Newham	Mr YI	2019	City of London and Hackney	MS	2021

In addition to published reviews, occasionally SABs report on completed reviews in annual reports that are otherwise not in the public domain. For example, Walsall SAB conducted a learning review that is only reported in its 2016/2017 annual report. Redbridge SAB completed a thematic review that is reported in its annual report for 2017/2018. Occasionally reports are undertaken by local authorities independent of a SAB. A review by Worcester City Council (2018) is such an example.[9]

Not all the individuals were rough sleeping at the time of their deaths; some were in hostels or temporary accommodation. Nonetheless, all had a history of experiencing homelessness. In line with SARs

---

7   Ms H and Ms I.
8   No date given.
9   Worcester City Council has responsibility for housing and homelessness but not adult social care.

generally (Preston-Shoot *et al.* 2020), most of the individuals whose cases were reviewed had died,[10] and there are more male than female subjects. The exact ages of the subjects were not always recorded, an imprecision that was also found in the national analysis (Preston-Shoot *et al.* 2020). However, where precise ages were given, the average age for men was 46 and for women 40. This compares with the average age of death reported in the Government's Rough Sleeping Strategy of 44 for men and 42 for women (MHCLH 2018a).

Thematic Analysis

The purpose of this section, and the one that follows, is to capture the learning from SARs and to organise it into an evidence base for understanding best practice in adult safeguarding and homelessness.

The reviews clearly show that there are multiple routes into homelessness. These may include relationship breakdown, poverty, unemployment, no recourse to public funds, domestic abuse, cuckooing[11] and/or an inability to sustain placements in hostels or temporary accommodation due to anti-social behaviour and/or aggression and exploitation by others. These routes into homelessness are often accompanied by a lived experience that includes adverse childhood experiences, loss and trauma, mental health problems, physical ill-health and/or disability, suicidal ideation, self-neglect and substance misuse. Adverse experiences in childhood can include abuse and neglect, domestic violence, poverty and parental mental illness or substance misuse (Public Health England 2018). These life events do not predict and are not necessarily precursors of homelessness but it is not unusual to find them within the human stories that are found within SARs. The brief case studies that follow serve to illustrate the complex comorbidities that people experiencing homelessness may present to statutory and third sector agencies.

Adult B – Milton Keynes SAB

Adult B was 33 and homeless when he died. The SAR outlines a childhood that included the loss of his parents and time spent in the care of a local authority. His longstanding drug and alcohol misuse

---

10   The Doncaster, Gateshead and Cornwall SARs are exceptions.
11   Where an individual's home is taken over to be used as a location for crime.

is understood as a coping mechanism in response to family trauma. There were signs and symptoms of autism.

A hostel place broke down due to his substance misuse, and tenancies were terminated on the grounds of anti-social behaviour and rent arrears. His mood was often low and there were episodes of self-harm. Attempts at rehabilitation to overcome his substance misuse proved unsuccessful. As the SAR observes, however, with the right support he could demonstrate some resilience and engage with the services on offer.

Paul – Solihull SAB

Paul had experienced long periods of being homeless. He was known to have an addiction to alcohol and drugs and was previously a victim of an arson attack and a serious sexual assault. At the time of his death, he was in a supported housing scheme for homeless persons.

Due to his trusting and friendly personality he was very vulnerable to being exploited. After the breakdown of a relationship Paul's vulnerability increased and over the following years he experienced some significant events. He lost his tenancy after two men took over his flat and bullied him; he began sleeping on the street. His tent was set on fire with him in it by a longstanding friend who was convicted for attempted murder. He was sexually and physically assaulted, bullied, robbed. He was alcohol and drug dependent. He attended detox treatments and was prescribed methadone to treat his opiate addictions. During 2018 he attended A&E approximately 40 times.

Ms I – Tower Hamlets SAB

Ms I had been homeless periodically since 2000 (aged 16). Details of her family background are patchy but include reports of the suicide of a brother, a mother with alcohol problems and unspecified childhood trauma. She had a history of depression and had been diagnosed as having an emotionally unstable personality disorder. Practitioners and services found her challenging and difficult to support, aggressive and non-compliant with hostel rules and/or medical treatment. She had also experienced domestic abuse. Her partner felt that, as a consequence of her experiences, her 'real self' was often 'hidden'.

She had a history of overdoses and was the subject of a suicide marker periodically. She had a longstanding history of alcohol and drug misuse. She experienced physical health problems, including TB, asthma, epilepsy, pneumonia and osteomyelitis. She had experienced cellulitis due to intravenous drug use, and alcohol-related pancreatitis. One necrotic finger had been amputated. She had also experienced deep vein thrombosis and ulcerated feet.

A hostel place was withdrawn because she was not using the room, which by then was unkempt. She was then homeless, except when accessing severe weather provision. Before the final hospital admission, when she died, she was using a temporary assessment hostel bed, although perhaps erratically.

Instances of good practice are reported in the cases. Reports comment positively on the rapport that practitioners develop with people experiencing homelessness, various demonstrations of humanity and the quality of support being offered. There are positive assessments of colocation, where practitioners from different disciplines work together to address a person's accommodation, physical and/or mental health needs, and/or care and support needs. Referrals to enlist the involvement of other agencies, including adult safeguarding, and the provision of emergency accommodation, also draw positive assessments. Good practice was also found regarding coordination of services, with clarity about the roles, remits and responsibilities of different services around the person.

However, there are consistent and repetitive findings of practice shortcomings. These include assumptions that individuals are making 'lifestyle choices' rather than showing professional curiosity to explore whether a person is unwilling and/or unable to address their circumstances. SARs consistently highlight how little has been known about a person's history and therefore the impact of their experiences on how they view their present circumstances. There are examples of missing or significantly delayed and incomplete assessments of risk, mental capacity, mental health and care and support needs. On mental capacity, SARs pinpoint that assessments should include a focus on executive functioning, especially where there are repetitive patterns. On mental health, SARs highlight the value of assessments even if people are not in acute crisis, and of exploring the interface between physical and mental wellbeing, and mental distress and substance misuse.

Pathways through which practitioners can seek to engage other services are too often unclear or, through use of thresholds and eligibility criteria, unavailable. Examples here include the availability of mental health support for people who are not in acute crisis, and the tendency of mental health and substance misuse services to cross-refer rather than to work together. Referrals of adult safeguarding concerns, using the criteria in section 42(1) Care Act 2014, do not result in enquiries using the provision in section 42(2), and the failure to escalate concerns is often noted. Adult safeguarding enquiries are one mechanism whereby the practitioners and services involved can come together.

Noteworthy in these SARs, however, is often the failure to convene the system, to bring those involved together to share information, assess needs and risks, agree upon a lead agency and key worker to coordinate a response, and devise and implement a risk management plan. Some SARs also note the failure to consider and use different legal options, such as provisions in the Homelessness Reduction Act 2017, especially the duty to refer, the Human Rights Act 1998 and the Court of Protection provision in the Mental Capacity Act 2005.

These themes are illustrated by the same three case studies from above.

Adult B – Signposts to Improvement

The review found that practitioners did not understand the signs and symptoms of autism. There were no recorded mental capacity assessments or consideration of the need for advocacy. There were no structured or completed risk and care and support assessments, and little evidence of professional curiosity. Agencies were working in silos. There was a lack of management guidance and direction, for example through supervision.

There were criticisms of the failure to share information and to record the outcomes of decision-making. Opportunities to refer and to complete assessments were missed. There was no consideration given to convening multi-agency safeguarding meetings, and little if any evidence of escalation of concerns.

Paul – Signposts to Improvement

Not all practitioners were aware of initiatives to support people experiencing homelessness. Referral routes and key individuals to contact were not widely known. Service enhancements to improve coordination and collaboration, including hospital discharge procedures and practice, enhanced access to tenancies and wrap-around support, were yet to be fully embedded.

Thresholds to access adult social care and mental health provision were high and decision-making was inconsistent. There were gaps in the knowledge, skills and confidence of staff regarding legislation and supporting people with multiple disadvantage, including homelessness, self-neglect, trauma, mental ill-health and substance misuse. No assessment had been undertaken of Paul's care and support needs despite substance misuse and mental health needs.

Ms I – Signposts to Improvement

Whilst some practitioners did attempt to 'stay alongside' Ms I, there was little evidence of a sense of exploration, inquiry and challenge regarding what lay behind suicidal ideation and/or substance misuse, or whether she could envisage a different life trajectory than the one into which she had become locked. Service refusal and non-engagement or disengagement appears often to have been seen as a lifestyle choice, however unwise, rather than a response occasioned by substance misuse, physical disability, mental ill-health or trauma. The case highlights the question of whether the impact of trauma and longstanding substance misuse on mind or brain is recognised and assessed, and most particularly whether executive capacity is considered. Potential legal options were not considered.

There does not appear to have been any sustained examination of whether and how any friends or partners could provide a circle of support. Repeating patterns do not seem to have been addressed. Responses to risks involving drug and alcohol misuse, homelessness, mental health and neglect of care and support needs were not addressed in an integrated, coordinated way. There was limited use of multi-agency risk management meetings, high-risk panels, multi-disciplinary meetings and section 42 enquiries. Use, monitoring and review of plans in response to risk and safeguarding concerns were variable. Given the repetitive pattern of non-engagement or non-compliance, there was an absence of contingency planning. There was information-sharing but arguably an absence of coordination between hospital and community provision, mental health and drug/alcohol services, and between statutory and third sector staff. There appears to have been an absence of parity of esteem of voices between statutory and third sector professionals.

An Evidence Base for Sector-Led Improvement

The learning from SARs translates into an evidence base that spans four domains (Preston-Shoot 2020a), which each have key components or characteristics – components of three of the four domains are outlined in Figures 10.1–10.3.

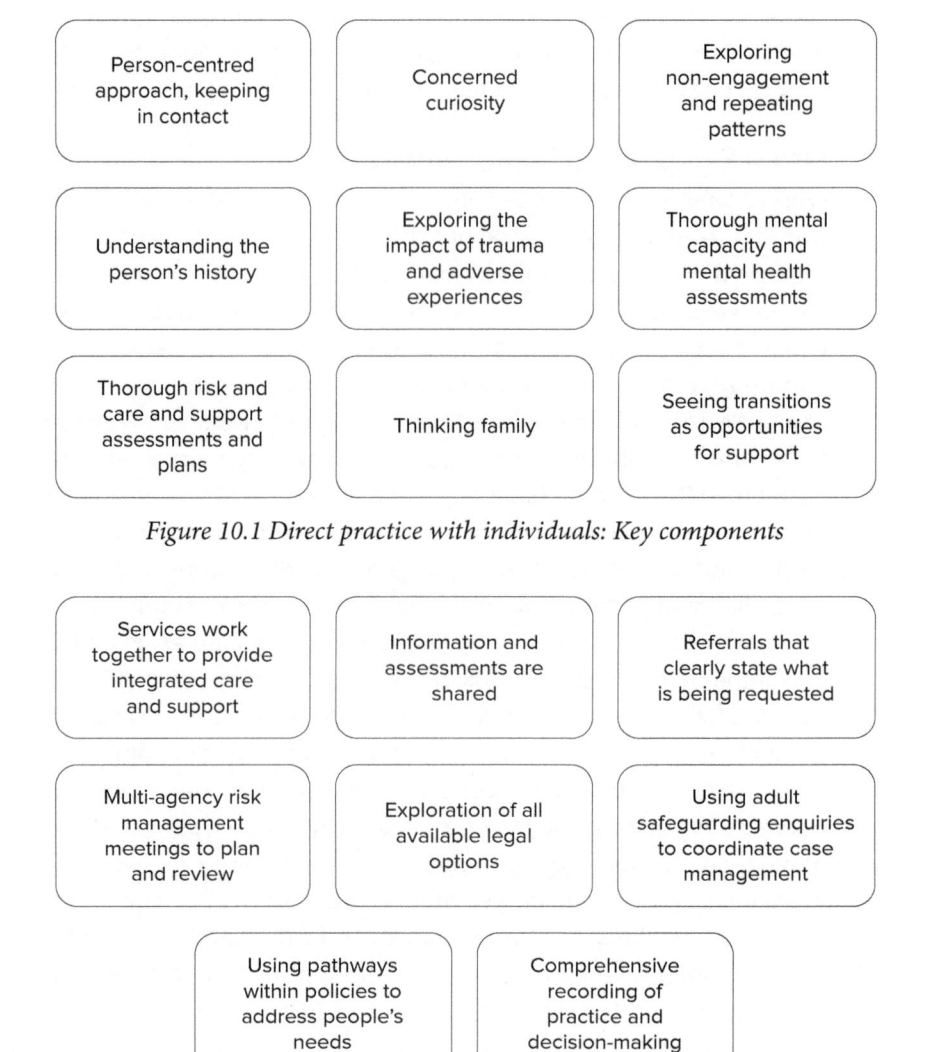

- Person-centred approach, keeping in contact
- Concerned curiosity
- Exploring non-engagement and repeating patterns
- Understanding the person's history
- Exploring the impact of trauma and adverse experiences
- Thorough mental capacity and mental health assessments
- Thorough risk and care and support assessments and plans
- Thinking family
- Seeing transitions as opportunities for support

Figure 10.1 Direct practice with individuals: Key components

- Services work together to provide integrated care and support
- Information and assessments are shared
- Referrals that clearly state what is being requested
- Multi-agency risk management meetings to plan and review
- Exploration of all available legal options
- Using adult safeguarding enquiries to coordinate case management
- Using pathways within policies to address people's needs
- Comprehensive recording of practice and decision-making

Figure 10.2 Multi-agency team around the person: Key components

Learning from Safeguarding Adults Reviews and Fatality Reviews

- Supervision to promote reflection and analysis of case management
- Supporting staff
- Management oversight of decision-making
- Access to specialist legal safeguarding, mental capacity and mental health advice
- Providing workforce development and ensuring that workplace culture and policies enable effective practice
- Developing commissioning to respond to the needs of people experiencing multiple exclusion homelessness

Figure 10.3 Organisational support for the team: Key characteristics

Finally, SABs should engage in governance conversations with Community Safety Partnerships, Health and Wellbeing Boards and other partnership bodies to ensure that strategic oversight and assurance of multi-agency partnership working is clearly located. There is no one model; what is decided will be determined locally. The SAB's role and responsibility thereafter is to promote best practice when working with adults experiencing multiple exclusion homelessness, via procedures and training for example, and to seek assurance that learning from SARs has been embedded in service development and practice.

Using this framework enables SABs and their partner agencies to explore what facilitates and what prevents good practice, and to take action accordingly. It is a framework for implementing a clear and shared vision. It adopts a whole system approach. This recognises that effective practice will only flourish and be sustained when there is alignment across the whole system, each component of the system working in an integrated way to support effective practice.

The evidence base translates across to the six adult safeguarding principles (DHSC 2020), as follows:

- *Empowerment:* Looking beyond the presenting problem to the backstory; making every adult matter; listening, hearing and acknowledging.

- *Prevention:* Commissioning to avoid revolving doors and to provide integrated wrap-around support; seeing transitions as opportunities.

- *Protection:* Addressing risks of premature mortality and from exploitation.

- *Partnership:* No wrong door; making every contact count.
- *Proportionality:* Minimising risk; judging the level of intervention required.
- *Accountability:* Getting the governance right.

It is fully supported by research that highlights, for example, local leadership that models effective partnership working and that commissions integrated provision (Cream *et al.* 2020; Weal 2020), and the importance of wrap-around support to help people maintain tenancies (Pleace 2013).

A Fifth Domain

Adult safeguarding and responding to homelessness are situated in a legal, policy and financial context. This has impacted, often unhelpfully, on services and practice. Legal rules and national policy, for instance with respect to people with no recourse to public funds, have restricted accommodation options and increased rather than decreased the risks associated with being homeless. In relation to housing and homelessness, and the interface with care and support, there is a fragmented rather than a coherent and aligned set of legal rules. The Housing Act 1996 uses concepts of vulnerability, priority need and intentionality for decision-making about access to provision, whereas the Care Act 2014 refers to wellbeing and eligibility (K. Mason *et al.* 2017, 2018). People with no recourse to public funds are excluded from the main homelessness provisions in housing law but may be entitled to social care support, including the provision of accommodation under certain circumstances. Housing and social care practitioners often find navigating this complex terrain in practice challenging (Preston-Shoot 2020a). Financial austerity combined with policies on social housing and welfare benefits have impacted adversely on the availability of services and also increased the risks of becoming locked into homelessness (Weal 2020). SARs comment only infrequently on this context (Preston-Shoot *et al.* 2020) and yet it severely restricts how SABs and partner agencies can make a difference for people experiencing multiple exclusion homelessness locally.

Government response to the Covid-19 pandemic regarding people experiencing homelessness has demonstrated what can be achieved when the legal, policy and financial context shifts, when combined action is taken to ensure that people have accommodation and the wrap-around support to sustain it.

Fatality Reviews

Whilst SARs have clearly been used to illuminating effect in respect of the organisational and operational policy and practice which can better safeguard people experiencing homelessness who have care and support needs, the duties of the Care Act 2014 fall short of providing a comprehensive approach to reviewing and learning from all homeless deaths. Partly this is because of differing interpretations of what constitutes care and support needs between housing and social care sectors, and partly because even with a unified definition not all people who die whilst rough sleeping would fit into any such definition.

Development of the Review Process

In 2018, a sharp increase in premature deaths of people experiencing homelessness in the London Borough of Haringey triggered an enquiry into the benefits of reviewing such deaths in the borough. The enquiry found that, whilst a number of deaths were picked up by existing statutory review processes (SARs, Learning Disability Mortality Reviews, Domestic Homicide Reviews and Drug-Related Deaths Reviews), homelessness was understood by these reviews as a contributory factor, rather than as a key pillar in the person's inability to remain safe or access appropriate support to reduce the risks they faced. Moreover, some deaths were not within the criteria of any review process and as such these lives and deaths were not explored at all, potentially missing vital opportunities to improve local practice and, crucially, to prevent further deaths.

In January 2019, Haringey Safeguarding Adults Board approved a proposal to develop a discrete review process, which would explore the deaths of anyone who died whilst rough sleeping, or homeless and/or living in hostels. The proposal's approach was based on the following principles:

- *Strengths-based:* Reviews will look at how the person, and the services that supported them, had been able to manage and avoid risks, focusing on periods where the person had been safer as a means of identifying positive practice to be built on further.

- *Practice-focused:* Reviews will focus on local operational and organisational practices and partnerships, identifying strengths and opportunities for improvement in the operational, commissioning and policy infrastructure around homelessness.

- *Action learning:* Reviews will be more concise and faster-paced than SARs, identifying learning and opportunities for change to be implemented immediately.

- *Human:* Using pen portraits and the involvement of friends and family, reviews would try to capture more than just the risks, needs and deficits related to someone's life and death, but also who they were, what they were good at and what they had achieved and offered to those around them.

- *Aligned:* Reviews would not supersede or duplicate other statutory review processes but contribute positively to them by gathering early evidence and insights.

Haringey's Homelessness Fatality Review Procedure was adopted using powers granted by section 44(4) of the Care Act. Henceforth, Fatality Reviews would act as one mechanism by which the SAB could prioritise the prevention of abuse and neglect affecting adults experiencing homelessness in the Borough. Adopting this review process ensured that Fatality Reviews could leverage and draw on the authority of the SAB partnership, encouraging participation from a range of partners and giving weight to review recommendations and outcomes.

The review process was agreed as a responsibility of the Borough's Strategic Lead for Homelessness and Vulnerable Adults, who leads commissioning, strategy and delivery of the Borough's work around rough sleeping and multiple exclusion homelessness. To account for the additional pressures on capacity, the review process had two discrete stages which would ensure all deaths were reviewed; those which highlighted an opportunity for preventative learning and practice development were taken to the second more in-depth stage, involving multi-disciplinary panel discussion, an outcome report and action plan. The agreed governance for the review process also recognised pressures on capacity, thus proposing an annual report be submitted to and published by the SAB, rather than the publication of every review as is the case with the SAR process. The annual report provides a thematic analysis of the completed reviews in the previous 12 months, and describes developments in partnership and practice which had arisen from them, as well as capturing other developments in the local system, such as commissioning and strategy activity, of relevance to the SAB's strategic priorities around homelessness.

Overview of Completed Reviews

Since January 2019, the Homelessness Fatality Review procedure has been employed to explore 14 deaths. Of those who passed away, 79% were men, with an average age at death of 41 years old, lower than the national average for homeless deaths.[12] Three women died, and their average age at death was 43 years old, this time slightly higher than the national average, although still shockingly young. Of those who died, 80% were from BAME backgrounds, with 33% of these being people from Eastern European nations, most commonly Poland. Whilst broadly representative of the population of single adults experiencing multiple exclusion homelessness in the Borough, it highlights the vast over-representation of BAME people and raises serious questions for local and national policy-makers about the racialised dynamics of homelessness and its most harmful effects. Of the people who died, 53% could be defined as experiencing multiple exclusion homelessness, with drug/alcohol dependency, mental and/or physical health issues and involvement with the criminal justice system factors affecting their ability to live healthy and satisfying lives.

Learning from Fatality Reviews

Homelessness Fatality Reviews have contributed similar evidence to that of SARs into the causes, contributors, positive practice and professional shortfalls surrounding the premature deaths of people experiencing homelessness and rough sleeping. However, implementation of a discrete homelessness review process has contributed additional learning and insight.

---

[12] www.ons.gov.uk/peoplepopulationandcommunity/birthsdeathsandmarriages/deaths/datasets/deathsofhomelesspeopleinenglandandwales

Grief

That anyone should die whilst homeless in one of the world's most developed economies should be cause for a national outcry. Yet, in the region of 1000 homeless people die prematurely in England and Wales every year, a fact largely ignored at the national level until the Bureau of Investigative Journalism and the Museum of Homelessness[13] captured the attention of mainstream media in 2017/2018, compelling the Ministry of Housing, Communities and Local Government/ONS to begin to collect and scrutinise data about this most deleterious of social phenomena.

Judith Butler (2009) has written about the idea of 'precariousness' and how it relates to 'ungrievable lives', where 'an ungrievable life is one that cannot be mourned because it has never lived, that is, it has never counted as a life at all'.[14] Although she was writing specifically about lives lost as part of war, there are obvious parallels in how deaths of other socially marginalised people are understood and accounted for, both by those around them and society at large. In the absence of a social outcry, and even in much of the media, academic and practice-based writing on the subject, there is a subtle tone of inevitability, even at times a deservedness, which is evoked to explain the deaths of people experiencing homelessness. This can be evidenced in the pervasive nature of phrases such as 'lifestyle choice', the focus on socially denigrated experiences such as addiction as opposed to those perceived as more deserving of sympathy such as childhood trauma and abuse, and in pervasive stereotypes about the types of people and experiences associated with street homelessness.

By contrast, Haringey's homelessness fatality review process has created space for exploring grief and loss experienced by peers, practitioners and family members alike. The reflective and human nature of the review, with its attempt to evoke a portrait of each person rather than just a summation of their needs, risks and vulnerabilities, has had the effect of evoking conversations that, as it became clear, were all too poignantly absent during the person's life. Talking about the unique things each person contributed to the world and the things that brought them joy illuminated the limitations of so-called 'professional' language when describing a human life.

---

13 www.theguardian.com/society/2018/oct/08/homeless-people-die-uk-2017
14 www.versobooks.com/blogs/2339-judith-butler-precariousness-and-grievability-when-is-life-grievable

In all reviews where a multi-disciplinary panel was convened, practitioners were encouraged to reflect on their relationship with the person who passed away, and how their memories of the relationship they had with the person highlighted opportunities for learning and improvement. The impact of creating this type of relational-reflective space for practitioners was not only that it gave an outlet for the grief involved in this type of interpersonal support work; this also afforded practitioners a meaningful insight into the motivations, limitations and frustrations of their colleagues.

Recognising Friends and Chosen Family

Many people affected by homelessness have challenging and fractured relationships with their biological families or legal next of kin. This is particularly the case for survivors of childhood abuse, people from the LGBTQ+ community and those with longstanding issues around addiction and dependency, who are vastly over-represented in the population of people affected by rough sleeping.

Whilst SARs do involve family members, sometimes with powerful influence on the outcome, there is an absence of recognition, and therefore involvement of, 'chosen family' and other friends/peers, whom many homeless people rely on heavily for emotional and practical support (Neale and Brown 2016). Notwithstanding the need and commitment to maintain the personal privacy of the person who died, the Haringey Homelessness Fatality Review procedure includes an invitation to the deceased's peers, friends and neighbours to share their memories and reflections of the person who had died, either 1:1 with the Panel Chair, or in a group with a trusted supporter as facilitator. The purpose of this invitation is to create space for grief, for talking about acts of remembrance and to provide an opportunity for people affected by homelessness to contribute to the conclusions and recommendations of the review.

This invitation was taken up as part of three reviews, leading to one group discussion in a night shelter and four 1:1 conversations with the Panel Chair. In all three reviews where this was a feature, the involvement of the person's chosen family and peers was significant and impactful. Not only did people reflect that it felt therapeutic and novel for them to be invited to share their memories and feelings, but it also felt important to talk about death in general, to describe their own fears and frustrations about the support available to people who were homeless and at risk. In all instances where people with lived experience were involved, their input led directly to changes in operational practice.

Transitions

Mr XX

Mr XX died in March 2019 after a long period of self-neglect related to alcohol dependency and depression. Although he had been supported by a number of statutory and third sector organisations, his health had declined steadily over several months and nothing practitioners offered had any positive effect on his health or state of mind.

The review identified a number of shortfalls in communication between social care, acute and primary health care teams, and included a recognition that the daily task of supporting this very unwell man had fallen predominantly on a single support worker in the supported housing service where Mr XX had lived.

In the review panel meeting, the support worker shared frustrations with other services and organisations, emotionally articulating the impact of feeling he had been left to all but watch a softly spoken, intelligent and caring former nurse drink himself to death.

The bravery with which this support worker spoke of his relationship with Mr XX and of his grief and frustration at his passing had a profound effect on everyone present. A health colleague made a personal apology to the support worker for failing to do more to understand the environment Mr XX was being discharged into, and the impact of this. Mr XX's GP, who had been very involved in his care for a number of years, also expressed his deep sadness and frustration at the loss of a man who in other circumstances would have been considered a colleague.

This experience at the first multi-disciplinary Homelessness Fatality Review panel in Haringey created an unexpected blueprint for those that followed, which was reflective, accountable and profoundly human. Continuity of care is now one of Haringey's strategic priorities for improving homelessness health outcomes, as is developing a palliative care pathway which recognises the specifics of enabling someone to die with choice and dignity whilst living in hostels and supported housing.

Conclusion

This chapter has outlined the contribution of SARs and Homelessness Fatality Reviews to the evidence base for working with people experiencing multiple exclusion homelessness, and the place of adult safeguarding within it. SABs may use this evidence base to hold partner agencies accountable for the degree to which organisational and multi-agency partnership cultures, policies and procedures, and relationships between commissioners and providers, provide an enabling context in which positive practice can flourish. Where barriers remain, SABs can seek assurance that these are being addressed. That mandate of 'holding to account' extends to national government, as to whether the climate it creates through legislative, policy and finance decisions upholds the right to life and the right to live free of inhuman and degrading treatment (Human Rights Act 1998).

Fundamentally, the focus of both SARs and Fatality Reviews is on learning and improvement across five domains – direct work with individuals, collaboration between members of the team around the person, organisational support for practitioners, SAB governance and the national legal, policy and financial context within which adult safeguarding and work with people experiencing homelessness is located. When all the domains are in alignment, each supporting best practice across the system, transformational change is achievable. That is one lesson that has been learned again in the national response to people experiencing homelessness during the first wave and lockdown of the Covid-19 pandemic.

A key challenge is to demonstrate the impact and the outcomes of this review activity, the difference that is achieved. In terms of the review process, experience with Fatality Reviews suggests that practitioners find the reflective discussions helpful, that the process can explore tensions, limitations and conflicting practices between organisations, and that accountability is a key pre-requisite for change. A further key outcome has been their influence on the SAB strategic priority setting, where multiple exclusion homelessness and rough sleeping are now clear priorities across prevention and workforce development workstreams. Further, gaps in service delivery and local systems identified in reviews have been used to inform successful bids for new funding from central government departments, resulting in the creation of a pioneering multi-disciplinary homelessness health and social care team. In acknowledging the emotional impact of reviewing deaths there is also now a commitment from the local authority to ensure all its frontline rough sleeping and housing support teams have access to regular reflective practice, something not previously available.

With SARs there has been little published evaluative enquiry on the process of reviewing. However, the national analysis (Preston-Shoot *et al.* 2020) highlighted the importance of compliance with the statutory guidance, for instance on family and practitioner involvement, with individual reports identifying what had been helpful, including reflective analysis by the agencies involved.

Research has identified the barriers to transferring learning into policy and practice (Rawlings *et al.* 2014; Preston-Shoot 2018). Change takes time and requires sustained leadership and focus within a learning culture. Some SARs do identify policy and practice change that has been accomplished during the review process (Preston-Shoot *et al.* 2020). Some SABs provide detailed accounts in annual reports of the outcomes of review findings and recommendations. What is clear, including from arrangements for Fatality Reviews, is that the SAB must be a guiding presence, seeking assurance and holding agencies to account through audits, learning development seminars and proportionate methodologies that explore and challenge where obstacles continue to block change. SABs and reviews, however, also need to be clear where outcomes are sought, whether this is in changes in attitudes, knowledge and skill acquisition, practice, organisational behaviour and/or policy (Preston-Shoot 2020c), and how the impact of change will be captured, not least in benefits for individuals and their families.

Chapter 11

Safeguarding Adults Boards and Multiple Exclusion Homelessness: The Challenges for System Leadership

Adi Cooper

Introduction

This chapter argues that Safeguarding Adults Boards (SABs) have a key role to provide local leadership regarding safeguarding and multiple exclusion homelessness. Demonstrating collaborative and transformative leadership through working with others, actively engaging new partners and connecting with other partnerships are essential practices for any SAB. Tackling the safeguarding risks for people who experience multiple exclusion homelessness can be regarded as a 'wicked issue'. 'Wicked issues' include those relating to social exclusion, particularly when mediating between the public sphere of government and government policy and the private sphere of people living their lives (De Corte *et al.* 2017). By definition, these sit at the interface of different legal, policy and partnership roles and responsibilities (Camillus 2008; De Corte *et al.* 2017). SABs can influence the actions of partners in this area. Responding to local needs through prioritising this improvement at a strategic level provides a clear message to practitioners and managers across partner organisations, agencies and sectors, recognising the work that is done. SABs can also validate people's lived experience through acknowledging the risks and needs that people face and recognising the additional barriers that people experiencing homelessness confront in accessing support. They can emphasise that the safeguarding needs of people who experience multiple exclusion homelessness are as valid as anyone else's in the community and are as important to address.

SABs became statutory partnerships under the Care Act 2014, although local partnerships had been established with a focus on adult protection since 'No Secrets' in 2000 (Department of Health and Social Care 2000). With senior representatives from relevant local organisations and sectors as members, SABs provide strategic leadership regarding safeguarding adults. They are a forum for both collaboration and holding partners to account, evidencing how partners are meeting their own statutory duties and responsibilities to ensure that local people are safeguarded (DHSC 2020).

The challenges in recognition of the safeguarding needs of people experiencing multiple exclusion homelessness are reflected throughout the chapters in this book. These people have often experienced marginalisation, trauma, institutional care and tri-morbidities of substance misuse, mental ill-health and physical ill-health as well as homelessness (Mason *et al.* 2018). The needs of people experiencing multiple exclusion homelessness have featured on the agendas and in the annual strategic plans of SABs where homelessness and rough sleeping have been longstanding local priorities, for example in central London (see City and Hackney Safeguarding Adults Board 2018, 2019; Safeguarding Adults Executive Board 2019), or where there have been deaths of people who were homeless that have led to Safeguarding Adults Reviews (SARs) (see Chapter 10). In response, local SABs have sought to improve multi-agency working across service and agency boundaries to safeguard people experiencing homelessness.

The Government's Rough Sleeping Strategy (MHCLG 2018a) raised the profile of people who experience homelessness within safeguarding policy and practice. Subsequently, during the Covid-19 pandemic, the raft of initiatives to move people off the streets has also attempted to address some of the longer-term needs of people who have been sleeping out. These activities frame the changing local responses to homelessness, including addressing the complex health needs that lead to the shocking life expectancy rates for this section of the population (see Chapter 5).

In this chapter, the roles and responsibilities of SABs are described and examples of how these apply to people experiencing multiple exclusion homelessness are provided. The collaborative leadership function of the SAB partnership is explored, as safeguarding is fundamentally and essentially a partnership responsibility. The governance functions for SABs are discussed, including the need for cross-partnership collaboration and transformational leadership, with reference to the leadership roles of elected members. The final section outlines the outcome of learning to date, presented as a 'reflection tool for SABs'. These indicate the success factors that can illustrate the collaborative innovation necessary in this area to support future development and achieve change.

Safeguarding Adults Boards: Roles and Responsibilities under the Care Act 2014

The role and responsibilities of SABs are set out in the statutory guidance (DHSC 2020, sections 14.133–14.161) and summarised in Table 11.1, with comments regarding people who experience multiple exclusion homelessness.

Table 11.1 Safeguarding Adults Boards: Responsibilities

	Detail of responsibilities	Implications regarding homelessness
SAB main objective (DHSC 2020, s.14.133, s.14.2).	'to assure itself that local safeguarding arrangements and partners act to help and protect adults in its area who meet the criteria set out in paragraph 14.2'. People who are eligible for safeguarding are defined as 'an adult who has care and support needs…is experiencing, or at risk of, abuse or neglect', and 'as a result of those care and support needs is unable to protect themselves from either the risk of, or experience of, abuse or neglect'	This can include people who experience multiple exclusion homelessness in the area, if their circumstances meet the criteria in paragraph 14.2 (although this is not specified in the statutory guidance)
SAB strategic role (DHSC 2020, s.14.134).	'it oversees and leads adult safeguarding across the locality' including prevention as well as protection	This can include people who experience multiple exclusion homelessness in the area (although this is not specified in the statutory guidance)

	Detail of responsibilities	Implications regarding homelessness
SABs should evidence the safeguarding principles (DHSC 2020, s.14.13, s.14.137).	'Partnership' is one of the six key principles of safeguarding adults described in the statutory guidance and this should be evidenced in leadership, collaboration and co-operation in delivering its responsibilities	The partnership can include representatives of organisations working with people experiencing homelessness, on the SAB, in its groups and any joint work (although this is not specified in the statutory guidance)
SABs have three key core statutory duties (DHSC 2020, s.14.136, ss.152–173).	To produce a strategic plan (annually or every three to five years), which sets out what the SAB and its partners intend to do to meet local safeguarding needs To produce an annual report which describes the SAB and its partners' activities during the period to achieve its objectives To arrange SARs in certain circumstances	This can include objectives, achievements and SARs related to work in safeguarding people experiencing homelessness in the area

Following the implementation of the Care Act 2014 and establishment of SABs as statutory partnerships, their main focus was on ensuring that they were functioning adequately and meeting their duties and responsibilities (National Network of Chairs of Safeguarding Adults Boards 2017).

Research on Safeguarding Adults Partnerships prior to the Care Act 2014 described core governance functions of: strategic leadership and planning; setting standards and issuing guidance, quality assurance, promoting participation; awareness-raising and publicity; capaciy-building and training; and relationship management (Braye *et al.* 2012, p.65). These are included in the broad range of responsibilities for SABs described in the statutory guidance. In addition the guidance specifies that the SABs have responsibilities for: reviewing what local data says about the prevalence of abuse and neglect; developing preventative strategies; developing strategies to deal with the impact of inequalities on abuse and neglect; holding partners to account for the quality and effectiveness of their safeguarding services; establishing mechanisms to develop policies and strategies, monitoring and reviewing them; as well as meeting the core duties described above (DHSC 2020, s.14.139).

Homelessness as an Emerging Challenge and Priority Area for SABs

The survey of Chairs of SABs shows that, between 2017 and 2019, safeguarding and homelessness had emerged as an issue for some partnerships. Homelessness was identified as an area for the SABs' 'broadened remit' following the implementation of the Care Act 2014, a future priority for SABs, and as a 'contemporary safeguarding challenge' (National Network of Chairs of Safeguarding Adults Boards 2019, pp.6, 24, 27). In terms of addressing the safeguarding needs of people who experience homelessness, the range of responsibilities described in the statutory guidance is relevant. In considering how SABs might respond to the safeguarding needs of their homeless populations (not just their resident populations), they can apply all the functions described previously. A further survey conducted in 2019, focused on homelessness and safeguarding, found that SABs were increasingly engaged with issues regarding safeguarding and homelessness: 36% of SABs responded and 76% of those said that homelessness and safeguarding had been discussed between June 2018 and the end of May 2019, and several had held dedicated meetings or development days on this topic (Lloyd-Smith and Bampton 2019).

Some SABs have taken the initiative in response to local need, for example in central London. The City and Hackney Safeguarding Adults Board set up a Homelessness/Rough Sleeping and Safeguarding Task and Finish group during 2017/2018, which aimed to improve the way that safeguarding needs of people who experienced homelessness or were rough sleeping were addressed (City and Hackney Safeguarding Adults Board 2018, 2019). The Safeguarding Adults Executive Board (SAEB) covering Westminster, Kensington and Chelsea prioritised this area of work following an increase in deaths of people who experienced homelessness. This workstream aimed 'to keep track of trends and to look for and share lessons learned, with a multi-agency approach and within a clear governance structure' and 'develop a new pathway to support people who are rough sleepers and those who are in hostels and supported housing who may be at high risk and eligible for safeguarding under the Care Act 2014' (SAEB 2019, p.22). They also reported the establishment of an 'enhanced vulnerabilities forum' in Westminster, which is 'a multi-agency problem solving forum to improve planning and coordination support for some people experiencing homelessness who have "fallen through cracks" and/or been very resistant to change' (SAEB 2019, p.22).

The extent and impact of homelessness will have local characteristics in any area, and understanding the local profile is essential for developing safeguarding work to support local people. In Norfolk, local Public Health officers undertook a joint strategic needs assessment, which identified the demographic profile, range of needs and existing services to meet the needs of people experiencing homelessness across the county (Ollett 2019). This identified safeguarding risks, particularly for young people vulnerable to exploitation, abuse or trafficking. This type of information provides helpful background for the SAB to consider when looking at the prevalence of abuse and neglect and identifying strategic priorities for its annual plans. It raises significant implications for working across partnership boundaries with Community Safety and Children's Safeguarding Partnerships.

The SAB has duties to develop relevant policies and strategies for safeguarding. In London, the addition of Appendix Seven to the 'London Multi-Agency Safeguarding Policy and Procedures' on safeguarding and homelessness provides a framework for London SABs (London Safeguarding Adults Board 2019). The purpose of this appendix is to provide an overview of what is considered current good practice in relation to individuals who experience multiple exclusion homelessness, and information about relevant legal rules. It includes how SABs might respond to increased media and public interest in this area and provides links to helpful resources. Since all London SABs, and all their members, are signed up to operate according to London Multi-Agency Safeguarding Policy and Procedures, this appendix supports a consistent approach across London.

In summary, these examples illustrate the ways in which SABs have started to develop safeguarding responses to meet the needs of people experiencing multiple exclusion homelessness within the remit of their duties and responsibilities. However, a major driver in many cases has been when the SAB has undertaken a SAR, which is the subject of the next section.

Safeguarding Adults Boards and Homelessness: Learning from Safeguarding Adults Reviews

A major prompt for SABs to engage in this area of safeguarding activity comes from SARs. A snapshot survey in 2019 found that there were a significant number of referrals to SABs to undertake SARs about people who had experienced homelessness to learn lessons from these tragic events (Lloyd-Smith and Bampton 2019). Given that SARs aim to shine a light on areas where partnership and multi-agency practices require improvement, there is growing evidence of activity in this area indicating that this is a priority for learning for SABs (see Chapter 10). If the challenge for SABs is to recognise the strategic implications and their leadership responsibilities for safeguarding people who are homeless, particularly those who experience multiple exclusion homelessness, SARs provide a robust evidence base and indicate clear priorities for improvement. Identifying barriers to effective practice, especially multi-agency practice, and addressing the barriers that frustrate effective practice are the key aims of any review. Following the SAR, the local SAB should ensure that recommendations arising from the SAR are responded to through action plans and the relevant agencies are held to account to deliver those recommendations. New policies and procedures, training and guidance are frequently recommended and can be helpful to support practice improvement, but culture and attitude changes are also required, and these can be modelled and led by SAB partners.

Relevant to safeguarding people who experience multiple exclusion homelessness is the learning from many SARs that there is limited understanding and recognition of self-neglect at a practice level. Further, there is a lack of recognition of it as a safeguarding category, as well as a reluctance to see substance misuse/alcohol abuse or substance dependency as self-neglect (Alcohol Change UK 2019; Leeds SAB and Safer Leeds 2020; Martineau and Manthorpe 2020, p.192). The national review of SARs found that self-neglect was the most common category of harm identified in the 231 SARs that were analysed: it is telling that the deaths of people who self-neglect have been the ones we have most to learn from, where most often things have gone wrong or could have been done differently (Preston-Shoot 2020d; Preston-Shoot *et al.* 2020). As with rough sleeping, substance misuse, alcohol abuse and other forms of self-neglect can all be (mis)construed as 'lifestyle choices', and their impact, in terms of risks to the person, then not identified or recognised (see Chapter 3). The interface between substance misuse, alcohol abuse, mental health and mental capacity are explored elsewhere (see Chapter 4); how they might affect someone's behaviour and ability to protect themselves from harm, as well as cause self-harm, are relevant to safeguarding. Further, as with substance misuse, homelessness continues to be perceived as a result of personal failure (see Chapters 2 and 3). The implications for SABs are similarly to recognise and 'see' these needs and risks in their local populations, and to then include them as priorities in their strategic plans. A SAR is likely to highlight these aspects as areas for learning and improvement (see Chapter 10). Although it could be argued that policy developed in response to tragedy can have disbenefits, the key message from SARs is that they provide opportunities for local learning and insight into what can change.

Where local SARs have not been commissioned about people with experience of homelessness, to learn lessons, the SAB can look at learning from national or thematic SAR analyses, and then review and audit the impact of these on their policies, procedures and practice in this area of safeguarding activity (Preston-Shoot 2020d). Indeed, an ongoing key challenge for SABs is how to demonstrate the effectiveness and impact of their work to improve safeguarding in the area, and auditing is one mechanism for achieving this (Preston-Shoot 2020c).

In summary, SARs have provided a catalyst for some SABs and highlighted where safeguarding for people experiencing multiple exclusion homelessness needs to change. They identify learning across all domains. They provide key insights and a framework for improvement through the action plans developed in response to SAR recommendations.

Safeguarding Adults Boards: Collaborative and Transformational Leadership

The core purpose of SABs is to provide strategic leadership for safeguarding adults in a specific location. How this is achieved is more than the content of its plans and strategies. Just as 'safeguarding is everyone's responsibility', similarly 'leadership is everyone's responsibility' (Preston-Shoot 2020a, p.5). This can then become 'no one's priority' and so the SAB's key role is to keep safeguarding at the forefront for all partners. During the Covid-19 pandemic SABs demonstrated this through highlighting emerging concerns and issues, promoting good practice and seeking assurance that partners were meeting their safeguarding responsibilities (Cooper 2020).

The value and importance of clear strategic leadership in terms of effectiveness, rather than structure or form, was recognised even before

SABs became statutory partnerships (Braye *et al.* 2012). For interagency partnerships such as SABs, collaborative and collective forms of leadership are necessary. Research has shown that 'collaboration between public agencies is critical to address social issues effectively' (Ramadass *et al.* 2018, p.749). Moreover, collaborative leadership is required, as the guidance states, 'in order to create a framework of inter-agency arrangements' (DHSC 2020, para.14.137). Collaborative partnership working is core to SAB functioning, and partnership is one of the six safeguarding principles in the statutory guidance.

SABs provide a governance mechanism for local leaders committed to improving the lives of people who may be at risk of or experiencing abuse or neglect. As such, governance network theory provides a paradigm for understanding how they operate and how collaboration can provide innovative solutions to complex social problems (Klijn and Koppenjan 2012). These types of networks require trust between partners because this 'reduces strategic uncertainty', as partners 'take each other's interests into account' (Klijn and Koppenjan 2012, p.593). Understanding the challenges and achievements of SAB partners is part of what happens through information-sharing at meetings, development days and contributions to SAB annual reports.

Ramadass *et al.* (2018) argue that successful achievement of desired collaboration outcomes in the public sector requires transformational leadership, collaborative governance frameworks and relational capital. This is particularly pertinent where there are 'wicked issues' to solve and innovative and different solutions are required, such as safeguarding people who experience multiple exclusion homelessness (Von Bueren *et al.* 2003; De Corte *et al.* 2017). Learning from examples of where health care for people who sleep rough has been effectively led, 'local leaders need to manage complex interdependencies across multiple organisations and sectors. This requires them to take shared ownership and responsibility for tackling rough sleeping and model partnership working across different professional cultures' (Cream *et al.* 2020, p.7). Further they need to model positive relationships and effective partnership working; raise the profile of the issues; set high expectations for staff; and give permission for staff to 'do the right thing', in order to be able to bridge the barriers between the different systems and structures of health, but also social care and safeguarding, and homelessness services (Cream *et al.* 2020). These desired leadership behaviours apply to SAB members when looking to improve partnership working in safeguarding people experiencing multiple exclusion homelessness. The benefits of inter-organisational networking and collaborative working can be realised both at operational and strategic levels in overcoming the fragmentation that exists due to different duties, responsibilities, organisational structures, systems and budget pressures. The SAB can be used as 'a forum for debate to challenge dominant conceptualisations of complex social problems across organisational and sectorial boundaries' (De Corte *et al.* 2017, p.524). This way of working applies to partners across the SAB and with partners who are not members of the SAB, for example local businesses, religious communities and others who have an interest in public spaces.

The SAB is a partnership or network of senior representatives of the partner agencies, and as such lends itself to more dispersed or distributive leadership styles with senior leaders leading together as a 'team'. Konradt (2013) describes the mechanics and effective impact of dispersed leadership in team working structures: distributive or dispersed leadership is about shared leadership and the interactions between people, influencing horizontally (Mandell and Keast 2009). Members of the SAB are senior officers within their own agencies, organisations or sectors. They not only participate in the SAB meetings but may undertake leadership roles on behalf of the SAB for sub-groups or particular projects or priority areas. Research has found that when public sector leaders lead networks other than in their own agency, they demonstrate people-orientated behaviours rather than the task-orientated behaviours they demonstrate within their own organisation (Silva and McGuire 2010). This echoes the findings regarding effectiveness of collaborative network leadership styles that highlight relational skills and competence in building trust to achieve collective goals (Mandell and Keast 2009). In the context of the leadership endeavour to shift multi-agency practice regarding a 'wicked issue', dispersed or distributive leadership is essential.

The local authority is the lead agency for safeguarding adults (DHSC 2020, Chapter 14) and local government is politically led. Elected councillors can hold a range of roles regarding safeguarding, including being members of SABs. These are 'crucial roles for councillors in examining how safeguarding is experienced by local people, how people were consulted and involved in developing policies and monitoring services, and how they were involved in their own safeguarding plans and procedures' (Local Government Association 2015, p.2). Councillors can hold officers and the SAB to account if they are not members of the SAB through scrutinising the work of the SAB (LGA 2015). They can make links to other local agendas, strategies and partnerships, including police and criminal justice, community safety and cohesion, housing and homelessness. They can also play a role in mediating the interface between the public (their constituents) and professionals working with or developing services for people experiencing homelessness. Whether elected councillors are SAB members or not, the questions at the end of this chapter are relevant.

Where there are two-tier councils (county councils and district councils) rather than unitary or metropolitan local authorities, responsibilities for safeguarding adults sit with the County Council Adult Social Care Services and housing and homelessness with the district councils. In these areas, the organisational structures can be barriers to joint working and the role of senior officer and elected members can be critical in modelling effective partnership working. Research has illustrated how local political leadership has played a critical role in prioritising homelessness issues in some places (Cream *et al.* 2020). At the Birmingham workshop (one of the series cited below), the closing remarks from Councillor Sharon Thompson, Cabinet Member for Homes and Neighbourhoods, evidenced the passionate leadership driving change in the city.[1]

Whilst the three statutory agencies – local authority, clinical commissioning group and police – are core members of the SAB, the SAB can include other organisations and individuals in its membership, and invite others to its meetings (DHSC 2020, paras.14.145–14.146). In the context of safeguarding people experiencing homelessness, a SAB can invite partners with responsibilities for policy development, commissioning or providing services in this area to attend their meetings. In particular, the local providers of outreach services, frequently from the voluntary and community sector, can offer critical insight into the issues faced. Further, asking for contributions from experts by experience or lay members can provide insights that are otherwise inaccessible (see Chapter 3). There are different ways of involving people in SABs and this is an area of critical challenge for them in Making Safeguarding Personal (Droy and Lawson 2017). Whilst a range of agencies may be drawn into participating in a Safeguarding Adults Review process

---

1   Available at www.youtube.com/watch?v=iUmfYC81JjI.

(SAR panel membership or learning event participations), longer-term engagement with the SAB is essential to achieve improvement and change.

Many SABs have appointed Independent Chairs, who can offer constructive challenge, help to hold partners to account, interface with other partnerships (see below) and provide additional reassurance that the SAB has some independence from the statutory partners (DHSC 2020, s.14.150). Independent Chairs can model the collaborative leadership style and be 'process catalysts' in their leadership of collaborative networks (Mandell and Keast 2009). Through initiating, facilitating and minding the process of collaboration, they can create an environment in which partners can access new learning and change their behaviours. This leadership can mean that there is the 'ability to find and develop a pool of shared meaning through a process of creating a new collective value' which leads to reframing the situation and producing new solutions (Mandell and Keast 2009, p.174). The leadership role 'centres on creating a space and the process to enable network members to understand and appreciate each other, push boundaries and discover leverage synergies and innovative outcomes' (Mandell and Keast 2009, p.175). This is what Independent SAB Chairs should aspire to, particularly given the challenges regarding safeguarding and homelessness.

A collaborative leadership style is conducive to effective partnership working. However, the responsibilities to hold partners to account and demonstrate accountability can be challenging to achieve within a collaborative approach. Skilful leadership, including the Independent Chair's, is critical to navigate what may appear to be contradictory forces.

In summary, SABs can provide strategic leadership, but need to do so in a way that enables and supports local leadership mechanisms. Collaborative, transformative and participatory leadership styles are conducive to effective partnership working. Local politicians can play a key role. Partners, including people with lived experience, can enrich the partnership.

Multi-Agency Governance Mechanisms and Partnership Relationships

Governance has been defined as: 'structures and processes designed to ensure accountability, transparency, responsiveness, rule of law, stability, equality and inclusiveness, empowerment and broad-based participation' (International Bureau of Education n.d.); or 'the process whereby public institutions conduct public affairs, manage public resources and guarantee the realisation of human rights...with due regard to the rule of law' (United Nations Human Rights, Office of the High Commissioner 2020). Prior to the Care Act 2014, good governance for SABs included accountability to external bodies as well as accountability on behalf of member agencies (Braye *et al.* 2012). The Care Act 2014 guidance describes a range of governance mechanisms: an Independent Chair of the SAB is accountable to the Chief Executive of the local authority; the Annual Report of the SAB must be sent to the Chief Executive and Leader of the local authority, the Police and Crime Commissioner and the Chief Constable, the local Healthwatch and the Chair of the Health and Wellbeing Board (DHSC 2020, s.14.150, s.14.160). Additionally, many SAB Annual Reports are reviewed by the local authority's scrutiny arrangements, and presented to the local community safety partnership as well as children's partnership, particularly where there are intersecting areas of interest and concern such as modern slavery, domestic abuse or transitional safeguarding.

When considering homelessness and safeguarding, new inter-partnership relationships and governance may be required. In Birmingham the Safeguarding Adults Board worked closely with the Homelessness Partnership Board in developing their workstreams (BSAB 2020). In Leeds the SAB and Community Safety Partnership undertook a joint review, which included information from a range of sources regarding people living street-based lives, following the deaths of ten people 'to identify what we need to do to enhance and improve how we work together as a city to bring about sustained change and improved life experiences for those of our citizens living in these circumstances' (Leeds Safeguarding Adults Board and Safer Leeds 2020, p.5).

The SAB has the lead for governance of safeguarding adults; however, the governance for safeguarding people who experience homelessness can be led by different partnerships in each area, depending on local arrangements, systems or structures, and could be the local Health and Wellbeing Board, Homelessness Reduction Board, Community Safety Partnership, SAB or their local equivalents. Whatever the type of local arrangements, they need to be supported by the key partners and politicians, who can provide the strategic leadership, agree on 'a common and shared vision alongside roles and responsibilities for assuring the quality of policies, procedures and practice', who are 'able to hold relevant organisations and system leaders to account for delivering strategic objectives and service improvement', and the 'local partnership delivery mechanisms will need to report regularly into the agreed governance arrangements on progress with improvement activity' (Preston-Shoot 2020a, p.28).

This governance oversight should include ensuring that lessons are learned from different types of reviews and improvements in practice promoted, for example through the development and subsequent review of policies and procedures that combine adult safeguarding and multiple exclusion homelessness (Preston-Shoot 2020a). Auditing practice can provide an evidence base of whether the changes in policy, procedure or protocol have been effective in practice and achieved the desired outcomes.

However, the culture and system changes that are necessary may not be able to be fully achieved through revising transactional processes and monitoring impact through performance management. Complex challenges, such as effectively safeguarding people experiencing homelessness, require more than the 'new public management' approach that has dominated the public sector in the last decades. Rather it has been argued that collaborative leadership of complex change requires 'system stewardship' roles and a 'human learning systems' approach (Lowe et al. 2020).

Governance oversight informs the nature of local improvement objectives, meeting the responsibilities of the SAB partner organisations and sectors, and leadership objectives, and can promote a sector-led improvement type approach (Local Government Association 2012). Shared values are necessary for effective networks to resolve 'wicked issues'; effective networks need to develop a common framework, or value base, with reference to human rights and principles of social justice (De Corte et al. 2017). This research implies therefore that SAB members, as a 'network', need also to have a common value base to support their leadership and achieve change.

Understanding the impact of structural inequalities and intersectionality on people's lives is also relevant to safeguarding people experiencing homelessness. The differential impact on people experiencing homelessness is influenced by different structural oppressions, for example Black, Asian and minority ethnic people are three times more likely to experience homelessness (Shelter 2017). A quarter of trans people have experienced homelessness (Stonewall 2017). The common value base can include an explicit commitment to challenging inequalities. People have multiple identities, and so understanding the personal experience of homelessness as well as discrimination is key (see Chapter 3).

Responding to the Challenge: Criteria for Success?

At a national level, the emerging interest in safeguarding adults and homelessness led to the establishment of an expert reference group in 2019. This group included: civil servants from the Department of Health and Social Care as well as the Ministry of Housing, Communities and Local Government; adult safeguarding and homelessness practitioners and managers from the statutory and voluntary sectors; SAB Independent Chairs; business managers; health and police representatives. This group advised on the development of a programme of four workshops, held in Autumn 2019, focused on safeguarding and homelessness. These were supported by the workstream on safeguarding adults within the Care and Health Improvement Programme (CHIP), which is funded by the Department of Health and Social Care and delivered by the Local Government Association, in collaboration with the Association of Directors of Adult Social Services (Preston-Shoot 2020a). The ethos and purpose of the CHIP programme is sector-led improvement (Local Government Association 2012). The workshops were well attended by practitioners and managers from a range of statutory and third sector services, including adult social care, health, police, housing and ambulance, as well as SAB Chairs and managers, and senior leaders with responsibilities for policy development and service improvement. The aims of the workshops were to hear from people working in this area and share good practice, discuss and understand the blocks and barriers to improvement, and identify what enables good practice to be developed and sustained (Preston-Shoot 2020a). Presentations evidenced that homelessness had become a key priority for some SABs, for example in Leeds, where a review into a number of deaths of people experiencing homelessness was underway, and in Birmingham, where there was a strong council commitment regarding tackling homelessness.

The product of the workshops was *Adult Safeguarding and Homelessness: A Briefing on Positive Practice* (Preston-Shoot 2020a), which contains a checklist for SABs who wish to know how well they are progressing in this area which can be used as a mechanism for self-assessment. Examples of questions used in the self-assessment reflection tool are as follows.

Key Questions for Safeguarding Adults Boards and Elected Members

> What level of reassurance do you have that services are aligned to deliver practice that corresponds with the evidence base presented in *Adult Safeguarding and Homelessness: A Briefing on Positive Practice*?
>
> How are you holding agencies and the multiagency partnership to account for policy and practice in the field of adult safeguarding and multiple exclusion homelessness?
>
> Are there gaps in policies, procedures and protocols that need to be filled?
>
> How have lessons from audits and Safeguarding Adults Reviews, completed locally or elsewhere, informed practice and service development?
>
> What examples of positive practice can you share?
>
> *(Preston-Shoot 2020a, p.5)*

At a more detailed level, actions could include:

- Reviewing any multi-agency agreements or multi-agency panel arrangements regarding working with people at high risk and other complex cases including safeguarding and multiple exclusion homelessness.

- Ensuring that there are the strategic agreements and leadership arrangements necessary for the cultural and service changes required to improve services to safeguarding people experiencing homelessness.

- Auditing the impact of policies and procedures regarding safeguarding people experiencing homelessness (which may be standalone or incorporated in others, e.g. self-neglect).

- Providing or arranging for the provision of training, workshops, workforce development regarding practice and the management of safeguarding practice with people experiencing homelessness.

- Establishing a system to review the deaths of people experiencing homelessness and learning from these deaths.
- Joint working with relevant local partnerships (Community Safety Partnerships, Health and Wellbeing Boards and partnership arrangements for safeguarding children and young people) to coordinate governance, namely oversight of the development and review of policies, procedures and practice.
- Invite the homelessness support sector into the SAB.
- Find ways to include the voices of people who experience homelessness and safeguarding risks in the SAB.

Conclusion

SABs are in a key position to take a leadership role in initiating and collaborating to achieve positive changes in practice that will benefit those people at risk of abuse or neglect who experience homelessness. SABs can respond to the challenge to recognise the strategic implications and take on leadership responsibilities for safeguarding people who are homeless, particularly those who experience multiple exclusion homelessness. The steps taken by each SAB will depend on the local situation. In addition, any response requires collaborative leadership, as it means working with different partners. Mature partnerships and a 'human learning systems' approach (Lowe *et al.* 2020) are needed in order to respond to 'wicked issues', and safeguarding people experiencing homelessness can be considered one of these. There is an evidence base from SARs, mortality reviews and other research regarding learning from poor practice, service gaps and system breakdowns that indicates what works and what can help. It is incumbent on SABs to ensure that people experiencing homelessness in their areas are supported to deal with and reduce their safeguarding risks, alongside addressing their other significant multiple needs. It is critical that SABs work with other local governance mechanisms to progress improvement in this area.

Chapter 12

Multiple Exclusion Homelessness and Safeguarding: Supporting Practitioners

Katy Shorten

Introduction
Ensuring practitioners working across the homelessness and safeguarding sectors are well supported is fundamental to enabling people who are homeless to express and reach their goals and aspirations. Fitzpatrick *et al.* (2018) make the link between practitioner wellbeing and support with the success of homelessness interventions. They completed an evidence map identifying issues associated with the implementation of homelessness interventions; 61% of responses mentioned 'staff and caseworkers' issues. The analysis suggested the enablers of implementation were: ensuring an optimum 'caseload', matching up the practitioner skillset with the needs of the person, and 'buy in' with the intervention the practitioner is working on.

This chapter explores key elements of what support could be offered within and across the large range of organisations, roles, responsibilities and duties of the homelessness and safeguarding sectors. Three common themes for effective support to practitioners permeate this chapter: the voice of lived experience throughout practice, the importance of culture and leadership, and developing the confidence of practitioners in their own practice. This chapter explores the evidence for fostering these and covers (not in any order of importance or priority) the following.

Developing knowledge, understanding and skills: 'Seeing the person', rather than the circumstances and homelessness, and attending to stigma or judgement are key to building trusting relationships with people who are homeless. This is a fundamental skill for effective work across the sector. There is an opportunity to share learning and experience of approaches to support (e.g. strengths-based working, trauma-informed practice and Psychologically Informed Environment). Developing legal literacy in particular helps with a shared understanding of safeguarding to develop confidence and competence.

Practitioner wellbeing: This is a complex area of work where the dynamic between 'keeping people safe' and upholding people's rights plays out daily. Creating opportunities for reflective practice and supervision is key to reconciling this complexity within different roles across the sector. Ensuring the involvement of feedback from people who are homeless is an important part of this practice.

Partnership working: Developing mechanisms for equal value and respect for different parts of the system is crucial. This can be achieved by a commitment across the sector to developing a shared understanding of different roles, responsibilities and language.

Organisational culture: Providing a clear and congruent strategic backdrop and culture in which practitioners can work is a way to support practitioners. Support for practitioners working in homelessness and safeguarding needs to reflect structural and role complexity. As a starting point Preston-Shoot (2020a) identifies the key components of the 'organisation around the team', and ensuring effective management and oversight of the 'system', as:

- Supervision and staff support – with particular attention to staff stress or silo working.
- Access to specialist support – for example legal, safeguarding, mental capacity, mental health and housing.
- Commissioning – reflecting on how to measure success, procurement cycles, involvement of people with lived experience, and aligning commission cycles and budgets across sectors.
- Workforce development – covering both statutory and voluntary sectors.
- Workplace development – challenges workplaces to adapt and align their processes to meet the needs of individual people and staff.

- Culture – following on from the above, this is about giving permission and autonomy to staff to respond in a person-centred way to people they are working with.

Developing Knowledge, Understanding and Skills
Seeing the Person: Perceptions of Homelessness

Maseele *et al.* (2013) describe the shift in society's opinion of homelessness from a historical perception of 'vagrancy' to a poverty problem, accompanied by an emphasis on a psycho-social approach to homelessness. It is a health and welfare concern and not just a state of 'rooflessness'. The definition of 'multiple exclusion homelessness' (MEH) used throughout this book supports this premise. As such, working in homelessness requires knowledge and skills across many generalist and specific areas. Being able to understand and work together with a person who is homeless in the context of their own lives and experiences is fundamental to this. Woodcock and Gill (2014, p.48) identify that 'although homelessness and housing support staff are not therapists, the nature of the work entails a need for understanding and sensitivity'. This is not without its challenges, as described below.

Arguably the most important skill is the ability to build trusting relationships in a context of individual and system complexity. Trust is the mark of a good practitioner to person relationship. People who experience homelessness have often had breaches of trust in previous relationships and may be suspicious, so it may sometimes feel difficult to achieve (Phipps *et al.* 2017). In parallel, practitioners often report 'difficulties with engagement' when working with people who are homeless (Martineau *et al.* 2019, p.5). Exploring these different starting points and positions may help to reach a closer alignment and support strong practitioner and person relationships. This would support the sense of efficacy and self-worth of practitioners working with people who experience homelessness – practitioners feel better if they know they are making a positive difference (Watson *et al.* 2019).

In addition, practitioners may interact and work with people differently if they are aware of certain things happening for that person. For example, Martineau *et al.* (2019) identified practitioner attitudes about people using substances might influence the way they work with them. This in part led Alcohol Change UK (2019) to recommend the development of national guidance on applying safeguarding thresholds to people who self-neglect due to alcohol misuse and suggest that 'free choice' is often an 'unhelpful paradigm'. Evidence also suggests that over time a realistic assessment of risk could prove difficult for practitioners as it becomes normalised (Martineau *et al.* 2019). One example is the Serious Case Review of Ms Y (Torbay Safeguarding Adults Board 2011, p.3), where a key finding was how 'an alcohol dependent individual, with serious health issues and in need of safeguarding, was consistently viewed as making lifestyle choices that appeared to determine the quality and level of services made available'. The consequences of this 'normalisation' in a safeguarding context mean opportunities to identify and work with people are missed. Specifically in relation to homelessness, Martineau *et al.* (2019) found 'this ranged from a lack of interest in the homeless person's "story", to a failure to see patterns in the person's record that might have triggered a safeguarding alert' (p.5). Guarding against judgement and keeping an open mind to the person is important to foster across the sector. Braye *et al.* (2020) suggest an approach which flows from building rapport and relationship, by finding the right tone, being honest and straight, and going at the person's pace, to then starting with practicalities and identifying actions.

Developing relationships with people who are homeless may be experienced differently across colleagues working in different parts of the sector. In their study of people experiencing MEH, K. Mason *et al.* (2017) suggest that social workers may find it difficult to view and understand how homeless people and their 'needs' fit in terms of mainstream social work. Simcock and Machin (2019) also identified a paucity of detailed research on the links between housing and social work practice, with practitioners reporting feeling ill-equipped to support service users with housing-related needs. They argue that educating social work students about housing-related matters not only reduces this reported practice knowledge gap but may also develop their understanding of social justice. In contrast, in their study around building connection and relationships, Watson *et al.* (2019) identified that voluntary community and social enterprise (VCSE) sector support workers understood their role in relationships to be restorative, focusing on drawing out strengths and skills, and a deliberate attempt to counter previous abuses of power. The opportunity to share learning and experiences between and across different organisations and roles seems apparent when looking to support practitioners through the development of knowledge and understanding and skills.

People who are homeless are not a homogenous group. Diverse groups have different experiences and are often disproportionately affected. Shelter (2020) report that a quarter (24%) of people making homelessness applications to local councils are from Black, Asian and minority ethnic (BAME) groups, even though they make up just over a tenth (11%) of all households in England. Centrepoint (2020) also report that LGBTQ+ young people are more likely to find themselves homeless than their non-LGBTQ+ peers and make up around 24% of the young homeless population. Common themes and feedback about what good support looks like frequently include person-centred and non-judgemental approaches. However, women who are homeless also report that women-only services can provide a sense of peace and safety (Cameron *et al.* 2016), and LGBTQ+ young people have reported that services they're referred to aren't always trained to deal with the issues that are specific to this community (Centrepoint 2020). The importance of 'seeing the person', particularly where there are different and diverse needs, is crucial.

All of this indicates the importance of recognising that personal culture and position may be impacting the views, judgements and decision-making of practitioners. Guthrie (2018) describes this as the sense of being in constant contact with our own thoughts and emotions when communicating with other people. The diversity of the homelessness population, the stigma and marginalisation experienced by people who are homeless and practitioners working in the sector, the range of different personal experiences of homelessness, and the emotional responses this can foster in practitioners all mean that being aware of how professional and personal identities are influencing work with people is particularly important in the homelessness and safeguarding sectors. The 'Inner Supervisor' is a concept which represents the part of the self which can hover above and observe the thoughts and feelings which are being experienced by the professional, personal and organisational selves. The inner supervisor is characterised by neutrality and an ability to see all parts equally, and comparing them in order to reach new conclusions (Guthrie 2018; adapted from 'Emotions Map', Reflective Supervision Toolkit (Hewson and Carroll 2016)).

The current legislative and policy backdrop responds to this body of evidence. Building on the 'personalisation' journey since Putting People First in 2009, the Care Act 2014 places individual wellbeing and person-centred practice at the heart of adult social care, including safeguarding through Making Safeguarding Personal (MSP) (DHSC

2020). Strengths-based practice is a more recent policy direction, again placing people's goals, aspirations and strengths as the starting point for any conversation.

Some areas for learning and development opportunities are identified in the Making Every Adult Matter (MEAM) Approach (2019), including developing and understanding trauma and strengths-based approaches. Advocating for making the best use of lived experience and peer support in order to enable practitioners to 'see the person' is also a key element of any learning and development offer.

Strengths-Based Working

A strengths-based approach explores, in a collaborative way, the entire individual's abilities and their circumstances rather than making the deficit the focus of the intervention. It gathers a holistic picture of the individual's life through working with the person and others involved in their life (Baron and Stanley 2019). The Department of Health and Social Care (DHSC) have developed a Practice Framework and Handbook to support the implementation of strengths-based working across adult social care and safeguarding.

www.gov.uk/government/publications/strengths-based-social-work-practice-framework-and-handbook

Trauma-Informed Care and Psychologically Informed Environments

Trauma-informed care (TIC) and Psychologically Informed Environments (PIEs) are related and complementary approaches to service delivery for people with complex needs. Both aim to improve the psychological and emotional wellbeing of people accessing, or working in, their services (Homeless Link 2017b).

www.homeless.org.uk/trauma-informed-care-and-psychologically-informed-environments

Developing Legal Literacy

Legal literacy in the adult social care context is the ability to connect relevant legal rules with the professional priorities and objectives of ethical practice.[1] It includes having a sound knowledge of the legal rules and understanding their relevance to practice, an engagement with professional ethics, and respect for principles of human rights, equality and social justice (Braye and Preston-Shoot 2016).

Understanding the legislative backdrop when working with people who are experiencing homelessness is an important part of the practitioners' knowledge base. Martineau *et al.* (2019) identified that application of the Housing Act 1996, Care Act 2014 and Mental Capacity Act 2005 were all areas for development and learning. In terms of the impact on practitioners, as well as learning and development offers, access to specialist support 'promotes confidence and competence and enables operational staff to find a way of "carrying on"' (Preston-Shoot 2019). This suggests the need for opportunities to reflect and review what potential there is for practitioners across both safeguarding and homelessness to access learning and development and check in with legal expertise as they practise.

This is particularly important when supporting practitioners who are working together but are individually in roles or organisations working to different legislative frameworks. For example, supporting practitioners working in the VCSE sector to understand duties under the Care Act 2014 around safeguarding referrals (Martineau *et al.* 2019), or supporting homelessness practitioners 'to become legally literate in order to support people who are homeless to access adult social care' (K. Mason *et al.* 2017, p.3). Social care practitioners who are well placed to identify housing issues, or risk of homelessness, may benefit from support to understand the 'duty to refer' under the Homelessness Reduction Act 2017 (Blood 2019). Legal literacy is therefore a critical issue for practitioner support and development across all parts of the homelessness and safeguarding sectors.

A specific area for development is self-neglect. This is a common factor in Safeguarding Adults Reviews (SARs) where homelessness is a part of the person's experience. In Waltham Forest (Martineau *et al.* 2019, p.23) the SAR found 'a universal sense of professional frustration

---

1 www.researchinpractice.org.uk/all/topics/legal-literacy

that was caught up in the confusion of not having a universal understanding of chronic alcohol use being self-neglect'.

The Care Act 2014 guidance requires Safeguarding Adults Boards (SABs) to seek assurance that relevant partners provide training for staff and volunteers on the policy, procedures and professional practices that are in place locally, which reflects their roles and responsibilities in safeguarding adult arrangements. Developing a shared understanding of what is and isn't safeguarding, and the mechanics of how it works, is a key area of needed support for practitioners.

The Care Act 2014 and MSP also both 'make it clear that adults at risk should be at the centre of safeguarding enquiries. SABs also need to consider how the experience of those adults can inform training in a meaningful and engaged way. If training solely focuses on processes, the principles of MSP may not be transferred into practice' (Leverton and Elwood 2018, p.8).

Making Safeguarding Personal Toolkit
The Making Safeguarding Personal Toolkit includes tools that support legal literacy.

www.local.gov.uk/msp-toolkit

Implications for Practice

- Get to know the person for who they are, being mindful of societal and personal influences on judgements and decisions.

- Share your experiences with colleagues and learn from them in return – particularly in light of the different legislative backdrops across the system.

Homelessness and Safeguarding Practitioner Wellbeing
The Challenges
Marginalisation: Scanlon and Adlam (2012) describe the complexity and parallels in the experiences of both being homeless and working

within homelessness. They articulate this as a 'double bind' (p.75) with both being caught between contradictory societal and individual demands around achieving 'resettlement' and the supply of appropriate resources to achieve this. The parallel between people who are homeless and practitioners' experience is also articulated by Watson *et al.* (2019), where practitioners identify the lack of value placed on their role (by society); they aligned themselves with residents, creating a sense that they had 'picked a side', and in turn experienced marginalisation by society.

Competing demands: Practitioners can experience these 'day to day dilemmas and conflicts about how to make sense of the work and so how to exercise a proper "duty of care"' (Watson *et al.* 2019, p.76). Daly (2017) also articulates the context of tension and pressure for practitioners working in homelessness; around the complexities of the emotionally challenging nature of their role and navigating organisational pressures around resources and success defined through targets. Watson *et al.* (2019) also describe the internal conflicts which 'occurred between attuning to residents' needs and meeting organisational demands' (p.132), which meant that value-driven practice proved at times more of an ideal than reality.

Role conflict: The consequences can lead to practitioners feeling 'alone in striving to gain residents access to resources and as a result [feeling] unsupported and let down by fellow professionals from external agencies and their organisation' (Watson *et al.* 2019, p.133). There is also a risk that in this context practitioners may adopt an advocacy role which has the potential to put them into a position of fighting against the system within which they are working (Scanlon and Adlam 2012; Watson *et al.* 2019).

Stevens *et al.* (2018) also identified conflicts which play out within safeguarding roles, in particular supporting autonomy against a sense of responsibility and duty of care. This is all in the broader safeguarding context, where social care practitioners working in day-to-day safeguarding roles report concerns around risk and their responsibility to minimise risk for the adult or carer they are working with.

Emotional impact: Working in homelessness demands knowledge of a range of issues, including welfare, health, social care, socio-cultural and rights-based practice, alongside skills in effective direct relational practice, and multi-agency working (Martin *et al.* 2012). This study also identified that most practitioners were motivated to work in the homelessness sector out of a desire to help others and to do something worthwhile. The work can also be challenging on an emotional level (Woodcock and Gill 2014). Secondary trauma is a common experience in practitioners working directly with people who are homeless (Petrovich *et al.* 2020).

Working in adult social care can also be emotionally challenging. Brown (2020) identifies that 'professional burnout, secondary trauma, vicarious trauma and compassion fatigue are some of the ever-present hazards that can affect social workers in any sphere of practice' (p.43). Specifically in relation to safeguarding work, Stevens *et al.* (2018, p.19) describe the complexity of some of the judgements that need to be made and the range of information and relationships that need to be taken into account when investigating a situation. They also identify tensions between the emphasis on autonomy whilst retaining a strong sense of duty of care.

Coupled with this, the way that adult safeguarding is set up within local authorities varies. Graham *et al.* (2017) suggest there are four critical features or variables which distinguish between the different models of safeguarding organisation: 1) the level of specialism, 2) centralisation of decision-making, 3) analysis and importance given to risk, and 4) the separation of coordination and investigative roles in each stage of the safeguarding process.

The experience of working in homelessness and safeguarding can be one where practitioners' values and system practicalities are in conflict. This, coupled with the emotional impact of the work and sense of investment and responsibility practitioners feel, is an important consideration in informing the way support is designed and delivered.

Reflective Practice and Supervision

Woodcock and Gill (2014) acknowledge this emotional impact of work with homeless young people, and encourage practitioners to explore the felt experience through an honest exploration of the emotional challenges of the work; this most importantly supports an awareness of project workers' personal challenges and vulnerabilities.

In these contexts, there are examples where practitioners and teams develop flexible, informal and compassionate support from one another and their immediate managers, providing a place of safety. Watson *et al.* (2019) identified that where project workers attended reflective practice and were provided with time to think about their own emotional responses, it was highly valued. Scanlon and Adlam (2012) conclude that in order to be able to work ethically, it is imperative that reflective spaces that can make sense of the potentially compromising challenges are provided. Reflective practice sessions were described as a safe space to take a step back from everyday tasks and think in detail about what might underlie resident difficulties; this allowed staff to see the 'bigger picture' of clients' lives and appreciate multiple perspectives (Phipps *et al.* 2017). In their study of PIEs, Woodcock *et al.* (2014) also identified that reflective practice, supervision and evaluation are essential tools in developing a 'learning organisation'. This is where the collective dynamics at an organisational level support the psychological work of the PIE. In their study investigating professional curiosity in adult safeguarding, Thacker *et al.* (2019) identify that 'participation in reflective supervision would have supported professionals in any of the agencies concerned to consider [this] case from a number of different perspectives and could have increased the likelihood of a holistic picture emerging' (p.259).

Specifically, more formal supervision can 'offer an opportunity for supervisees to reflect upon their own personal attitudes to risk, and the ways in which they may influence their approach to working collaboratively. Supervision can also support defensible decision making, by offering a formal opportunity for managers to be involved in decision making, and to record this' (Guthrie 2020, p.18). Maguire *et al.* (2017) investigated the impact of a CBT and supervision package developed from the Kolb (1984) reflective cycle for people working in the homelessness sector. It was found that burnout significantly reduced after the training and supervision package, and the CBT training package reduced negative beliefs and increased confidence in facilitating change.

Part of reflective practice and supervision is gathering feedback from residents and acknowledging success: 'Some project workers spoke about focusing on residents' strengths and holding onto hope as a means of sustaining themselves' (Watson *et al.* 2019, p.133), with clear examples of the value and fulfilment workers gain when the people they support achieve their dreams and goals. Phipps *et al.* (2017) identified that some staff in their study of PIEs reported 'distress at thinking about client trauma but also particular reward when residents were doing well, sometimes against the odds' (p.32). Using the voice of lived experience and this feedback in reflective practice could be a powerful way to support practitioner wellbeing by understanding their impact in order to grow and learn.

Reflective practice and supervision are well-established disciplines amongst adult social care practitioners. However, 'voluntary sector culture was described as privileging "doing" things for others; thinking about one's own feelings was regarded by some as an unnecessary luxury' (Phipps *et al.* 2017, p.37). When working across the sector of homelessness and safeguarding, being mindful of the different cultural backdrops and approaches to supporting reflective practice may provide opportunities for sharing learning and development.

Practice Supervision

Although developed to support the implementation of the Post Qualifying Standards for Practice Supervisors in Adult Social Care, the open access Supervisor Development Programme website features tools and learning resources that could be transferable across the homelessness sector.

https://adultsdp.researchinpractice.org.uk

Implications for Practice

- Recognise you are working in a context of individual and system complexity.
- Take the opportunity for individual reflection, and reflection with colleagues.

Partnership Working

Working in the homelessness sector means working with people who may benefit from support in a number of different areas simultaneously, which extends beyond housing to include physical health, mental health, and care and support (Preston-Shoot 2020a). This inevitably involves working with practitioners across different organisations and disciplines. As well as responding to the needs of individuals there are statutory duties requiring different agencies to work together when supporting people who are homeless (Housing Act 1996; Care Act 2014; Homelessness Reduction Act 2017) which provide a clear unequivocal backdrop for partnership working. Relating to safeguarding more specifically, the Care Act Statutory Guidance (DHSC 2020) includes six key principles that underpin all safeguarding activity: empowerment; prevention; proportionality; protection; partnership; and accountability. The partnership principle is described as 'Local solutions through services working with their communities. Communities have a part to play in preventing, detecting and reporting neglect and abuse', and the corresponding lived experience 'I' statement is 'I know that staff treat any personal and sensitive information in confidence, only sharing what is helpful and necessary. I am confident that professionals will work together and with me to get the best result for me' (DHSC 2020, para.14.13).

Evidence suggests that there are some areas where practitioners could be supported to develop and encourage partnership working. Martineau *et al.* (2019) reviewed 14 SARs where homelessness was a factor and identified five broad themes for learning and practice improvement. One of the themes was 'cooperation, coordination and leadership'. Specifically, issues around 'care coordination' and the identification of a lead agency or professional, and multi-agency meetings, communication and feedback between agencies.

Providing the conditions for confident and competent partnership working is an important part of supporting practitioners. The impact of an uncoordinated or unclear system of partnership working can lead to practitioners feeling overwhelmed, fatigued and frustrated (Martineau *et al.* 2019), which in turn affects the quality of care and support provided to an individual. There is some evidence that project workers, in particular from the housing sector, can feel 'undervalued by other professionals creating distance within working relationships, and as a result, an "us against them" dynamic seemed to develop' (Watson *et al.* 2019, p.133). Preston-Shoot (2020a) identifies as important: 'flexible working across agency boundaries, rather than buck passing; professional respect and trust; and collaboration that recognises the contribution that can be made by statutory and third sector agencies' (p.21).

Recruitment and retention of practitioners across teams is also an important consideration for partnership working. K. Mason *et al.* (2017) 'noted the high turnover of social work staff and the problems this posed in terms of establishing stable and meaningful interprofessional practice' (p.7). This impacted on the ability to support people who are homeless to make referrals between agencies, and impacted on how people who are homeless were able to engage with support. There may be an opportunity to work together in partnership across organisations to think about how teams are recruited and supported together. Co-location can also support practitioners with greater knowledge and understanding, ensuring a good 'fit' across disciplines; 'for example, embedding health practitioners in street outreach teams, and mental health practitioners in emergency response teams' (Braye *et al.* 2020, p.21). MEAM (2019) suggests that considering arrangements such as colocation of services and expertise enhances existing responses and supports joint working (e.g. a mental health worker within probation, or a homeless outreach worker in the hospital discharge team).

The Care Act 2014 widened the right to an assessment to anyone 'where it appears that adult may have needs for care and support'. It also includes a broad underpinning principle of 'wellbeing' and that all activities completed under the Care Act 2014 duties should be with a focus on the 'needs and goals of the person concerned' (DHSC 2020). Cornes *et al.* (2016) argued that this is 'good news' for people experiencing homelessness as it clarified grey areas which could lead to an 'inadequate response' from adult social care in the past. However, K. Mason *et al.* (2017, p.6) highlight challenges for successful implementation. Alongside workload and resource issues, this includes 'interprofessional challenges and opportunities' borne from the perception of the adult social care and safeguarding systems being 'configured around how people could fit into the system, rather than how the system could meet people's need'. Martineau *et al.* (2019) also identified a discrepancy between statutory and VCSE practitioners' positions when it came to knowing when safeguarding was appropriate or applicable.

A potential area where different parts of the sector may diverge or come together in partnership is around the concept of 'risk'. 'Risk' is an underlying narrative in work with people who are homeless and in safeguarding. 'The inherent complexity of a person's life, with all its interlocking threads, means there is often no simple action to reduce risk or improve wellbeing. Uncertainty is inevitable' (Baim *et al.* 2018, p.54). Practitioners working in adult social care may be familiar with the need to strike the difficult balance between a 'duty to protect' and a 'duty to enable' (Finlayson 2015). In particular, practitioners in safeguarding will be familiar with striking this balance by 'working together to prevent and stop both the risks and experience of abuse or neglect, while at the same time making sure that the adult's wellbeing is promoted including, where appropriate, having regard to their views, wishes, feelings and beliefs in deciding on any action' (DHSC 2020, para.14.7). The underpinning legislation and this balance may not be so well understood among other partners. Bridging any gap is important to facilitate smooth and joined-up support for people. Guthrie (2018, p.3) encourages practitioners to 'hold in mind the underlying aim of adult social care; to support individual wellbeing and to help people live their lives in a way which reflects their wishes and choices', and Baim *et al.* (2018) suggest that 'in order to work fully with complexity, we must engage creatively with two key concepts – citizenship and freedom – to find the most appropriate solutions and help people stay safe as they shape their own lives' (p.54). Developing a shared understanding and language around risk underpinned by the concepts of citizenship and freedom may be a powerful unifier across the sector.

A 'communities of practice' (CoP) approach has been shown to improve partnership working across the homelessness and safeguarding sectors. Mason *et al.* (2018) identified some key areas in which the CoP supported practitioners in meeting partnership challenges:

- *Language:* Harnessing the language of the Care Act 2014 to optimise the likelihood of referrals being accepted by adult social care. This means reframing stories away from narratives of 'vulnerability' towards terminology around eligibility and wellbeing.

- *Self-neglect:* Understanding the concept of self-neglect in relation to people experiencing homelessness and ensuring it is explicitly referenced in communication between agencies. Self-neglect is included under the definition of safeguarding in the Care Act 2014.

- *Risk and choice:* Developing understanding of the balance between supporting the autonomy/consent of a person who is homeless and 'protection' against risk of harm or abuse. Establishing consent of the person and also 'respectfully challenging why the person was refusing care and support' are suggested frames to explore where this balance is under debate.

Communities of Practice

Anderson *et al.* (2013) developed a toolkit for practitioners who are interested in establishing communities of practice in health, housing, criminal justice and social care agencies. It draws on the experience of instigating and supporting six communities of practice in England in 2012. It includes the experience and views of facilitators and members of those communities of practice collected over the lifetime of the project and during the evaluation.

www.kcl.ac.uk/scwru/res/roles/copdp/cptoolkit-final.pdf

Care Act Toolkit

The Care Act Multiple Needs Toolkit was developed in response to a theoretically informed case study relating to the access to care and support needs assessment for people with experiences of homelessness and multiple exclusion (Ornelas *et al.* 2018). The toolkit provides a form with detailed accompanying guidance which people with multiple needs and their supporters can complete to help them articulate their needs within the context of the Care Act 2014 (Ornelas *et al.* 2018).

www.voicesofstoke.org.uk/care-act-toolkit

Implications for Practice

- Recognise and value colleagues for the different outlook and experience they bring to supporting people who are homeless.

- Consider setting up a community of practice with colleagues working across the sector to share experience and develop ways of working.

Organisational Culture

Guthrie (2020) suggests an organisational culture that supports positive approaches to risk is one that has clear values and principles that run through both the formal (policy and process) and informal (ways of working) elements of an organisation, one that is collaborative and uses respectful language.

Unfortunately, some evidence suggests that this is not the case in all areas of homelessness and safeguarding: 'shortcomings in direct practice are often related to the ways in which organisational systems, processes, cultures and constraints directly impact upon the work of an organisation's staff' (Braye and Preston-Shoot 2017, p.65). Specific examples include the discrepancy between the overarching values – in particular around wellbeing and strengths-based working – and expectations of the Care Act 2014 and what is possible in practice. This has been described as demoralising, for example where the context of resource limitations is cited as impacting on access to support and the ability to spend time developing relationships (K. Mason *et al.* 2017). More specifically Martineau *et al.* (2019) suggest that legal or organisational financial risk could contribute to the quality of service provision, in particular the 'professional curiosity' of practitioners.

An opportunity to articulate and make real the positive values and principles of homelessness and safeguarding for practitioners is through local Homelessness Strategies. These are required under the Homelessness Act 2002. A review completed by Martineau *et al.* (2019) identified a range of references to safeguarding within a selection of these but question whether, in the light of the apparent lack of local policy and guidance linking homelessness and safeguarding, agencies and practitioners generally conceive of people who are homeless in safeguarding terms. MEAM (2020) note that effective coordination requires the support and engagement of the strategic and operational partnerships in local areas. There is an opportunity to provide a clear leadership position through these key documents, giving an important supportive foundation for practitioners to shape and frame their practice positively.

There is also an opportunity for SABs to support and develop a positive culture, through learning and development together across all organisations involved in homelessness and safeguarding.

SARs (and their predecessors, Serious Case Reviews) have been criticised for their failure to examine macro-level factors such as 'poverty, organisational culture and the impact on staff and services of financial austerity' (Preston-Shoot 2016, p.140), and so there is a potential opportunity to improve this – in particular by ensuring and enabling both practitioners and people with lived experience to have a stake. Accounts of these (SAR learning) events certainly give the impression of professionals having a stake in the review rather than being the passive recipients of recommendations, and give SARs a feeling of the lived experience of those concerned and the difficulties they faced (Martineau *et al.* 2019).

Resilience is a term that has evolved from a focus on the individual to one that encompasses an organisational culture and responsibility. It has been conceptualised as being a dynamic interplay between a personal trait that helps people adapt positively to adversity and an aspect of the external environment that enables people to thrive (Grant and Kinman 2014). Sharing the responsibility for the resilience of individual practitioners, teams and systems at an organisational level could underpin the way organisations develop and support practitioners.

Resources to Support Making Safeguarding Personal – for SABs

This resource offers support to Boards both in their assurance role and in actively supporting and leading a culture change towards MSP. The resources describe what 'good' might look like in MSP for a range of organisations and promote ownership of this agenda within and across all organisations. The full suite of documents comprises:

- Support for Boards across the Safeguarding Adults Partnership.
- What might 'good' look like for health and social care commissioners and providers?
- What might 'good' look like for the police?
- What might 'good' look like for advocacy?
- What might 'good' look like for those working in the housing sector?
- Supporting the involvement of service users.

www.local.gov.uk/our-support/our-improvement-offer/care-and-health-improvement/making-safeguarding-personal/resources

Social Work Organisational Resilience Diagnostic

The Social Work Organisational Resilience Diagnostic (or 'SWORD') was developed and designed for the social care sector in order to support the move away from individual responsibility for resilience to organisational responsibility. Five domains were identified:

- *Secure base:* A sense of protection and safety; constructive challenge to explore change.

- *Sense of appreciation:* Feeling valued and appreciated, where leaders are approachable, trusted and understand the pressure of work.

- *Learning organisations:* Shared goals and beliefs; opportunities for reflection, learning and change as part of the culture.

- *Mission and vision:* Clear and understood direction of travel, communicated well and sharing a sense of ownership.

- *Wellbeing:* Where the wellbeing of people working in the organisation is prioritised.

https://sword.researchinpractice.org.uk (Adapted from Grant and Kinman 2019)

Implications for Practice

- Seek out the vision or strategy for the homelessness and safeguarding systems in your local area.

- Utilise organisational approaches to supporting resilience for individual practitioners and across the system.

Conclusion

The experience of working in homelessness and safeguarding can be one where practitioners' values and system/societal practicalities are in conflict. This, coupled with the emotional impact of the work and sense of investment and responsibility practitioners feel, can inform the way support is designed and delivered. Support to explore through reflective practice and supervision is a key mechanism for this, and the involvement of feedback from people who are homeless is an important part of the practice. It is also worth being mindful that practitioners working across different organisations will have different experiences and levels of comfort with reflective practice – with adult social care practitioners likely to be more familiar than colleagues across the VCSE.

Supporting practitioners to build trusting relationships with people who are homeless is fundamental, especially when working with safeguarding risks. Practitioners across the sectors may experience this differently depending on their organisation, role and experience. There is an opportunity to share learning and experience in terms of approaches to support strengths-based working, trauma-informed practice and PIE, and legal literacy, in particular a shared understanding of safeguarding to develop confidence and competence. Crucially this is about all practitioners having an overview of the different legal frameworks and duties that are at play when working with people who are homeless and working together to identify what the best solution for the individual will be with the legal duties and levers available.

Support for practitioners has to be in the context of the partnerships in which they are inevitably working. Ensuring there is value and respect for different parts of the system is crucial. This can be achieved by a commitment across the sector to developing a shared understanding of different roles, responsibilities and language. Some suggestions for how this can be achieved include co-location and/or communities of practice.

Providing a clear and congruent strategic backdrop and culture in which practitioners can work is a way to support practitioners in their work, underpinning this and making it real through local Homelessness Strategies, systems working (e.g. MEAM) and taking organisational responsibility for supporting and developing resilience.

The importance of involving the voice of lived experience is a golden thread throughout.

Chapter 13

Commissioning Services: Safeguarding and Homelessness

Rebecca Pritchard

Introduction

This chapter demonstrates how good commissioning practice can support the safeguarding of people facing homelessness, whilst acknowledging the challenges arising from austerity, for commissioners and providers alike, as well as the diversity and complexity of people facing homelessness. Commissioning involves the processes by which services are planned, purchased and monitored (Wenzel and Robertson 2018). This will include:

- *Analysis:* Defining the change needed, the problem that needs solving, and the desired outcome.

- *Planning:* Designing a range of options that will work to address the issues identified against the desired outcome.

- *Securing (purchasing) services:* The process of funding the option or range of options agreed to deliver the defined outcome, via an agreed funding method, whether grant funding or contracting. Commissioners also need to consider how to shape the market supplying those services. Capacity and demand management are key aspects of procurement.

- *Reviewing:* Evaluating the chosen option(s) to see what has worked well and what can be improved further.

Safeguarding should run through all these key stages and activities of commissioning.

What good looks like in commissioning to safeguard people who are homeless

Having a vision for 'what good looks like' is essential (Institute of Public Care 2018), alongside a culture of collaboration and inclusive approaches. Commissioning for Better Outcomes (Health Services Management Centre 2015) sets out 12 key standards that should be achieved by good commissioning (see Table 13.1).

Table 13.1 Twelve key standards for good commissioning

Domain	Standards
Person-centred and outcome-focused	1. Person-centred and outcome-focused 2. Promotes health and wellbeing for all 3. Delivers social value
Inclusive	4. Coproduced with local people, their carers and communities 5. Positive engagement with providers 6. Promotes equality
Well-led	7. Well-led 8. A whole system approach 9. Uses evidence about what works
Promotes a sustainable and diverse marketplace	10. A diverse and sustainable market 11. Provides value for money 12. Develops the workforce

Source: Health Services Management Centre 2015

Integrated Commissioning for Better Outcomes (Local Government Association 2018) built on this framework, highlighting the importance of closer working between local government and the NHS, with health and wellbeing closely intertwined.

Safeguarding Is Everyone's Business: The Role and Contribution of Commissioning in Safeguarding People Who Are Homeless

People facing homelessness are a heterogeneous group, with diverse strengths and experiences. Many are driven to the brink by systemic factors that arise from policy decisions, including a lack of affordable housing supply; a welfare benefits system that doesn't cover the costs of renting; and insecure employment. Not every person facing homelessness has complex needs or requires safeguarding support. However, for the thousands of individuals who do, homelessness can be both a result of needs and risks that go unaddressed or can exacerbate those needs and risks and create additional barriers for people (Mackie *et al.* 2017; Downie *et al.* 2018).

People facing homelessness who have additional needs for care and support often have contact with many different agencies across statutory and voluntary sectors, in health, social care, criminal justice, housing and homelessness, and welfare benefits services, and this generates a lack of clarity about who is responsible. Homeless Link (2019) found that only 3% of accommodation providers said their clients had no needs beyond housing.

Individuals with complex and multiple needs may fall between different statutory services, and the 'cumulative' impact of multiple needs is not always recognised or sufficient for them to access services (MHCLG 2018a; Preston-Shoot 2020a). This can increase the risk for them and others and increases the complexity of approaches needed to adequately safeguard people experiencing homelessness with complex needs. Different thresholds for access to services create further barriers to safeguarding and advocacy, and case management is essential to help safeguard individuals and navigate pathways.

People facing homelessness who have complex needs will particularly benefit from integrated commissioning. In order to safeguard and meet their needs, commissioners need to shape markets across a wide range of organisations: the voluntary and community sectors, small-scale local enterprises, housing providers, and larger public, private and social enterprises to meet needs and enable individuals to realise their potential.

Commissioning approaches, which are systemic rather than focused on separate services, are essential. Commissioners should also consider service designs which include co-location in multi-agency hubs to reduce silos and increase exposure and access between professionals. Where this is not possible, commissioners need to design-in regular multi-agency meetings at the strategic, operational and individual client levels (Cream *et al.* 2020).

Safeguarding people who are homeless is not the sole responsibility of adult social care, housing options or housing and support providers, but is everyone's business. What is needed is a holistic, collaborative partnership approach that recognises the diverse routes into homelessness in order to avoid further preventable deaths (see Chapter 10).

Commissioners are well-placed to design and convene these partnership approaches and bring people and agencies together at both operational and systems levels to safeguard people who are homeless.

Barriers and Challenges for Commissioning to Safeguard People Facing Homelessness
Lack of Visibility and Evidence Gaps

We commission in order to achieve outcomes for our citizens, communities and society as a whole, based on knowing their needs, wants, aspirations and experience (Local Government Association 2018). A challenge for commissioners of services that will safeguard people who are homeless is knowing their needs, wants and aspirations. Although some forms of homelessness are visible, namely people sleeping rough or those in commissioned services, many people who experience homelessness may be relying on insecure temporary arrangements such as B&B hotels or private hostels, sofa surfing, sleeping on public transport, or in private vehicles, tents or non-residential buildings. These forms of 'hidden' homelessness are harder to quantify and plan for, so may be overlooked (Maciver 2018).

The variety of forms of homelessness also mean that safeguarding has to take place in a variety of settings, from hostels and supported housing to people's own homes, where they have secured accommodation, and in public spaces where there may be community safety considerations. Services and partnerships need to be designed to safeguard people facing homelessness in non-traditional settings, where people may be unwilling to engage and where their capacity to make decisions is not always clear; however, an assertive trauma-informed approach rather than an enforcement-led approach is essential (Scanlon and Adlam 2012).

Women's homelessness may be less visible, in part because of the greater risk of exploitation and abuse if sleeping rough, or in 'mainstream' services that are often mixed (Homeless Link 2017c). Commissioners need to develop gendered approaches to ensure women who are homeless and at risk of abuse have their needs understood and services designed to meet them (Young and Horvath 2018).

There are additional challenges for commissioners in meeting the needs of couples who are homeless. Many accommodation-based services have been designed for single people, and the welfare system makes providing rooms for couples complicated. There are also practical considerations in terms of room sizes and where facilities are shared. From a safeguarding perspective, it is important to work with people as individuals and as a household. Where domestic abuse is a concern, specialist support and input will be required to safeguard individuals and reduce the risks of homelessness (Homeless Link 2017d).

'Self-neglect' is a form of abuse or neglect that is seen by staff supporting people who are homeless but is not always understood or recognised by statutory services, as it can be less visible or normalised when people are sleeping rough or in temporary accommodation, and assessments of capacity can be complicated (Preston-Shoot 2019). Commissioners need to design services that are person-centred, seek to understand the individual's history and perspectives, work at their pace and do not 'penalise' individuals or providers for persistent non-engagement. Commissioners should work with SABs to ensure self-neglect in people who are homeless is recognised and addressed (Preston-Shoot 2020a).

Homeless people may also be perceived to have only tenuous 'local connections' and not be owed the full duty of housing by a local authority under the Homelessness Reduction Act 2017 or meet other residency requirements (Cream *et al.* 2020).

Whilst the importance of housing is recognised as a core component of health and wellbeing, this is often focused upon the quality and suitability of accommodation in terms of insulation or physical adaptations (Buck and Gregory 2018). Relatively little attention is given to one key group of citizens: people with no home, who may have an often fragile and contested link to a specific place.

Furthermore, commissioning also involves prioritising which hitherto collective unmet needs should be met, or which needs to continue to meet (Wenzel and Robertson 2018). People who are homeless and hidden or 'hard to reach' can often fall between traditional statutory services, but commissioners need to be mindful of equality and diversity in meeting the needs of people facing additional disadvantage. Whilst decisions on priorities should be evidence-based, linked to an analysis of individual and community needs, such choices also have political dimensions, and when resources are finite the needs of less-established groups may not be considered (Homeless Link 2013).

Some homeless services operate within two-tier authorities where the upper tier, the county council, holds the responsibility and budget for social care, and the lower tier authority, at borough or district council level, holds the responsibility for homelessness and housing duties. The visibility and recognition of the needs of people facing homelessness can be further impacted by the division of responsibilities for homelessness/housing allocations and the funding of housing-related support (Cornes *et al.* 2015). Many homeless people with complex needs are still overlooked (Preston-Shoot and Cooper 2020).

There is growing recognition of the importance of designing services to reflect the evidence of 'what works' (Teixeira and Cartwright 2020). Whilst there is emerging evidence on the effectiveness of service models such as Housing First for people whose needs have not been met through traditional shared housing pathways, and Critical Time Interventions (CTIs) that support people who are leaving institutional care to avoid homelessness (Downie *et al.* 2018), the quality and availability of evidence for other services and interventions remains patchy (Teixeira and Cartwright 2020) and is not always clearly linked to the range of outcomes commissioners wish to achieve – including ensuring people facing homelessness are safeguarded and supported to improve their quality of life.

People with No Recourse to Public Funds

A significant challenge for commissioners is meeting the needs of and safeguarding people who are homeless and have no recourse to public funds (see Chapter 9). Having no recourse to public funds presents barriers to accessing usual housing provision and puts people at greater risk of ill-health and exploitation. There are non-commissioned service solutions but these are often temporary, and people in acute need may be assisted under the Human Rights legislation to access social care and health provision. During the Covid-19 pandemic local authorities were 'permitted' to accommodate people with no recourse to public funds on a temporary basis. However, commissioners continue to face restrictions on the services they can offer to this group.

Impacts of Austerity

Many providers, commissioners and people at risk of homelessness have been affected by austerity since the recession of 2008. This has seen a reduction in spending on non-statutory services – most keenly reflected in the changes to the former Supporting People programme where a 48.8% reduction in funding and provision occurred between 2010/2011 and 2014/2015 (Bramley *et al.* 2015). Homeless Link's 2019 survey of provision for homeless people noted an overall decrease in homelessness bedspaces of 22% since 2010. This reduction in provision for homeless people has been accompanied by a 134% increase in the number of people sleeping rough since 2010 (GLA 2010–2020; Downie *et al.* 2018).

Homeless Link reported in 2013 that 70% of organisations working in homelessness relied upon local authorities as their primary source of funding (Homeless Link 2013). The reduction in Supporting People Grant from central government, together with the loss of the ring-fencing, increased pressures to submit lower and more price-competitive tenders in order to retain and secure new business. Providers responded by reducing salaries and/or increasing the contracted hours staff were required to work for the same wage. Caseloads have increased and the levels of cover in accommodation-based services reduced, with implications for staff retention, recruitment and safety and quality of services, especially where clients experience frequent changes in their support workers. Downward pressures on costs are exacerbated by shorter tendering cycles and contracts, and where longer-term contracts are awarded, 'price held' contracts (often without uplifts during the contract period for inflation) reduce providers' ability to invest in services (Homeless Link 2013), as many report year-on-year declines in funding (Fitzpatrick 2017; Homeless Link 2018c).

Commissioning teams have also been affected: they have been reduced in size or absorbed into generic adult social care commissioning teams or central procurement teams, resulting in a loss of understanding of the needs and experiences of the people for whom services were designed (Homeless Link 2013). Reduced monitoring and quality assurance activities and a loss of the relational aspect of scrutiny increased the risk of poorer outcomes for service users, and also presented implications for quality and safety. It is important that commissioners are visible and accessible to both providers and the people who use services. This creates the opportunity to build relationships based on trust, partnership and a shared responsibility for service delivery and safeguarding that ensures all parties are able to raise challenges and concerns and work collaboratively to address them, celebrate successes and share learning (Taylor 2021).

The loss of the Supporting People ring-fencing also impacted on the governance arrangements that had been established to manage the programme. Supporting People Commissioning Bodies brought together housing and homelessness, health, social care and criminal justice, and services for people who faced homelessness were a specific group within Supporting People commissioning strategies. Health and Wellbeing Boards and Joint Strategic Needs Assessments support integrated commissioning approaches, but services for housing-related support and the dedicated commissioning teams that understood homelessness, multiple exclusion and the safeguarding implications of these have been significantly reduced as a result of austerity and the removal of the ring-fencing (Cornes et al. 2015).

Payment By Results
A further challenge for some providers has been the development of Payment By Results (PBR) contracts which can disproportionately transfer risk to the provider. Performance measures drive practice approaches and may inadvertently distort outcomes (Lowe 2013).

Case Study: Important Role of Voluntary Sector Organisations within Multi-Disciplinary Approaches
In one PBR contract for drug treatment services, payments were triggered by clients accepting dry blood tests and blood-borne virus (BBV) inoculations. Whilst this was motivated by public health concerns, the need to promote this element of the service cut across establishing a relationship with the clients, with a greater drop-out rate than before the contract commenced. The author was involved in the review and subsequent re-tendering of the service and worked with the commissioner (and with service users) to design a more person-centred, recovery-focused model. This involved establishing the 'therapeutic relationship' and asking new clients about their aspirations and priorities – what mattered to them – to inform treatment and psycho-social support plans. The focus of the new service was on recovery and improved quality of life, using the self-assessment scales within the Treatment Outcome Profile dataset used by the National Drug Treatment Monitoring Service (NDTMS). Whilst no longer the focus of the key performance indicators (KPIs), a more person-centred relational focused service ultimately improved retention rates and BBV delivery levels.

Growth of Exempt Accommodation

A recent trend linked to the reduction of the Supporting People programme has been the growth of non-commissioned support-exempt provision. Exempt accommodation is a sub-set of supported housing that is funded directly by the Department for Work and Pensions. Due to landlords providing loosely defined care and support services, their tenants can be exempt from housing benefit caps and associations can charge much higher rents when compared with normal landlords. It is often used as a means of housing those with very few other housing options, including people at risk of homelessness with support needs.

Exempt accommodation was first introduced into housing benefit regulations in January 1996, after the rules were tightened to limit the amount paid to claimants outside of the regulated social rented sector (Raisbeck 2018; MHCLG 2020e). Exempt accommodation is defined as accommodation which is provided by a non-metropolitan county council, a housing association, a registered charity or a voluntary organisation where that body or a person acting on its behalf also provides the claimant with care, support or supervision (Housing Benefit Regulations 1996; Booth *et al.* 2010). Research commissioned by the Birmingham Safeguarding Adults Board (Raisbeck 2018) found that placements were made outside established pathways and risks were not always well managed or understood either by the providers or by those placing vulnerable clients.

Although a level of assurance is provided because exempt accommodation is delivered by charities or voluntary organisations, many smaller organisations (and sometimes sole traders) have developed with relatively little internal governance and no external scrutiny, as they are outside commissioning frameworks. Even where larger registered providers deliver such services, their regulator, Homes England, is focused on the financial viability of social housing providers and the regulation of consumer standards that protect the rights of tenants and the services provided to tenants, rather than the quality of the care, support or supervision (Raisbeck 2018; Regulator of Social Housing 2020). The issues with the provision of services to people who were homeless and had needs for care and support outside commissioned frameworks have been recognised in a 'statement of expectations on supported housing' (MHCLG 2020e), where Birmingham City Council's approach was used as a case study for other authorities to consider in order to safeguard people who may be in exempt supported accommodation.

Case Study: Non-Commissioned Services in Birmingham

Following a study undertaken on behalf of the Birmingham Safeguarding Adults Board (SAB), the Council established a Multi-Agency Task and Finish Group to consider issues relating to the exempt sector and to develop an action plan for delivery, bringing together key partners such as adult safeguarding, planning, the fire service and police. When complaints and safeguarding alerts are received, the group shares intelligence and agrees actions and responsibility between agencies.

A dedicated team oversees support-exempt providers to improve standards. One landlord, who continuously failed to provide evidence of support in an ongoing review, was warned that their claims could be refused if they did not comply.

The team also reviews providers where there are concerns around governance and finances. Since April 2020 the team have reviewed nine landlords who supply supported accommodation, and are undertaking further reviews.

Birmingham is also taking appropriate action to protect the wellbeing of the people living in the support-exempt accommodation to ensure their needs are recognised and they are not put at risk of further homelessness.

The author has had experience of supporting staff to raise safeguarding alerts for clients living in exempt accommodation with local authorities in the North East, West Midlands and South London. These alerts concerned financial abuse and institutional and psychological abuse of vulnerable people, albeit where this was sometimes due to lack of training rather than deliberate malpractice. In one case, the landlord had not understood the impact of controlling the tenant's money on their ability to exercise choice and control and their emotional wellbeing; the tenant was left to sleep rough rather than stay in what they felt was a controlling and demeaning situation. In another situation, inexperienced and untrained staff were unable to understand or respond effectively to an individual's behaviour that was rooted in trauma. They imposed a series of sanctions that restricted the individual's choice and control, including freedom of movement, and made them fearful and anxious.

Proactively engaging with such providers through commissioning activities such as training and attending key meetings and forums would increase awareness on both sides and better safeguard the people living in such provision. MHCLG has funded five pilot areas, including Birmingham (as well as Blackpool, Hull, Bristol and Blackburn), to develop collaborative working between local partners and test different approaches to greater oversight of the sector to improve the quality of non-commissioned provision in priority areas (MHCLG 2020e).

Commissioning and Safeguarding: The Quality and Safety Interface

To achieve any degree of quality, services must be safe. Within the health sector, safety is often defined as the absence of avoidable harm resulting from the use of services. In Adult Social Care, Quality Matters (DHSC 2019) defines quality as having the following key dimensions:

- *Positive experience:*
  - *Caring:* Providers treat people with compassion, dignity and respect.
  - *Responsive:* Services respond to citizens' diverse needs, meeting the needs that people themselves have identified, in ways they have chosen, with support from professionals.
- *Safety:* People are protected from avoidable harm, neglect and abuse. When mistakes happen lessons are learned.
- *Effectiveness:* People's care promotes a good quality of life and is based on best practice.
- *Well-led:* They promote a culture that is open, transparent and committed to learning and improvement.
- *Use resources sustainably:* Resources are used responsibly, providing fair access.

The role of commissioners in ensuring quality and safety of services is described by the Social Care Institute for Excellence (SCIE 2012), although its focus is on the commissioning of care homes. Their guidance states that commissioners should ensure that providers:

- incorporate safeguarding principles into recruitment, induction and supervision

- provide a safe environment and can demonstrate good practice on health and safety
- provide (or access) good quality training on quality standards and safeguarding for all care and support staff
- demonstrate good leadership and a culture of dignity and respect
- encourage staff to question poor practice, to develop learning and avoid a blame culture
- encourage connections with the wider community and access support (e.g. befriending) for people who are at risk of social isolation
- actively promote empowerment, providing education about risks and enabling [people] to protect themselves
- properly support and monitor [people] who may present a risk to others
- can demonstrate how they learn from mistakes.

SCIE also recommend that commissioners should take an active interest in the quality of *all* care service provision in their area, including the integration of health and social care, whether or not it is commissioned by them and whatever the method of funding.

As indicated above, this should include non-commissioned (support-exempt) provision, and commissioners should develop protocols with housing benefit teams to identify addresses where claims are made, ensure providers are engaged in local safeguarding training and systems, and put in place arrangements to consider how all provision for people who are homeless with needs for support and care fit with wider local support pathways, including health and social care referral pathways.

MHCLG (2020h) developed a National Statement of Expectations for Supported Housing intended to ensure residents of supported housing have safe, appropriate accommodation which meets their needs, and which delivers positive outcomes. The guidance is aimed primarily at the managers of the accommodation, rather than support-only providers. It does include expectations around training, safer recruitment and oversight by relevant local authority commissioners to safeguard residents.

Case Study: The Plymouth Alliance

The Plymouth Alliance was commissioned by Plymouth City Council to achieve transformational change and better responses and outcomes for homeless people with complex needs. A single contract for an alliance of providers replaced traditional siloed contracts that added to challenges of sharing information and managing risks. A contractual environment has been designed where suppliers share responsibility for achieving outcomes and are mutually supportive, making decisions based on the best outcome for the individual using services. Partners and people who use services have co-designed the future complex needs system as one which will enable people to be supported flexibly, receiving the right care, at the right time, in the right place. The Plymouth Alliance also has a small number of subcontracted partners who provide a range of supported lodgings, supported accommodation and leased properties. These partners adhere to the same principles as the Alliance to provide good-quality, affordable and sustainable accommodation. Key principles include 'no handing off', with all partners taking collective responsibility for risk and delivery, and decisions being centred on what is best for the people using services.

(Plymouth City Council 2019b; Preston-Shoot 2020a)

Safeguarding in Pathways and Transitions

Many people at risk of homelessness are required to engage with multiple agencies to access the support they need, especially at the point of transitions from institutional care which can increase the risk of further homelessness (Downie *et al.* 2018).

There is emerging evidence of the effectiveness of CTIs, which provide structured support for people leaving institutional care such as hospitals, National Asylum Seekers Service accommodation, Children's Care, custody or large hostels to help each person to access appropriate health and/or social care services to reduce the risk of readmission and support their reintegration into the community (Downie *et al.* 2018). This reflects the importance of commissioners understanding pathways into homelessness and working with partners across local areas and systems (Cream *et al.* 2020). However, CTI is a time-limited model and may not be appropriate for those people with multiple needs, including those at risk of abuse, who require a trauma-informed and less time-bound approach (Hough 2020).

Recognising the complexities faced by some people who are homeless as well as the providers within a local area has prompted some commissioners to establish pathways navigators or complex case panels to bring key partners together to safeguard people experiencing homelessness.

Case Study: Brent

Brent has established a Complex Case Panel to bring together multiple services around people who need multi-disciplinary support. A multi-disciplinary team led by social care helps identify and meet the support needs of single homeless people. The targeted group of service users supported by the service are frequent users across the 'system'. A major focus has been understanding where prior engagement has failed and where a multi-disciplinary team approach may be able to deploy a reflective/creative approach towards personal outcomes. Joined-up working with the person is at the forefront of assessments, and decision-making ensures there is increased expertise in assessing service users' mental health needs and potential to manage, and identifying housing (London Borough Brent 2021).

Commissioning: Power Balances, Reciprocity and Safeguarding

From a provider's perspective, traditional commissioning can feel transactional and top-down, with targets imposed that do not always take account of the complexity of the individual's situation (Robertson and Ewbank 2020). This can fail to make use of the provider's ability to innovate and may not utilise the creativity, insight and experience of the people using services (Field and Miller 2017). Many commissioners use a suite of KPIs to monitor providers. Typical KPIs may include:

- Service utilisation – the occupancy level of accommodation-based services or the number of people supported by an organisation against the contracted caseload.

- The number of assessments or support plans completed or reviewed within a timescale.

- The number or proportion of people whose support is concluded within an agreed contracted (but often arbitrary) timescale (one or two years is common).

Without a collaborative approach that involves providers and people who are homeless in defining outcomes that are meaningful to them, this can lead to the balance of power sitting with the commissioner and unintended consequences may occur:

- Providers may be pressed to accept referrals even where the individual's needs are complex and may be beyond the capacity of the service. This can increase risks, and in residential services reduce the choice and control of other residents. In smaller less-intensive services without staff on duty, safeguarding issues may arise unseen.

- A focus on the number of plans or assessments undertaken within agreed timescales can push providers towards process-focused activity and 'tick box' approaches rather than quality measures, for example whether safeguarding needs have been identified and acted upon or the extent to which clients co-produced and felt positive about the process and actions agreed.

- Contracted targets around closing cases within prescribed periods work against person-centred approaches and could push providers into an optimism bias, where they don't identify more complex underlying longer-term needs.

To deliver person-centred and safe care, commissioners need to allow providers flexibility in meeting KPIs and tailoring service delivery to individuals, rather than demand fixed hours or activities in every case. This includes being open to conversation and challenge where things are complex and sometimes contested before closing cases.

The emergence of Social Impact Bonds (SIBs) within the sector has brought partners together to focus on defining outcomes that are both stretching and meaningful to the people services are designed to assist. SIBs use social investors to bring in additional funding alongside the commissioner's resources, to deliver agreed outcomes, often for groups and individuals with complex needs and barriers. The investor takes the risk, unlike a PBR contract where the provider is not paid if results are not achieved. In return for their investment and risk, the investor is paid a premium if outcomes are met or exceeded (Dear *et al.* 2016). This creates a focus on 'what works' to achieve outcomes, rather than processes and outputs, and allows innovation and holistic approaches. A SIB for 'entrenched rough sleepers' used personal budgets to incentivise individuals and support them to achieve recovery and health-related goals as well as to secure accommodation. SIB development often involves competitive dialogue approaches that ensure potential providers can shape service designs and the outcome measures used; this reduces the risk of driving the wrong behaviours (P. Mason *et al.* 2017).

Commissioning which requires potential providers to compete with each other to retain or gain contracts can hinder partnership approaches. The author has also had experience of more collaborative approaches to designing service specifications, albeit still too rarely. In one London borough, providers were brought together, including people with lived experience, to develop a new specification for an assertive street outreach service, ahead of it being competitively tendered. In this example, the quality:price ratio for evaluation of tenders was set at 70:30, reflecting the feedback about the importance of quality from those involved in informing the specification.

In an ideal situation, commissioners should understand the services they commission through regular visits, access to service users to hear their experiences and priorities, and engagement with staff at all levels in addition to reliance on KPIs. This is resource-intensive but provides additional 'triangulation' and assurance about a safety and quality of services. Whilst this does take place in many local authorities, the loss of expertise in homelessness services and the pressures of reduced resources experienced by some commissioners is a challenge. Where commissioners do not have the staff and time to invest in this aspect of commissioning, this can impede effective co-production and safeguarding (Cream *et al.* 2020).

The power imbalance can also manifest in statutory professionals not recognising the voluntary provider as a significant source of support in an individual's care, leading to a failure to provide them with key information. Unless such agencies are invited to and included in case conferences, a complete picture of an individual's strengths and capabilities, needs and current risks may be impossible, putting individuals at greater risk. Fragmented services and referral pathways, with a perceived failure to involve and 'hear' voluntary sector providers, requires tenacity and the escalation of concerns to break through and safeguard homeless people (Preston-Shoot and Cooper 2020).

Voluntary sector organisations need to be recognised as equal partners and respected parts of the local ecosystem of services. This leverages their ability to forge relationships with people who might be less willing to engage with statutory services, and brings different insights and experiences of individuals (Cream *et al.* 2020). This improves information-sharing, person-centred multi-agency planning and safeguarding outcomes for people who are homeless.

Case Study: John

John (a pseudonym) was a single man in his 50s with a history of abuse, poor physical health and severe and enduring mental health problems. His statutory support network had broken down and he was struggling. His developing relationship with a voluntary sector provider was not informed by formal duties and obligations and focused on his priorities. He felt heard and expressed more hope for his future.

John had a tenancy but was sleeping rough as he felt this was safer than staying in his flat, where he was at risk of physical and financial abuse from neighbours. The voluntary agency took on an advocacy role and convened a multi-disciplinary team meeting, with social services, housing options, the registered social landlord, police and the street outreach team. An action plan was put in place to safeguard John, hearing his wish to be rehoused and accepting this as the best way forward to safeguard him. His wider needs were also addressed through multi-disciplinary team meetings until John was rehoused in a new location with a care package and an appointee who would safeguard him from future financial abuse.

This case study shows the power of multi-agency working, and the important role voluntary sector agencies can play in working alongside an individual and advocating for them. Although there was some initial resistance and delay to a voluntary sector agency playing this role, the local authority commissioner was committed to safeguarding being an integral part of their response to homelessness and was supportive of the voluntary sector convening to get the best outcomes for John. Often, contracts and commissioning arrangements set out the (appropriate) duty and expectations of third sector agencies to attend case conferences called by statutory agencies, but these expectations are rarely reciprocal.

Commissioners should ensure contracts and structures are in place that explicitly support the convening of multi-agency case conference arrangements, including where these are requested by voluntary sector organisations.

They should promote the inclusion of voluntary sector providers in multi-agency meetings, and should ensure training is provided (or funded) in key areas such as the Care Act 2014 and the operation of MAPPA (multi-agency public protection arrangements) and MARAC (multi-agency risk assessment conference) arrangements so that organisations can participate effectively in multi-agency safeguarding activity.

More promisingly, some voluntary sector homelessness providers have positive experiences of the commissioning process, as highlighted in Cream *et al.*'s (2020) study of four areas' approaches to meeting the health and care needs of people sleeping rough.

Commissioners must be cognisant of this power imbalance and seek to create a culture of collaboration and open dialogue to promote safeguarding, building trust and providing improvement support across a system (Robertson and Ewbank 2020; see Table 13.2).

Table 13.2 A changing approach to commissioning in three case study sites

From	To
Health care focus	Population health focus
Organisational focus	System focus
Contract enforcer	System enabler
Transactions	Relationships and behaviours
Decision-maker	Convener for collective decisions
High bureaucracy, low trust	Low bureaucracy, high trust
Monitoring organisational performance	Monitoring system-wide performance and providing improvement support

Source: Robertson and Ewbank 2020, p.59

The Skills Needed to Safeguard People Who Are Homeless

Safeguarding people who are homeless requires a blend of interpersonal and professional skills and knowledge (Sheikh and Teeman 2018; Skills for Care 2018; Cream *et al.* 2020; Preston-Shoot 2020a), and access to training, learning and development for staff is something commissioners need to ensure is available. This may be through a combination of contractual requirements and expectations on providers, and delivery via commissioners and Safeguarding Adults Boards. Learning and development needs to build capacity for staff working in homelessness who do not have specific professional qualifications, and support continued professional development for regulated staff.

People and interpersonal skills are essential; the ability of staff to work in a person-centred manner is key. This will involve recognising an individual's strengths and working alongside them to enable and empower them to exercise choice and control. This requires well-developed active listening and communication skills. Communication skills include quality, objective and timely recording of contacts (or lack of contact) with clients and appropriate sharing of information. Information-sharing with confidence is important, and as many SARs have shown, a failure to share information has been a contributory factor to many safeguarding failures.

Staff need the ability to work 'in the grey' and with complexity, where there is no simple solution. Access to reflective practice is important to help people work in a person-centred way whilst being able to recognise the constraints and pressures on partners, including statutory services (Scanlon and Adlam 2012). This helps shape communications, advocate effectively for clients and present the contribution of one's own organisation. This latter is important to avoid using the referrals process to 'hand on' responsibility, rather than as the starting point for collaboration (Preston-Shoot 2020a).

Professional judgement and risk management skills are important. Whilst operating in a non-judgemental way, professional judgement must be exercised and staff need the ability to analyse a situation, question what they are hearing, recognise their own inherent role (and the possibility of optimism bias) and undertake dynamic risk assessments. Professional curiosity is of paramount importance and should, where possible, be built into service design (Preston-Shoot 2020a). For example, if someone discloses domestic abuse as a reason for homelessness, there should be protocols, training and reflective supervision that ensure follow-up questions include 'Is there anyone still at the home who could be at risk, either children or other adults with care and support needs?'

A degree of healthy scepticism (checking what you have been told and seeking to triangulate or verify information) is also important.

Knowledge and understanding of legislation are further key areas. Understanding mental capacity and how this fluctuates and varies between different decisions is important (Cream *et al.* 2020; Preston-Shoot 2020a). Being able to use and refer to the relevant legislation and guidelines (such as the Care Act 2014 and NICE guidance) can help establish the credibility of staff working for voluntary sector organisations with other professionals (SCIE 2012).

However, the impact of austerity on commissioning has actively worked against the ability of providers to invest in and develop the skills needed to ensure services are as safe and high quality as the people using and relying upon them need and deserve (Homeless Link 2013).

Commissioning: Place-Based and Systems-Wide Approaches

Place-based commissioning across a system is important to safeguarding people who are homeless and ensure co-ordinated and effective responses for this client group. A failure to commission on this basis and recognise the interplay between health, adult social care, welfare benefits and housing can leave vulnerable individuals falling through the gaps created by the fragmentation of responsibilities defined by housing, health and social care legislation (Cream *et al.* 2020; Robertson and Ewbank 2020).

Case Study: London Borough of Haringey

A whole system approach to commissioning to safeguard homeless people has been developed by Gill Taylor, from the London Borough of Haringey (see Figure 13.1). They have built integrated commissioning practices into each key area of the commissioning process, seeking to build in porous boundaries between services, including system-wide performance indicators and putting co-production at the heart of planning and review to understand what works and drive improvements.

Their approach is built upon five key pillars for integrated commissioning: housing, health, social care, harm and safety and wellbeing and community. Safeguarding practices and concerns are embedded in this structure, particularly in the social care and safety pillars, and linked through joint commissioning activities.

Source: Taylor 2021

Whole system approach

| Housing | Health | Social care | Harm and safety | Wellbeing and community |

Joint commissioning activities: partnerships, communities of practice, joint protocols, pathways and assessments, data systems, lead practitioner approaches...

↑

Coproduction and peer support

Figure 13.1 Integrated commissioning: A whole system approach
Source: Taylor 2021

Given that people who are homeless may move across boundaries, commissioners need to understand services and customers' journeys across sectors and with neighbouring places (Cream *et al.* 2020). Shared outcomes should be designed across a system, so that collaboration and safe transfer of care between services is central. This is described in Figure 13.2.

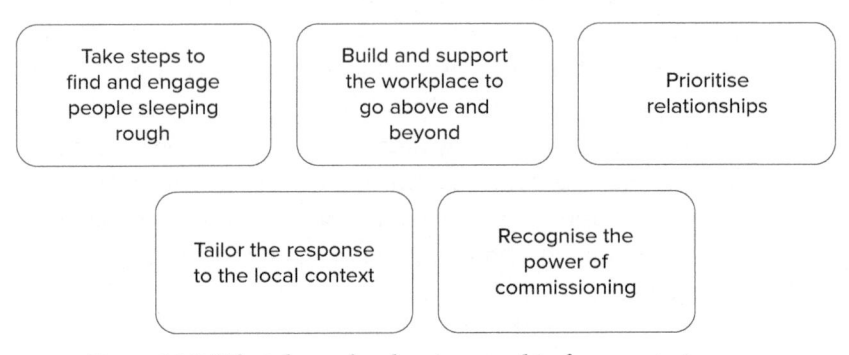

- Take steps to find and engage people sleeping rough
- Build and support the workplace to go above and beyond
- Prioritise relationships
- Tailor the response to the local context
- Recognise the power of commissioning

Figure 13.2 What does a local system need to focus on to improve health and care outcomes for people sleeping rough?
Source: Cream *et al.* 2020, p.71

Population health approaches can also be useful in drawing together a range of partners with the focus of improving the health and wellbeing of a given population (Robertson and Ewbank 2020). These approaches champion:

- Shared narratives which identify common objectives and promote the crossing of organisational and professional boundaries.
- Relationships which are based on trust (an assumption of good faith) and which are the building blocks of strong partnerships and allow distributed leadership and responsibility.
- Deep engagement of staff from all agencies and communities, focused around the principles of compassion and inclusion.

Place-based approaches require political leadership, vision and support to bring together the key organisations and the people within them at the strategic and operational levels to design and deliver effective services.

Case Study: A Strategic Approach – Liverpool City Council and Merseyside SAB

> Commissioning should promote the wellbeing for all, including safeguarding those at risk and be focused upon resolving the barriers in people's lives that affect their quality of life and ability to realise their potential. Accommodation is a key part of enabling people to maximise their life chances. (Farran 2020)

Safeguarding is integral to Liverpool's approach to addressing homelessness and rough sleeping in the city, where it was recognised that to achieve zero suicides and avoidable deaths, rough sleeping, as the most extreme form of homelessness, needed to be addressed by ensuring there were better offers and alternatives. The city brought together voluntary and statutory sector partners, including housing associations, around a strategic commissioning approach that recognises the importance of prevention; addresses the causes and not just the symptoms of homelessness and vulnerability; and seeks to reduce the time people spend in supported housing and hostels, and move demand away from temporary accommodation and increase community-based support.

During lockdown, Liverpool City Council worked with partners to place rough sleepers and people from a large night-centre (an earlier partial response to the challenge of providing people with an immediate alternative to sleeping rough, including those with no recourse to public funds) into apart hotels within the city, with support from voluntary sector agencies. The response of some individuals to being treated with dignity and respect and having basic needs met has been very positive, with several exhibiting increased practical self-care and tenancy management skills that they were able to demonstrate in self-contained space, and the overall level of assessed needs of some individuals for care and support has reduced. By September 2020, 350 people had been placed in permanent accommodation. Being able to undertake assessments away from the streets has enabled better informed co-produced assessments with some referred into the Housing First provision funded through the city region authority to ensure their longer term safeguarding and wellbeing (Farran 2020).

Liverpool is part of the Merseyside SAB which has taken a number of initiatives to promote the safeguarding of people facing homelessness. In the interview, Martin Farran advised that where the SAB feels the criteria for a Safeguarding Adult Review are not met, but homelessness was a factor in a case, the council has committed to undertake a senior management review. This ensures homelessness as an issue and a risk factor is not overlooked and embeds continued self-challenge and scrutiny to support the council's continuous improvement, and builds upon the good practice developed by the London Borough of Haringey on Homelessness Fatality Reviews (Preston-Shoot 2020a).

The SAB also takes a place-based (not sector-specific) and collaborative approach, as stated in the Merseyside SAB handbook:

> The SAB will need intelligence on safeguarding in all providers of health and social care in its locality (not just those with whom its members commission or contract). It is important that SAB partners feel able to challenge each other and other organisations where it believes that their actions or inactions are increasing the risk of abuse or neglect. This will include commissioners, as well as providers of services. (Merseyside Safeguarding Adults Board 2018, p.8)

The SAB's commitment to addressing safeguarding and homelessness extends to before the pandemic of 2020, and has been characterised by a series of events that focused upon the voices of clients and staff with experience of homelessness[1] and a resource pack on their website to promote better practice, including links to the King's College reports on SARs for homeless people and explicit endorsement of the Multiple Exclusion Homelessness Tools.

Conclusion

Safeguarding people facing homelessness remains a challenge for commissioners. People facing homelessness may be less visible, and the diversity of their needs may be harder to recognise, quantify and meet than others in the community. These challenges have been made more acute by the impact of austerity. However, there are examples of innovation and good practice in commissioning that respond to these challenges.

This remains an exciting and challenging time for commissioners, interested in safeguarding people facing homelessness. NICE is working on evidence-based guidelines for the integrated health and social care solutions for people who are homeless; but the White Paper on health and social care has no mention of homelessness (DHSC 2021).

Commissioners and SABs have a key role in leading the way to mitigate the exclusion and barriers people experiencing homelessness face by convening partnerships across places and systems, to drive collaboration and learning, and focus on the wellbeing and safeguarding of the individual.

---

1 For example, see www.youtube.com/watch?v=Kz7WFTAj61E.

References

Alcohol Change UK (2019) *Learning from Tragedies: An Analysis of Alcohol-Related Safeguarding Adult Reviews Published in 2017*. London: Alcohol Change UK.

Aldridge, R., Story, A., Hwang, S., Nordentoft, M., et al. (2018) 'Morbidity and mortality in homeless individuals, prisoners, sex workers, and individuals with substance use disorders in high-income countries: A systematic review and meta-analysis'. *The Lancet, 391*, 10117, 241–250.

Aldridge, R.W., Menezes, D., Lewer, D., Cornes, M., et al. (2019) 'Causes of death among homeless people: A population-based cross-sectional study of linked hospitalisation and mortality data in England'. *Wellcome Open Research, 4*. doi: 10.12688/wellcomeopenres.15151.1.

All Party Parliamentary Group on Domestic Violence and Abuse (APPG) (n.d.) *A Safe Home for Every Survivor: Extending Priority Need to All Survivors of Domestic Abuse*. Accessed on 03/01/2021 at www.crisis.org.uk/media/240051/appgeh-domestic-abuse-campaign-briefing.pdf.

Anderson, S., Cornes, M., Hennessy, C. and Manthorpe, J. (2013) *Toolkit: Developing a Community of Practice: Using Communities of Practice to Improve Front Line Collaborative Responses to Multiple Needs and Exclusions*. London: King's College.

Antonacopoulou, E. and Chiva, R. (2007) 'The social complexity of organizational learning: The dynamics of learning and organizing'. *Management Learning, 38*, 3, 277–295.

Archer, N. (2017) 'We at Sisters Uncut have occupied Holloway prison. Why? Domestic violence'. *The Guardian*, 1 June. Accessed on 09/06/2021 at www.theguardian.com/commentisfree/2017/jun/01/domestic-violence-services-occupying-holloway-prison-sisters-uncut-cuts-women.

Asmussen, K., Fischer, F., Drayton, E. and McBride, T. (2020) *Adverse Childhood Experiences: What We Know, What We Don't Know, and What Should Happen Next*. London: Early Intervention Foundation.

Baim, C., Duffy, S., Ford, D., Griffiths, R., et al. (2018) *Working with Complexity: Evidence Review*. Dartington: Research in Practice.

Barker, S.L. and Maguire, N. (2017) 'Experts by experience: Peer support and its use with the homeless'. *Community Mental Health Journal, 53*, 5, 598–612.

Barnett, P., Mackay, E., Matthews, H., Gate, R., et al. (2019) 'Ethnic variations in compulsory detention under the Mental Health Act: A systematic review and meta-analysis of international data'. *The Lancet Psychiatry, 6*, 4, 305–317.

Baron, S. and Stanley, T. (2019) *Strengths Based Approach Practice Framework and Handbook*. London: Department of Health and Social Care.

Basran, J. (2019) *Cover the Cost: How Gaps in Local Housing Allowance Are Impacting Homelessness*. Crisis. Accessed on 22/01/2021 at www.crisis.org.uk/media/240377/cover_the_cost_2019.pdf.

Bassot, B. (2016) *The Reflective Practice Guide: An Interdisciplinary Approach to Critical Reflection*. London: Routledge.

Bateman, F. (2019) *Mr Yi Safeguarding Adult Review, for City and Hackney, Islington, Newham and Lambeth Safeguarding Adults Boards*. London: Lambeth Safeguarding Adults Board.

BBC (2016) *Nottingham Anti-Begging Posters Banned by Advertising Authority*. BBC. Accessed on 09/06/2021 at www.bbc.co.uk/news/uk-england-nottinghamshire-37488612.

References

Bimpson, E., Reeve, K. and Parr, S. (2020) *Homeless Mothers: Key Research Findings*. UK Collaborative Centre for Housing Evidence. Accessed on 20/01/2021 at https://housingevidence.ac.uk/wp-content/uploads/2020/02/200211-homeless-mothers-findings-report.pdf.

Bion, W. (1961) *Experiences in Groups*. New York: Basic Books.

Birmingham Safeguarding Adults Board (BSAB) (2020) *BSAB Summer Newsletter June 2020*. BSAB. Accessed on 09/06/2021 at www.bsab.org/downloads/file/127/bsab-summer-newsletter-june-2020.

Blood, I. (2019) *Successful Relationships: Working Together across Housing and Social Care – Practice Tool*. Dartington: Research in Practice.

Blood, I., Copeman, I. and Finlay, S. (2016) *Supported Accommodation Review: The Scale, Scope and Cost of the Supported Housing Sector*. Research Report No. 927. The Stationery Office. Accessed on 21/01/2021 at www.gov.uk/government/publications/supported-accommodation-review.

Blood, I., Copeman, I., Goldup, M., Pleace, N. and Dulson, S. (2017) *Housing First Feasibility Study for Liverpool City Region*. Crisis. Accessed on 22/01/2021 at www.crisis.org.uk/media/237545/housing_first_feasibility_study_for_the_liverpool_city_region_2017.pdf.

Blood, I., Goldup, M., Birchall, A., Dulson, S. and Hands, C. (2020a) *Housing-Led Feasibility Study for Oxfordshire*. Crisis. Accessed on 03/01/2021 at www.crisis.org.uk/ending-homelessness/homelessness-knowledge-hub/housing-models-and-access/oxfordshire-feasibility-study.

Blood, I., Pleace, N., Alden, S. and Dulson, S. (2020b) *'A Traumatised System': Research into the Commissioning of Homelessness Services in the Last Ten Years*. The Riverside Group Ltd. Accessed on 21/01/2021 at www.riverside.org.uk/wp-content/uploads/2020/03/A_Traumatised_System_FULL-REPORT_v8_webFINAL.pdf.

Boath, M., Baker, E. and Wilkinson, H. (2010) *'Exempt' and Supported Accommodation*. Research Report No. 714. The Stationery Office. Accessed on 22/01/2021 at https://assets.publishing.service.gov.uk/government/uploads/system/uploads/attachment_data/file/214489/rrep714.pdf.

Boddy, J. and Dominelli, L. (2017) 'Social media and social work: The challenges of a new ethical space'. *Australian Social Work, 70*, 2, 172–184.

Boobis, S., Sutton-Hamilton, C. and Albanese, F. (2020) *'A Foot in the Door': Experiences of the Homelessness Reduction Act*. Crisis. Accessed on 22/01/2021 at www.crisis.org.uk/media/241741/a_foot_in_the_door_2020_es.pdf.

Booth, M., Baker, E. and Wilkinson, H. (2010) *Exempt Supported Accommodation: A Research Report*. London: Department of Work and Pensions.

Bradley, J. (2018) 'There is no excuse for homelessness in Britain'. *The British Medical Journal, 360*. doi: https://doi.org/10.1136/bmj.k902.

Bramley, G. and Fitzpatrick, S. (2018) 'Homelessness in the UK: Who is most at risk?' *Housing Studies, 33*, 1, 96–116.

Bramley, G., Fitzpatrick, S., Edwards, J., Ford, D., et al. (2015) *Hard Edges: Mapping Severe and Multiple Disadvantage in England*. Lankelly Chase. Accessed on 02/12/2020 at https://lankellychase.org.uk/resources/publications/hard-edges.

Braye, S. and Preston-Shoot, M. (2016) *Legal Literacy: Practice Tool*. Dartington: Research in Practice.

Braye, S. and Preston-Shoot, M. (2017) *Learning from SARs: A Report for the London Safeguarding Adults Board*. London: ADASS.

Braye, S., Orr, D. and Preston-Shoot, M. (2012) 'The governance of adult safeguarding: Findings from research'. *Journal of Adult Protection, 14*, 2, 55–72.

Braye, S., Orr, D. and Preston-Shoot, M. (2020) *Working with People Who Self-Neglect: Practice Tool*. Dartington: Research in Practice.

Bretherton, J. and Pleace, N. (2015) *Housing First in England: An Evaluation of Nine Services – Research Report*. York: Centre for Housing Policy, University of York.

Bretherton, J. and Pleace, N. (2018) *Women and Rough Sleeping: A Critical Review of Current Research and Methodology*. York: University of York, Centre for Housing Policy.

Bretherton, J., Hunter, C. and Johnsen, S. (2013) '"You can judge them on how they look…" Homelessness officers, medical evidence and decision-making in England'. *European Journal of Homelessness, 7*, 1, 69–92.

British Association of Social Workers (2018) *BASW Policy: Social Media*. Birmingham: BASW.

Brown, G. (2019) 'Beyond the pale: Psychotherapy with people who spell'. In G. Brown (ed.), *Psychoanalytic Thinking on the Unhoused Mind*. Abingdon: Routledge.

Brown, M. (2020) 'Hazards of our helping profession: A practical self-care model for community practice'. *Social Work*, 65, 1, 38–44.

Buck, D. and Gregory, S. (2018) *Housing and Health: Opportunities for Sustainability Transformation Partnerships*. London: King's Fund.

Bureau of Investigative Journalism (2019) *Local Stories*. BIJ. Accessed 27/04/2021 at www.thebureauinvestigates.com/projects/homelessness/local-stories.

Butler, I. and Drakeford, M. (2005) *Scandal, Social Policy and Social Welfare* (2nd edn). Bristol: Policy Press.

Butler, J. (2009) *Frames of War: When Is Life Grievable?* London: Verso Books.

Cambridgeshire Insight (2020) *Broad Market Rental Areas, Valuation Office Agency*. Accessed on 27/04/2021 at https://data.gov.uk/dataset/81a61cf3-ccad-4ba2-8945-74a2e6cbe4f9/broad-rental-market-areas-brma.

Cameron, A., Abrahams, H., Morgan, K., Williamson, E. and Henry, L. (2016) 'From pillar to post: Homeless women's experiences of social care'. *Health and Social Care in the Community*, 24, 93, 345–352.

Cameron, E. and Codling, J. (2020) 'When mental capacity assessments must delve beneath what people say to what they do'. *Community Care*, 28 October. Accessed on 09/06/2021 at www.communitycare.co.uk/2020/10/28/mental-capacity-assessments-must-delve-beneath-people-say.

Camillus, J. (2008) 'Strategy as a wicked problem'. *Harvard Business Review*, May. Accessed on 09/06/2021 at https://hbr.org/2008/05/strategy-as-a-wicked-problem.

Centrepoint (2020) *Creating Safe Spaces for the Young and Homeless in the LGBTQ+ Community*. Centrepoint. Accessed on 09/06/2021 at https://centrepoint.org.uk/about-us/blog/creating-safe-spaces-for-homeless-lgbtqplus-youths/#.

CFE Research (2018) *Fulfilling Lives: Promising Practice: Key Findings from Local Evaluations to Date*. CFE Research. Accessed on 03/01/2021 at www.fulfillinglivesevaluation.org/wp-admin/admin-ajax.php?juwpfisadmin=false&action=wpfd&task=file.download&wpfd_category_id=324&wpfd_file_id=5645&token=9a660a5917c050cc3fef5b0aedb3598c&preview=1.

Changing Lives (2018) *Too Complex for 'Complex Needs'? Learning from Work with Victims of Domestic Abuse, Who Also Have Multiple and Complex Needs – Final Report*. Changing Lives. Accessed on 03/01/2021 at www.changing-lives.org.uk/wp-content/uploads/2019/03/Too-Complex-Evaluation-Final-Nov-2018.pdf.

Charity Commission for England and Wales (2019) *Decision: Charity Inquiry: Bristol Sheltered Accommodation and Support Ltd*. The Stationery Office. Accessed on 03/01/2021 at www.gov.uk/government/publications/charity-inquiry-bristol-sheltered-accommodation-support-limited/charity-inquiry-bristol-sheltered-accommodation-support-limited.

City and Hackney Safeguarding Adults Board (CHSAB) (2018) *CHSAB Annual Report 2017/18*. Accessed on 09/06/2021 at https://drive.google.com/file/d/1Z96-yX2mTJ7takOlrIo36AP9GxbgLUCU/view?usp=sharing.

City and Hackney Safeguarding Adults Board (CHSAB) (2019) *CHSAB Annual Report 2018/19*. Accessed on 09/06/2021 at https://drive.google.com/file/d/1CrlE-jZwgyNOLBhJc1jqs6rOFvc_Qlfw/view.

Clark, M., Cornes, M., Manthorpe, J., Hennessy, C. and Anderson, S. (2015) 'Releasing the grip of managerial domination: The role of communities of practice in tackling multiple exclusion homelessness'. *Journal of Integrated Care*, 23, 5, 287–301.

Cockersell, P. (2018a) 'Social exclusion, complex needs and homelessness'. In P. Cockersell (ed.), *Social Exclusion, Compound Trauma and Recovery: Applying Psychology, Psychotherapy and PIE to Homelessness and Complex Needs*. London: Jessica Kingsley Publishers.

Cockersell, P. (2018b) 'A psychological perspective on recovery'. In P. Cockersell (ed.), *Social Exclusion, Compound Trauma and Recovery: Applying Psychology, Psychotherapy and PIE to Homelessness and Complex Needs*. London: Jessica Kingsley Publishers.

Cole, I., Green, S., McCarthy, L. and Pattison, B. (2015) *The Impact of the Existing Right to Buy and the Implications for the Proposed Extension of Right to Buy to Housing Associations*. Project Report. Communities and Local Government Select Committee. Accessed on 21/01/2021 at www.parliament.uk/globalassets/documents/commons-committees/communities-and-local-government/Full-Report-for-Select-Committee-141015final.pdf.

References

Colomina, C. and Pereira, T. (2019) *Strengths Based Approach: Practice Framework and Practice Handbook*. London: Department of Health and Social Care.

Connor, P. and Passel, J.S. (2019) *Europe's Unauthorized Immigrant Population Peaks in 2016, Then Levels Off*. Pew Research Center. Accessed on 11/02/2021 at www.pewresearch.org/global/2019/11/13/europes-unauthorized-immigrant-population-peaks-in-2016-then-levels-off.

Cooper, A. (2019) *'Myths and Realities' about Making Safeguarding Personal*. London: Local Government Association.

Cooper, A. (2020) 'Safeguarding adults and COVID-19: A sector-led improvement response'. *Journal of Adult Protection*, 22, 6, 401–413.

Cooper, A. and White, E. (eds) (2017) *Safeguarding Adults Under the Care Act 2014: Understanding Good Practice*. London: Jessica Kingsley Publishers.

Cooper, V. and McCulloch, D. (2017) 'Britain's dark history of criminalising homeless people in public spaces'. *The Conversation*, 10 March. Accessed 07/12/2020 at https://theconversation.com/britains-dark-history-of-criminalising-homeless-people-in-public-spaces-74097.

Cordis Bright (2020) *MEAM Approach Evaluation: Year 3 Report*. MEAM: London.

Corner, J., Mullen, P., Johns, D., Shildrick, T. et al. (2021) *The Knot: Responding to Poverty, Trauma and Multiple Disadvantage*. Lankelly Chase. Accessed on 09/06/2021 at https://lankellychase.org.uk/wp-content/uploads/2021/02/RDA_The-Knot_Essay-collection_FINAL.pdf.

Cornes, M., Joly, L., Manthorpe, J., O'Halloran, S. and Smythe, R. (2011) 'Working together to address multiple exclusion homelessness'. *Social Policy and Society*, 10, 4, 513–522.

Cornes, M., Mathie, H., Whiteford, M., Manthrope, J. and Clark, M. (2015) *The Care Act, Personalisation and the New Eligibility Regulations: A Discussion Paper about the Future of Care and Support Services for Homeless People in England*. London: King's College London, and Social Care Work Force Unit.

Cornes, M., Mathie, H., Whiteford, M., Manthrope, J. and Clark, M. (2016) 'The Care Act 2014, personalisation and the new eligibility regulations: Implications for homeless people'. *Research, Policy and Planning*, 31, 3, 211–223.

Cornes, M., Ornelas, B., Bennett, B., Meakin, A., et al. (2018) 'Increasing Access to Care Act 2014 assessments and personal budgets among people with experiences of homelessness and multiple exclusion: A theoretically informed case study'. *Housing, Care and Support*, 21, 1, 1–12.

Cornes, M., Aldridge, R., Tinelli, M., Whiteford, M., et al. (2019) *Transforming Out-of-Hospital Care for People Who Are Homeless: Support Tool and Briefing Notes – Complementing the High Impact Change Model for Transfers between Hospital and Home*. London: NIHR Policy Research Unit in Health and Social Care Workforce, The Policy Institute, King's College London.

Cream, J., Fenney, D., Williams, E., Baylis, A., et al. (2020) *Delivering Health and Care for People Who Sleep Rough: Going Above and Beyond*. London: King's Fund.

Crisis (2011) *Homelessness: A Silent Killer*. London: Crisis.

Crisis (2019) *The Lived Experience of Homelessness*. London: Crisis.

Croley, L.S. (1995) 'A working distinction: Vagrants, beggars, and the laboring poor in mid-Victorian England'. *Prose Studies*, 18, 1, 74–104.

Crowson, N.J. (2012) 'Revisiting the 1977 Housing (Homeless Persons) Act: Westminster, Whitehall, and the Homelessness Lobby'. *Twentieth Century British History*, 24, 3, 424–447.

Daly, A. (2017) 'Embodied austerity: Narratives of early austerity from a homelessness and resettlement service'. *Ethics and Social Welfare*, 12, 1, 1–13.

Dear, A., Helbitz, A., Khare, R., Lotan, R., et al. (2016) *Social Impact Bonds: The Early Years*. Social Finance UK. Accessed on 09/06/2021 at www.socialfinance.org.uk/sites/default/files/publications/sibs-early-years_social_finance_2016_final.pdf.

De Corte, J., Verschuere, B., Roets, G. and De Bie, M. (2017) 'Uncovering the double-edged sword of inter-organisational networks of welfare services: Tackling wicked issues in social work'. *British Journal of Social Work*, 47, 2, 524–541.

Department for Work and Pensions (DWP) (2014) *Local Housing Allowance Guidance Manual*. London: The Stationery Office.

Department of Health (DoH) (2018) *Post-Qualifying Standards for Social Work Practice Supervisors in Adult Social Care*. London: Department of Health.

Department of Health and Social Care (DHSC) (2000) *No Secrets: Guidance on Protecting Vulnerable Adults in Care*. London: Department of Health and Social Care.
Department of Health and Social Care (DHSC) (2019) *Adult Social Care: Quality Matters*. London: Department of Health and Social Care.
Department of Health and Social Care (DHSC) (2020) *Care and Support Statutory Guidance: Issued under the Care Act 2014*. London: The Stationery Office.
Department of Health and Social Care (DHSC) (2021) *Integration and Innovation: Working Together to Improve Health and Social Care for All*. London: The Stationery Office.
Dobie, S., Sanders, B. and Teixeira, L. (2014) *Turned Away: The Treatment of Single Homeless People by Local Authority Homelessness Services in England*. Crisis. Accessed on 21/01/2021 at www.crisis.org.uk/media/20496/turned_away2014.pdf.
Dobson, R. (2019a) 'Policy responses to "rough sleepers": Opportunities and barriers for homeless adults in England'. *Critical Social Policy*, 39, 2, 309–321.
Dobson, R. (2019b) 'Complex needs in homelessness practice: A review of "new markets of vulnerability"'. *Housing Studies*. doi: doi.org/10.1080/02673037.2018.1556784.
Dorling, D. (2014) *All that Is Solid: How the Great Housing Disaster Defines Our Times, and What We Can Do about It*. London: Penguin.
Dorney-Smith, S., Schneller, K., Aboim, S., Radcliffe, M., et al. (2018) 'Meeting the healthcare needs of people experiencing homelessness'. *Nursing Standard*. doi: 10.7748/ns.2018.e11455.
Downie, M., Gousy, H., Basran, J., Jacob, R., et al. (2018) *Everybody In: How to End Homelessness in Great Britain*. London: Crisis.
Droy, R. and Lawson, J. (2017) *Making Safeguarding Personal: Supporting Increased Involvement of Service Users*. London: Local Government Association and Association of Directors of Adult Social Services.
EASL and Homeless Link (2018) *Homelessness Guidance for Mental Health Professionals*. Accessed on 09/06/2021 at www.homeless.org.uk/sites/default/files/site-attachments/Homelessness%20guidance%20for%20mental%20health%20professionals%20June18.pdf.
Ecola, C. (2018) 'LGBT and homeless: A cycle of intimidation and ridicule'. *The Guardian*, 21 February. Accessed on 09/06/2021 at www.theguardian.com/housing-network/2018/feb/21/homeless-queer-over-sexualised-laughed-at-abused-intimidated-ridiculed.
Equality & Human Rights Commission (2018) *Housing and Disabled People: Britain's Hidden Crisis*. London: Equality & Human Rights Commission.
European Observatory on Homelessness (2015) *Local Connection Rules and Access to Homelessness Services in Europe*. FEANTSA. Accessed on 20/01/2021 at www.feantsaresearch.org/download/feantsa-studies_05_web7437249621511918755.pdf.
Farran, M. (Director of Adult Social Care and Housing for Liverpool City Council) (2020) Interview, 18 August, Liverpool.
Field, R. and Miller, C. (2017) *Asset-Based Commissioning: Better Outcomes, Better Value*. Bournemouth: Bournemouth University.
Finlayson, S. (2015) *Stop Worrying about Risk*. The Centre for Welfare Reform. Accessed on 09/06/2021 at www.thistle.org.uk/blog-articles/stop-worrying-about-risk.
Fitzpatrick, S. (2006) 'Explaining homelessness: A critical realist perspective'. *Housing, Theory and Society*, 22, 1, 1–17.
Fitzpatrick, S. (2017) *Can Homelessness Happen to Anyone? Don't Believe the Hype*. London School of Economics Blogs, 5 July. Accessed on 27/04/2021 at https://blogs.lse.ac.uk/politicsandpolicy/can-homelessness-happen-to-anyone.
Fitzpatrick, S., Johnsen, S. and White, M. (2011a) 'Multiple exclusion homelessness in the UK: Key patterns and intersections'. *Social Policy and Society*, 10, 4, 501–512.
Fitzpatrick, S., Pleace, N. and Quilgars, D. (2011b) *Multiple Exclusion Homelessness across the UK: A Quantitative Survey, Economic and Social Research Council (ESRC)*. End of Award Report, RES-188-25-0023-A. ESRC. Accessed on 09/06/2021 at www.bl.uk/collection-items/multiple-exclusion-homelessness-across-the-uk-a-quantitative-survey#.
Fitzpatrick, S., White, H. and Wood, J. (2018) *Evidence and Gap Maps on Homelessness: A Launch Pad for Strategic Evidence Production and Use. Part 2: Global Evidence and Gap Map of Implementation Issues*. London: Centre for Homelessness Impact.

References

Foster, D. and Bellis, A. (2019) *Right to Rent: Private Landlords' Duty to Carry Out Immigration Status Checks*. House of Commons Library Briefing Paper: Number 7025. Accessed on 09/06/2021 at https://commonslibrary.parliament.uk/research-briefings/sn07025.

Fransham, M. and Dorling, D. (2018) 'Homelessness and public health'. *The British Medical Journal*, 360. doi: https://doi.org/10.1136/bmj.k214.

Gallos, J.V. (ed.) (2006) *Organisation Development: A Jossey-Bass Reader*. San Francisco, CA: Jossey-Bass.

Garratt, E. and Flaherty, J. (2020) *Homelessness in Oxford: Risks and Opportunities across Housing and Homeless Transitions*. Nuffield College, Centre for Social Investigation. Accessed on 18/01/2021 at http://csi.nuff.ox.ac.uk/wp-content/uploads/2020/08/Homeless-in-Oxford-26-August-2020.pdf.

Gibbs, G. (1988) *Learning by Doing: A Guide to Reading and Learning Method*. Oxford: Further Education Unit, Oxford Polytechnic.

Golden Key (2020) *The Launch of 'Change for Good'*. Golden Key. Accessed on 31/01/2021 at www.goldenkeybristol.org.uk/news/announcing-the-launch-of-change-for-good.

Gousy, H. (2016) *Home: No Less Will Do – Improving Access to Private Renting for Single Homeless People*. Crisis. Accessed on 22/01/2021 at www.crisis.org.uk/media/237168/home_no_less_will_do_access_crisis.pdf.

Gowan, T. (2010) *Hobos, Hustlers, and Backsliders: Homeless in San Francisco*. Minneapolis, MN: University of Minnesota Press.

Graham, K., Stevens, M., Norrie, C., Manthorpe, J., *et al.* (2017) 'Models of safeguarding in England: Identifying important models and variables influencing the operation of adult safeguarding'. *Journal of Social Work*, 17, 3, 255–276.

Grant, L. and Kinman, G. (2014) *Developing Resilience for Social Work Practice*. London: Macmillan.

Grant, L. and Kinman, G. (2019) *The Social Work Organisational Resilience Diagnostic (SWORD)*. Dartington: Research in Practice.

Greater London Authority (GLA) (2010–2020) *Annual Reports 2010–2020*. Accessed on 27/04/2021 at https://data.london.gov.uk/dataset/chain-reports.

Greater London Authority (GLA) (2020) *CHAIN Annual Report, Greater London, April 2019–March 2020*. GLA. Accessed on 27/04/2021 at https://data.london.gov.uk/dataset/chain-reports.

Greaves, F. (2019) *Rethinking Allocations*. Chartered Institute of Housing. Accessed on 22/01/2021 at https://thinkhouse.org.uk/site/assets/files/1378/cih0919.pdf.

Groundswell (2018) *An End to Street Homelessness? A Peer-Led Research Project for the Hammersmith and Fulham Commission on Rough Sleeping*. Groundswell. Accessed on 18/01/2021 at https://groundswell.org.uk/wp-content/uploads/2020/06/Groundswell-HF-Rough-Sleeper-Commission-Report-Final-1.pdf.

Groundswell (2021) *Monitoring the Impact of COVID-19 on People Experiencing Homelessness*. London: Groundswell.

Guthrie, L. (2018) *Risks, Rights, Values and Ethics: Frontline Briefing*. Dartington: Research in Practice.

Guthrie, L. (2020) *Positive Approaches to Risk: Strategic Briefing*. Dartington: Research in Practice.

Hafford-Letchfield, T. and Carr, S. (2017) 'Promoting safeguarding: Self-determination, involvement and engagement in adult safeguarding'. In A. Cooper and E. White (eds), *Safeguarding Adults Under the Care Act 2014*. London: Jessica Kingsley Publishers.

Haigh, R., Harrison, T., Johnson, R., Paget, S. and Williams, S. (2012) 'Psychologically Informed Environments and the "Enabling Environments" initiative'. *Housing, Care and Support*, 15, 1, 34–42.

Hall, L. (2020) *Coronavirus (COVID-19): Letter from Minister Hall to Local Authorities on Plans to Protect Rough Sleepers*. Ministry of Housing, Communities and Local Government. Accessed on 28/03/2020 at https://assets.publishing.service.gov.uk/government/uploads/system/uploads/attachment_data/file/928780/Letter_from_Minister_Hall_to_Local_Authorities.pdf.

Hansard HC Deb. (2021) *Topical Questions*, vol. 687, col. 18, 11 January. UK Parliament. Accessed on 11/02/2021 at https://hansard.parliament.uk/Commons/2021-01-11/debates/254992CE-7A3B-4317-91FC-AD2674C0B73D/TopicalQuestions.

Hattestone, S. and Lavelle, D. (2019) 'The empty doorway'. *The Guardian*. Accessed 27/04/2021 at www.theguardian.com/cities/series/the-empty-doorway.

Health Services Management Centre (2015) *Commissioning for Better Outcomes: A Route Map*. Birmingham: Institute of Local Government Studies, University of Birmingham.

Healthy London Partnership (HLP) (2020) *Mini CHRISP Plus Tool*. Accessed 27/04/2021 at www.healthylondon.org/wp-content/uploads/2020/11/Mini-CHRISP-Plus-Tool-Final-191120_.pdf.

Healthy London Partnership (HLP) (2021) *Homeless Health during COVID-19*. Accessed 27/04/2021 at www.healthylondon.org/resource/homeless-health-during-covid-19.

Heffernan, M. (2011) *Wilful Blindness: Why We Ignore the Obvious*. New York: Simon and Schuster.

Henderson, R. (2020) *Treading New Territory: Getting 'Everyone In' during the Covid-19 Crisis*. Homeless Link Blog. Accessed 07/12/2020 at www.homeless.org.uk/connect/blogs/2020/apr/14/treading-new-territory-getting-everyone-in-during-covid-19-crisis.

Henderson, R. and Pochin, M. (2001) *A Right Result? Advocacy, Justice and Empowerment*. Bristol: Bristol University Press.

Herman, D., Susser, E., Struening, E. and Link, B. (1997) 'Adverse childhood experiences: Are they risk factors for adult homelessness?' *American Journal of Public Health*, 87, 2, 249–255.

Herring, J. (2017) 'Care, vulnerability and the law'. In A. Brammer and J. Boylan (eds), *Critical Issues in Social Work Law*. Basingstoke: Palgrave.

Hewson, D. and Carroll, M. (2016) *Reflective Supervision Toolkit*. Hazelbrook: Moshpit.

Home Office (2004, updated 2018) *Asylum Seekers with Care Needs*. London: Home Office.

Home Office (2020, updated 2021) *EU Settlement Scheme Quarterly Statistics, September 2020*. London: Home Office.

Home Office (2021) *Grounds for Refusal: Rough Sleeping*. London: Home Office.

Homeless Link (2013) *Who Is Supporting People Now? Experience of Local Authority Commissioning after Supporting People*. Homeless Link. Accessed on 09/06/2021 at www.homeless.org.uk/sites/default/files/site-attachments/Who%20is%20supporting%20people%20now%20Report%20Jan13_0.pdf.

Homeless Link (2017a) *Housing First in England: The Principles*. Homeless Link. Accessed on 03/01/2021 at https://hfe.homeless.org.uk/sites/default/files/attachments/The%20Principles%20for%20Housing%20First.pdf.

Homeless Link (2017b) *Trauma Informed Care and Psychologically Informed Environments*. Homeless Link. Accessed on 21/01/2021 at www.homeless.org.uk/trauma-informed-care-and-psychologically-informed-environments.

Homeless Link (2017c) *Supporting Women Who Are Homeless: Briefing for Homelessness Services*. London: Homeless Link.

Homeless Link (2017d) *Supporting Couples in Homelessness Services: An Introduction for Accommodation Teams*. London: Homeless Link.

Homeless Link (2018a) *Using the Mental Capacity Act: Guidance for Homelessness Services*. London: Homeless Link.

Homeless Link (2018b) *The Future Hostel: The Role of Hostels in Helping to End Homelessness*. London: Homeless Link.

Homeless Link (2018c) *Support for Single Homeless People in England, Annual Review 2017*. London: Homeless Link.

Homeless Link (2019) *Tackling Homelessness Together*. London: Homeless Link.

Homeless Link (2020) *Support for People Experiencing Single Homelessness in England, Annual Review 2019*. London: Homeless Link.

Hough, J. (2020) *Adopting a Critical Time Intervention Model through Fulfilling Lives Newcastle Gateshead: An Evaluation May 2020*. Fulfilling Lives. Accessed on 21/01/2020 at www.fulfillinglives-ng.org.uk/wp-content/uploads/2020/06/FLNG-CTI-Final-Evaluation-Executive-Summary.pdf.

Housing, Communities and Local Government (HCLG) Committee (2020) *Protecting Rough Sleepers and Renters: Interim Report*. London: House of Commons.

Housing, Communities and Local Government (HCLG) Committee (2021) *Impact of Covid-19 on Homelessness and the Private Rented Sector, HC 309*. House of Commons. Accessed on 11/02/2021 at https://committees.parliament.uk/oralevidence/1523/html.

Housing First England (2020) *The Picture of Housing First in England 2020, Headline Report*. Homeless Link. Accessed on 03/01/2021 at https://hfe.homeless.org.uk/sites/default/files/attachments/Picture%20of%20Housing%20First%202020_Headline%20Report.pdf.

Housing First Europe Hub (2021) *The Evidence for Housing First*. Housing First. Accessed on 29/04/2021 at https://housingfirsteurope.eu/guide/what-is-housing-first/the-evidence-for-housing-first.

Humphreys, R. (1999) *No Fixed Abode: A History of Responses to the Roofless and the Rootless in Britain*. Basingstoke: Palgrave Macmillan.

Institute of Public Care (2018) *LGA – Stepping Up to the Place, Part B Evidence Review*. Oxford: Oxford Brookes University.

International Bureau of Education (n.d.) *Concept of Governance*. IBE. Accessed on 09/06/2021 at www.ibe.unesco.org/en/geqaf/technical-notes/concept-governance.

Isle of Wight Safeguarding Adults Board and Preston-Shoot, M. (2018) *Howard: A Safeguarding Adult Review*. Isle of Wight Safeguarding Adults Board. Accessed on 22/01/2021 at www.iowsab.org.uk/wp-content/uploads/2019/01/2880-IoW-SAB-Howard-SAR-FINAL-FOR-PUBLICATION.pdf.

Johnsen, S. and Teixeira, L. (2010) *Staircases, Elevators and Cycles of Change: 'Housing First' and Other Housing Models for Homeless People with Complex Support Needs*. Crisis. Accessed on 22/01/2021 at www.crisis.org.uk/media/20498/staircases_elevators_and_cycles_of_change_es2010.pdf.

Johnstone, M., Jetten, J., Dingle, G.A., Parsell, C. and Walter, Z.C. (2015) 'Discrimination and well-being amongst the homeless: The role of multiple group membership'. *Frontiers in Psychology*, 6, 739, 1–9.

Klijn, E.-H. and Koppenjan, J. (2012) 'Governance network theory, past, present and future'. *Policy and Politics*, 40, 4, 587–606.

Knott, C. and Scragg, T. (eds) (2013) *Reflective Practice in Social Work* (3rd edn). London: Sage Publications.

Kolb, D. (1984) *Experiential Learning: Experience as the Source of Learning and Development*. Englewood Cliffs, NJ: Prentice-Hall.

Konradt, U. (2013) 'Towards a theory of dispersed leadership in teams: Model, findings, and directions for future research'. *Leadership*, 10, 3, 289–307.

Kowalewska, H. (2018) *Ethnicity and Social Housing Allocation in England: An Exploratory Analysis of CORE*. Southampton: University of Southampton and MHCLG.

Lambeth Safeguarding Adults Partnership Board (2012) *Annual Report September 2011–September 2012*. Accessed on 27/04/2021 at https://moderngov.lambeth.gov.uk/documents/s50149/03b%20Safeguarding%20Annual%20Report%20Appendix%20B.pdf.

Lawson, J. (2017) *Making Safeguarding Personal: For Safeguarding Adults Boards*. London: Local Government Association.

Leeds Safeguarding Adults Board and Safer Leeds (2020) *Executive and Oversight Report City-Wide Learning: Understanding and Progressing the City's Learning of the Experience of People Living a Street-Based Life in Leeds*. Accessed on 27/04/2021 at https://democracy.leeds.gov.uk/documents/s210886/Street%20Based%20Life%20Report%20Appendix%20091020.pdf.

Leverton, C. and Elwood, A. (2018) *Ensuring Effective Training for Safeguarding Adults Boards (SABs): Strategic Briefing*. Dartington: Research in Practice.

Levin, N.J., Kattari, S.K., Piellusch, E.K. and Watson, E. (2020) '"We just take care of each other": Navigating "chosen family" in the context of health, illness, and the mutual provision of care amongst queer and transgender young adults'. *International Journal of Environmental Research and Public Health*, 17, 19, 7346.

Levy, J.S. (2017) 'Principles and practice in psychology and homelessness: Case skills in pretreatment, trauma informed care and Psychologically Informed Environments'. In J.S. Levy and R. Johnson (eds), *Cross Cultural Dialogues on Homelessness: From Pretreatment Strategies to Psychologically Informed Environments*. Milton Keynes: Loving Healing Press.

Lewer, D., Braithwaite, I., Bullock, M., Eyre, M.T. *et al.* (2020) 'COVID-19 among people experiencing homelessness in England: A modelling study'. *The Lancet*, 23 September. Accessed on 07/12/2020 at www.thelancet.com/journals/lanres/article/PIIS2213-2600(20)30396-9/fulltext.

Lewer, D., Menezes, D. and Cornes, M. (2021) 'Hospital readmission among people experiencing homelessness in England: A cohort study of 2772 matched homeless and housed inpatients'. *Journal of Epidemiology and Community Health.* doi: 10.1136/jech-2020-215204.

Lloyd-Smith, W. and Bampton, L. (2019) *Homelessness and Safeguarding: A Survey of Safeguarding Adults Board Managers.* Unpublished.

Loach, K. (dir.) (1966) *Cathy Come Home.* BBC.

Local Government Association (2012) *Sector-Led Improvement in Local Government.* London: Local Government Association.

Local Government Association (2015) *Councillors Briefing 2015: Safeguarding Adults.* London: Local Government Association.

Local Government Association (2018) *Integrated Commissioning for Better Outcomes: A Commissioning Framework.* Accessed on 09/06/2021 at www.local.gov.uk/sites/default/files/documents/25.70_Integrated%20Commissioning%20for%20Better%20Outcomes_final.pdf.

Local Government Association (2020a) *Making Safeguarding Personal Toolkit.* London: Local Government Association.

Local Government Association (2020b) *Understanding What Constitutes a Safeguarding Concern and How to Support Effective Outcomes.* London: Association of Directors of Adult Social Services/Local Government Association.

Local Government Association (2021) *LGA Responds to NAO Report on Housing Rough Sleepers during COVID-19.* Local Government Association. Accessed on 12/02/2021 at www.local.gov.uk/lga-responds-nao-report-housing-rough-sleepers-during-covid-19.

Local Partnerships (2020) *Local Authority Briefing: Housing People Who Were Rough Sleeping and Those At Risk Who Have Been Accommodated Due to Covid-19.* Local Partnerships. Accessed on 11/02/2021 at https://localpartnerships.org.uk/wp-content/uploads/2020/06/Rough-sleeper-accommodation-guidance-final.pdf.

London Borough Brent (2021) *Homelessness and Rough Sleeping Strategy Update.* Accessed on 09/06/2021 at www.brent.gov.uk/your-council/about-brent-council/council-structure-and-how-we-work/strategies-and-plans/homelessness-and-rough-sleeping-strategy.

London Safeguarding Adults Board (2019) *Appendix Seven, Adult Safeguarding and Homelessness.* Association of Directors of Adults Social Services London. Accessed on 27/04/2021 at https://londonadass.org.uk/safeguarding.

Longmate, N. (2003) *The Workhouse.* London: Pimlico.

Lowe, T. (2013) 'New development: The paradox of outcomes – the more we measure, the less we understand'. *Public Money & Management,* 33, 3, 213–216.

Lowe, T., French, M., Hawkins, M., Hesselgreaves, H. and Wilson, R. (2020) 'New development: Responding to complexity in public services – the human learning systems approach'. *Public Money and Management.* doi: 10.1080/09540962.2020.1832738.

Maciver, C. (2018) *Lifting the Lid on Homelessness.* London: Lankelly Chase.

Mackay, K. (2018) 'The UK context for safeguarding adults: Rights-based v public protection?' In G. MacIntyre, A. Stewart and P. McCusker (eds), *Safeguarding Adults: Key Issues and Themes.* Basingstoke: Palgrave.

Mackie, P., Johnsen, S. and Wood, J. (2017) *Ending Rough Sleeping: What Works? An International Evidence Review.* London: Crisis.

Maguire, J. (2018) *How Byname Lists Help Communities End Homelessness.* Community Solutions Blog. Accessed on 24/04/2021 at https://community.solutions/the-by-name-list-revolution.

Maguire, N.J., Johnson, R., Vostanis, P., Keats, H. and Remington, R.E. (2009) *Homelessness and Complex Trauma: A Review of the Literature.* Southampton: University of Southampton.

Maguire, N.J., Johnson, R., Vostanis, P. and Keats, H. (2010) *Meeting the Psychological and Emotional Needs of Homeless People.* London: National Mental Health Development Unit.

Maguire, N.J., Grellier, B. and Clayton, K. (2017) 'The impact of CBT training and supervision on burnout, confidence and negative beliefs in a staff group working with homeless people'. *Behavioural and Cognitive Psychotherapy* (Submitted).

Making Every Adult Matter (MEAM) (2019) *The MEAM Approach.* MEAM. Accessed on 09/06/2021 at http://meam.org.uk/wp-content/uploads/2019/02/HOMJ6444-MEAM-wheel-190208-WEB.pdf.

Making Every Adult Matter (MEAM) (2020) *Submission to Comprehensive Spending Review 2020*. MEAM. Accessed on 05/11/2020 at http://meam.org.uk/wp-content/uploads/2020/10/CSR-response-design-version.pdf.

Making Every Adult Matter (MEAM) (n.d.) *About Multiple Disadvantage*. Accessed on 29/04/2021 at http://meam.org.uk/multiple-needs-and-exclusions.

Mandell, M. and Keast, R. (2009) 'A new look at leadership in collaborative networks: Process catalysts'. In J. Raffel, P. Leisink and A. Middlebrooks (eds), *Public Sector Leadership, Challenges and Perspectives*. Cheltenham: EE.

Manthorpe, J., Rapaport, J. and Stanley, N. (2008) 'The Mental Capacity Act 2005 and its influences on social work practice: Debate and synthesis'. *Practice*, 20, 3, 151–162.

Manthorpe, J., Cornes, M., O'Halloran, S. and Joly, L. (2015) 'Multiple exclusion homelessness: The preventive role of social work'. *British Journal of Social Work*, 45, 2, 587–599.

Marmot, M. (2020) 'Health equity in England: The Marmot Review 10 years on'. *The British Medical Journal*, 368. doi: https://doi.org/10.1136/bmj.m693.

Marmot, M. and Bell, R. (2012) 'Fair society, healthy lives'. *Public Health*, 126, S4–S10.

Marquet, L.D. (2015) *Turn the Ship Around!* London: Portfolio Penguin.

Martin, B., Philips, R. and Xiang, N. (2012) *Developing an Effective Homelessness Workforce*. Brisbane: Institute for Social Science Research, University of Queensland.

Martineau, S. and Manthorpe, J. (2020) 'Safeguarding Adults Reviews and homelessness: Making the connections'. *Journal of Adult Protection*, 22, 4, 181–197.

Martineau, S., Cornes, M., Manthorpe, J., Ornelas, B. and Fuller, J. (2019) *Safeguarding, Homelessness and Rough Sleeping: An Analysis of Safeguarding Adult Reviews*. London: NIHR Policy Research Unit in Health and Social Care Workforce, The Policy Institute, King's College London.

Maseele, T., Roose, R., Bouverne-de Bie, M. and Roets, G. (2013) 'From vagrancy to homelessness: The value of a welfare approach to homelessness'. *British Journal of Social Work*, 44, 7, 1717–1734.

Mason, K. and Evans, T. (2020) 'Social work, inter-disciplinary cooperation and self-neglect: Exploring logics of appropriateness'. *British Journal of Social Work*, 50, 3, 664–681.

Mason, K., Cornes, M. and Dobson, R. (2017) 'Multiple exclusion homelessness and adult social care in England: Exploring the challenges through a researcher-practitioner partnership'. *Research, Policy and Planning*, 33, 1, 3–14.

Mason, K., Cornes, M., Dobson, R., Meakin, A., et al. (2018) 'Multiple exclusion homelessness and adult social care in England: Exploring the challenges through a researcher-practitioner partnership'. *Research, Policy and Planning*, 33, 1, 3–14.

Mason, P., Lloyd, R. and Nash, F. (2017) *Qualitative Evaluation of the London Homelessness Social Impact Bond – Final Report*. London: DCLG.

Mattinson, D., Knox, A., Downes, N., Nichols, C., et al. (2019) *Social Housing in England after Grenfell: Final Report*. Britain Thinks. Accessed on 03/01/2021 at https://assets.ctfassets.net/6sxvmndnpn0s/1VZVTin61VJ92NiKGuEkRH/582a388ff91653f6ee77fa8c08b7b076/Britain_Thinks_final_report.pdf.

Mayor of London, NHS, Public Health England and London Councils (2019) *Our Vision for London*. Accessed on 09/06/2021 at www.england.nhs.uk/london/wp-content/uploads/sites/8/2019/10/London-Vision-2019-FULL-VERSION-1.pdf.

McClenaghan, M. (2020) *No Fixed Abode: Life and Death among the UK's Forgotten Homeless*. London: Picador.

Medicins Sans Frontiers (2020) *High COVID-19 Rates Found among People Living in Extreme Hardship in Paris*. MSF, 6 October. Accessed on 27/04/2021 at www.msf.org/high-coronavirus-covid-19-rates-found-amongst-people-living-hardship-paris.

Mental Health Foundation (2017) *Psychologically Informed Support for Homeless People: What It Means and Why It's Crucial*. London: Mental Health Foundation.

Menzies Lyth, I. (1960) 'Social systems as a defence against anxiety: An empirical study of the nursing service of a general hospital'. *Human Relations*, 13, 95–121.

Menzies Lyth, I. (1979) 'Staff support systems: Task and anti-task in adolescent institutions'. In I. Menzies Lyth (ed.), *Containing Anxiety in Institutions: Selected Essays*. London: Free Association Books.

Merseyside Safeguarding Adults Board (2018) *Members Handbook*. Accessed on 09/06/2021 at www.merseysidesafeguardingadultsboard.co.uk/wp-content/uploads/2018/06/Members-Handbook-Final-2018.pdf.

Migration Observatory (2020) *People with Valid Leave to Remain Other than ILR or Citizenship at the End of 2019 (for Those Issued Visas from 2004 Onwards) and with Their Asylum Application Pending*. University of Oxford. Accessed on 11/02/2021 at https://migrationobservatory.ox.ac.uk/resources/charts/people-with-valid-leave-to-remain-other-than-ilr-or-citizenship-at-the-end-of-2019-for-those-issued-visas-from-2004-onwards-and-with-their-asylum-application-pending.

Miller, R. and Appleton, S. (2015) 'Multiple exclusion homelessness: Is simplicity the answer to this complexity?' *Journal of Integrated Care*, 23, 1, 23–34.

Miller, R.M. and Rollnick, S. (2013) *Motivational Interviewing: Helping People to Change*. London: The Guilford Press.

Ministry of Housing, Communities and Local Government (MHCLG) (2018a) *The Rough Sleeping Strategy: Policy Paper*. London: MHCLG.

Ministry of Housing, Communities and Local Government (MHCLG) (2018b, updated 2020) *Homelessness Code of Guidance for Local Authorities*. London: MHCLG.

Ministry of Housing, Communities and Local Government (MHCLG) (2019) *Domestic Abuse Services, Future Delivery of Support to Victims and their Children in Accommodation-Based Domestic Abuse Services*. London: The Stationery Office.

Ministry of Housing, Communities and Local Government (MHCLG) (2020a) *COVID-19: Guidance for Commissioners and Providers of Hostel Services for People Experiencing Homelessness and Rough Sleeping*. London: MHCLG.

Ministry of Housing, Communities and Local Government (MHCLG) (2020b) *Local Authority Housing Statistics Data Returns, England 2019–20*. London: The Stationery Office.

Ministry of Housing, Communities and Local Government (MHCLG) (2020c) *Statistical Release: Housing, Social Housing Lettings, April 2019 to March 2020, England*. London: The Stationery Office.

Ministry of Housing, Communities and Local Government (MHCLG) (2020d) *Evaluation of the Housing First Pilots: Interim Process Evaluation Report*. London: The Stationery Office.

Ministry of Housing, Communities and Local Government (MHCLG) (2020e) *New Funding and Guidance to Improve Housing Support for Vulnerable People*. Accessed on 09/06/2021 at www.gov.uk/government/news/new-funding-and-guidance-to-improve-housing-support-for-vulnerable-people.

Ministry of Housing, Communities and Local Government (MHCLG) (2020f) *Rough Sleeping Snapshot in England: Autumn 2019*. London: MHCLG.

Ministry of Housing, Communities and Local Government (MHCLG) (2020g) *Council Tax Base 2020 in England*. London: MHCLG.

Ministry of Housing, Communities and Local Government (MHCLG) (2020h) *Supported Housing: National Statement of Expectations*. Accessed on 09/06/2021 at www.gov.uk/government/publications/supported-housing-national-statement-of-expectations/supported-housing-national-statement-of-expectations.

Ministry of Housing, Communities and Local Government (MHCLG) (2021) *Coronavirus (COVID-19) Emergency Accommodation Survey Data: November 2020*. London: MHCLG.

Ministry of Housing, Communities and Local Government (MHCLG) and Luke Hall MP (2020) *Letter from Minister Hall to Local Authorities on Plans to Protect Rough Sleepers*. MHCLG. Accessed on 22/04/2021 at www.gov.uk/government/publications/letter-from-minister-hall-to-local-authorities.

Ministry of Justice (2018) *Guidance: The Homelessness Reduction Act 2017 Duty to Refer*. London: Ministry of Justice.

Ministry of Justice (2019) *Safety in Custody Statistics, England and Wales: Deaths in Prison Custody to June 2019, Assaults and Self-Harm to March 2019*. London: Ministry of Justice.

Ministry of Justice (2020a) *Proven Reoffending Statistics Quarterly Bulletin, October 2018 to December 2018*. London: Ministry of Justice.

Ministry of Justice (2020b) *Her Majesty's Prison and Probation Service Offender Equalities Annual Report, 2019/20*. London: Ministry of Justice.

Morris, N. (2019) *Scrap the Act: The Case for Repealing the Vagrancy Act (1824)*. Crisis. Accessed on 09/06/2021 at www.crisis.org.uk/media/240635/scrap_the_vagrancy_act_2018.pdf.

Mullins, L.J. (2002) *Management and Organisational Behaviour*. London: Pitman Publishing.

Museum of Homelessness (2020) *Dying Homeless*. Museum of Homelessness. Accessed on 09/06/2021 at https://dying-homeless.museumofhomelessness.org.

National Audit Office (NAO) (2021) *Investigation into the Housing of Rough Sleepers during the COVID-19 Pandemic*. House of Commons. Accessed on 11/02/2021 at www.nao.org.uk/report/the-housing-of-rough-sleepers-during-the-covid19-pandemic.

National Network of Chairs of Safeguarding Adults Boards (2017) *Safeguarding Adults Boards, Auditing the Impact of Becoming Statutory*. London: Local Government Association.

National Network of Chairs of Safeguarding Adults Boards (2019) *Survey of Safeguarding Adults Boards in England*. London: Local Government Association.

National Records of Scotland (2021) *Homeless Deaths 2019*. Accessed on 27/04/2021 at www.nrscotland.gov.uk/statistics-and-data/statistics/statistics-by-theme/vital-events/deaths/homeless-deaths/2019.

Neale, J. and Brown, C. (2016) '"We are always in some form of contact": Friendships among homeless drug and alcohol users living in hostels'. *Health and Social Care in the Community*, 24, 5, 557–566.

Newburn, T. and Rock, P. (2006) 'Urban homelessness, crime and victimisation in England'. *International Review of Victimology*, 13, 2, 121–156.

NHS Digital (2020) *Safeguarding Adults England (2019–20) Data Returns*. Accessed on 09/06/2021 at https://digital.nhs.uk/data-and-information/publications/statistical/safeguarding-adults/2019-20/author-and-copyright.

NHS England (n.d.) *Improving Access and Outcomes to Health Services for Inclusion Health Groups*. Accessed on 27/04/2021 at www.england.nhs.uk/ltphimenu/improving-access.

NICE (2018a) *People's Experience in Adult Social Care Services: Improving the Experience of Care and Support for People Using Adult Social Care Services*. London: NICE.

NICE (2018b) *Decision Making and Mental Capacity*. London: NICE.

NICE (2021) *Integrated Health and Social Care for People Experiencing Homelessness: In Development [GID-NG101170]*. London: NICE.

No Accommodation Network (NACCOM) (2020) *Impact Report 2020*. NACCOM. Accessed on 11/02/2021 at https://naccom.org.uk/launching-our-2019-2020-impact-report.

Nobel, J. (2019) 'Finding connection through "chosen family"'. *Psychology Today*, 14 June. Accessed on 28/11/2020 at www.psychologytoday.com/us/blog/being-unlonely/201906/finding-connection-through-chosen-family.

NRPF Network (2018) *Assessing and Supporting Adults with No Recourse to Public Funds: Practice Guidance for Local Authorities*. Islington Council. Accessed on 11/02/2021 at http://guidance.nrpfnetwork.org.uk/reader/practice-guidance-adults.

NRPF Network (2020) *NRPF Connect – Annual Data Report 2019–2020: Local Authority Support for People with No Recourse to Public Funds (NRPF)*. Islington Council. Accessed on 11/02/2021 at www.nrpfnetwork.org.uk/-/media/microsites/nrpf/documents/nrpf-connect/data-report-201920.pdf.

Oakley, M. and Bovill Rose, C. (2020) *Local Authority Spending on Homelessness: 2020 Update*. St Mungo's. Accessed on 20/01/2021 at www.mungos.org/publication/local-authority-spending-on-homelessness-2020-update.

O'Conner, J. and McDermott, I. (1997) *The Art of Systems Thinking*. London: HarperCollins.

Office for National Statistics (ONS) (2018) *UK Private Rented Sector: 2018*. London: ONS.

Office for National Statistics (ONS) (2019a) *Deaths of Homeless People in England and Wales – 2019 Registrations*. London: ONS.

Office for National Statistics (ONS) (2019b) *Measuring Illegal Migration: Our Current View*. London: ONS.

Office for National Statistics (ONS) (2019c) *Comparing Affordable Housing in the UK: April 2008 to March 2018*. ONS. Accessed on 22/01/2021 at www.ons.gov.uk/peoplepopulationandcommunity/housing/articles/comparingaffordablehousingintheuk/april2008tomarch2018.

Office for National Statistics (ONS) (2020) *Deaths of Homeless People in England and Wales: 2020 Registrations.* London: ONS.

O'Leary, C. and Simcock, T. (2020) 'Policy failure or f***up: Homelessness and welfare reform in England'. *Housing Studies.* doi: 10.1080/02673037.2020.1849573.

Ollett, A.-L. (2019) *Joint Strategic Needs Analysis Briefing Document, Homelessness.* Norwich: Norfolk County Council.

Ornelas, B., Murinas, D., Hine, R., Whittaker, S., et al. (2018) *The Care Act Multiple Needs Toolkit.* Voices of Stoke. Accessed on 09/06/2021 at www.voicesofstoke.org.uk/wp-content/uploads/2018/02/CareActToolKit.pdf.

Ornelas, B., Bateman, F., Meakin, A., Cornes, M. and Pritchard-Jones, L. (2019) *Multiple Exclusion Homelessness: A Safeguarding Toolkit for Practitioners.* Accessed on 09/06/2021 at www.qni.org.uk/wp-content/uploads/2020/05/SafeguardingToolkitDRAFT-PDF.pdf.

Padgett, D. (2007) 'There's no place like (a) home: Ontological security among persons with serious mental illness in the United States'. *Social Science and Medicine,* 64, 9, 1925–1936.

Parry, I. (2013) 'Adult safeguarding and the role of housing'. *Journal of Adult Protection,* 15, 1, 15–25.

Parry, I. (2014) 'Adult serious case reviews: Lessons for housing providers'. *Journal of Social Welfare and Family Law,* 36, 2, 168–189.

Parsell, C. and Parsell, M. (2012) 'Homelessness as a choice'. *Housing, Theory and Society,* 29, 4, 420–434.

Pathway (2017) *Mental Health.* Pathway. Accessed on 09/06/2021 at www.pathway.org.uk/resources/learning-resources/mental-health-resource.

Pathway (2018) *Homeless and Inclusion Health Standards for Commissioners and Service Providers.* Pathway. Accessed on 09/06/2021 at www.pathway.org.uk/wp-content/uploads/Version-3.1-Standards-2018-Final-1.pdf.

Pathway (2020) *COVID-19: Clinical Homeless Sector Plan: Triage – Assess – Cohort – Care.* London: Pathway.

Pattison, B. and McCarthy, L. (2020) 'The role of mental health in multiple exclusion homelessness'. *Social Policy and Society,* 1–17. doi: 10.1017/S147474642000069X.

Payne, M. (2021) *Modern Social Work Theory* (5th edn). London: Red Globe Press.

Petrovich, J., Twis, M.K. and Evans, S. (2020) 'Practice with people experiencing homelessness: An analysis of secondary traumatic stress in the workplace'. *Journal of Social Distress and Homelessness.* doi: 10.1080/10530789.2020.1763574.

Phipps, C., Seager, M., Murphy, L. and Barker, C. (2017) 'Psychologically Informed Environments for homeless people: Resident and staff experiences'. *Housing, Care and Support,* 20, 1, 29–42.

Pleace, N. (2013) *Measuring the Impact of Supporting People: A Scoping Review.* Cardiff: Welsh Assembly Government.

Plymouth City Council (2019a) *Creative Solutions Forum Terms of Reference.* Accessed on 06/11/2020 at www.plymouth.gov.uk/sites/default/files/CsfTermsRef_0.pdf.

Plymouth City Council (2019b) *Homelessness Strategy 2019–2024.* Accessed on 06/11/2020 at www.plymouth.gov.uk/sites/default/files/Homelessness_Strategy_4web.pdf 2019.

Preston-Shoot, M. (2016) 'Towards explanations for the findings of serious case reviews: Understanding what happens in self-neglect work'. *Journal of Adult Protection,* 18, 3, 131–148.

Preston-Shoot, M. (2018) 'Learning from safeguarding adult reviews on self-neglect: Addressing the challenge of change'. *Journal of Adult Protection,* 20, 2, 78–92.

Preston-Shoot, M. (2019) 'Self-neglect and safeguarding adult reviews: Towards a model of understanding facilitators and barriers to best practice'. *Journal of Adult Protection,* 21, 4, 219–234.

Preston-Shoot, M. (2020a) *Adult Safeguarding and Homelessness: A Briefing on Positive Practice.* London: LGA and ADASS.

Preston-Shoot, M. (2020b) *Manchester Safeguarding Partnership Homelessness Thematic Review.* Manchester: Manchester Safeguarding Partnership.

Preston-Shoot, M. (2020c) 'Making any difference? Conceptualising the impact of Safeguarding Adults Boards'. *Journal of Adult Protection,* 22, 1, 21–34.

Preston-Shoot, M (2020d) 'Safeguarding Adults Reviews: Informing and enriching policy and practice on self-neglect'. *Journal of Adult Protection,* 22, 4, 199–215.

Preston-Shoot, M. (2021) *Adult Safeguarding and Homelessness: Experience-Informed Practice (2nd Briefing)*. London: Local Government Association and Association of Directors of Adults Social Services.
Preston-Shoot, M. and Cooper, A. (2020) *Oxfordshire Safeguarding Adults Board Thematic Review – Homelessness*. Oxford: OSAB.
Preston-Shoot, M., Braye, S., Preston, O., Allen, K. and Spreadbury, K. (2020) *Analysis of Safeguarding Adult Reviews April 2017–March 2019: Findings for Sector-Led Improvement*. London: Local Government Association and the Association of Directors of Adult Social Services.
Psychology Today (2020) *Bias*. Psychology Today. Accessed on 13/11/2020 at www.psychologytoday.com/gb/basics/bias.
Public Health England (2018) *Evidence Review: Adults with Complex Needs (with a Particular Focus on Street Begging and Street Sleeping)*. London: Public Health England.
Public Health England (2019) *Homelessness: Applying All Our Health*. Accessed on 27/04/2021 at www.gov.uk/government/publications/homelessness-applying-all-our-health/homelessness-applying-all-our-health.
Public Health England and Health Education England (2018) *Making Every Contact Count (MECC): Implementation Guide*. London: Public Health England.
Pyper, D., Sturge, G. and Cromarty, H. (2019) *Rough Sleepers and Anti-Social Behaviour (England): Research Briefing*. London: House of Commons Library.
Quilgars, D.J. and Pleace, N. (2018) *The Threshold Housing First Pilot for Women with an Offending History: The First Two Years*. York: Centre for Housing Policy, University of York.
Raisbeck, T. (2018) *Risk, Safety and Wellbeing in Shared Exempt Accommodation in Birmingham: Full Report*. Birmingham Safeguarding Adults Board. Accessed on 03/01/2021 at www.housinglin.org.uk/_assets/Resources/Housing/OtherOrganisation/Risk-Safety-and-Wellbeing-in-Shared-Exempt-Accommodation-in-Birmingham-Full-Report.pdf.
Raisbeck, T. (2019) *Exempt from Responsibility? Ending Social Injustice in Exempt Accommodation: Research and Feasibility Report for Commonweal Housing*. Spring Housing. Accessed on 21/01/2021 at www.commonwealhousing.org.uk/static/uploads/2019/11/Exempt-from-Responsibility-Full-Report-November-2019.pdf.
Ramadass, S.D., Sambasivan, M. and Xavier, J.A. (2018) 'Collaboration outcomes in a public sector: Impact of governance, leadership, interdependence and relational capital'. *Journal of Management and Governance, 22*, 749–771.
Raman, S. (2019) *Attitudes towards Homeless People, Beliefs and Burnout among NHS Staff in Physical and Mental Health Work Settings*. Unpublished, Doctoral Thesis, University of Southampton.
Rawlings, R., Paliokosta, P., Maisey, D., Johnson, J., Capstick, J. and Jones, R. (2014) *A Study to Investigate Barriers to Learning from Serious Case Reviews and Identify Ways to Overcome these Barriers*. London: Department for Education.
Redbridge Safeguarding Adults Board (2019) *Annual Report 2018/19*. London: Redbridge SAB.
Reeson, C. (2019) 'Intentional homelessness and affordability of accommodation'. *Journal of Social Welfare and Family Law, 41*, 4, 483–486.
Reeve, K., Casey, R. and Goudie, R. (2006) *Homeless Women: Still Being Failed, Yet Striving to Survive*. Crisis. Accessed on 20/01/2021 at www4.shu.ac.uk/research/cresr/sites/shu.ac.uk/files/homeless-women-striving-survive.pdf.
Regulator of Social Housing (2020) *Regulatory Standards, Economic and Consumer Standards that Registered Providers of Social Housing Must Comply With*. London: Regulator for Social Housing.
Reid, C. (2018) 'What the people say'. In P. Cockersell (ed.), *Social Exclusion, Compound Trauma and Recovery: Applying Psychology, Psychotherapy and PIE to Homelessness and Complex Needs*. London: Jessica Kingsley Publishers.
Richardson, S. and Asthana, S. (2006) 'Inter-agency information sharing in health and social care services: The role of professional culture'. *British Journal of Social Work, 36*, 4, 657–669.
Ritchie, C. (2015) 'Prevent rough sleeping: Create a Psychologically Informed Environment'. *Therapeutic Communities: The International Journal of Therapeutic Communities, 36*, 1, 7.
Robertson, M. (2017) 'The great British housing crisis'. *Capital & Class, 41*, 2, 195–215.

Robertson, R. and Ewbank, L. (2020) *Thinking Differently about Commissioning*. London: King's Fund.
Rogans-Watson, R., Shulman, C., Lewer, D., Armstrong, M. and Hudson, B. (2020) 'Premature frailty, geriatric conditions and multimorbidity among people experiencing homelessness: A cross-sectional observational study in a London hostel'. *Housing, Care and Support, 23*, 3/4, 77–91.
Rowe, S. and Wagstaff, T. (2017) *Moving On: Improving Access to Housing for Single Homeless People in England*. Crisis. Accessed on 22/01/2021 at www.thinkhouse.org.uk/site/assets/files/1104/crisis.pdf.
Rumlet, R. (2017) *Good Strategy/Bad Strategy*. London: Profile Books.
Safeguarding Adults Executive Board (SAEB) (2019) *Annual Report 2018/2019*. Accessed on 21/01/2021 at www.peoplefirstinfo.org.uk/media/10197/safeguarding-adult-executive-board-report_2018-19.pdf.
Sanders, B. and Albanese, F. (2016) *'It's No Life At All': Rough Sleepers' Experiences of Violence and Abuse on the Streets of England and Wales*. Crisis. Accessed on 22/01/2021 at www.crisis.org.uk/media/20502/crisis_its_no_life_at_all2016.pdf.
Satir, V., Banmen, J., Gerber, J. and Gomori, M. (1991) *The Satir Model*. Palo Alto, CA: Science and Behaviour Books.
Scanlon, C. and Adlam, J. (2012) 'The (dis)stressing effects of working in (dis)stressed homelessness organisations'. *Housing Care and Support, 15*, 2, 74–82.
Scanlon, C. and Adlam, J. (2019) 'Housing unhoused minds'. In G. Brown (ed.), *Psychoanalytical Thinking on the Unhoused Mind*. London: Routledge.
Scanlon, K. and Whitehead, C. (2020) *London Local Government Expenditure on 'Everyone In'*. London: LSE. Accessed on 11/02/2021 at https://blogsmedia.lse.ac.uk/blogs.dir/119/files/2020/11/Costs-of-Everyone-In-LSE-London.pdf.
Schon, D. (1983) *The Reflective Practitioner: How Professionals Think in Action*. New York: Basic Books.
Scottish Government (2018) *Health and Homelessness in Scotland: Research. Study Exploring the Relationship between Homelessness and Health*. Scottish Government. Accessed on 09/06/2021 at www.gov.scot/publications/health-homelessness-scotland.
Scurfield, J., Rees, P. and Norman, P. (2009) 'Criminal victimisation of the homeless: An investigation of Big Issue vendors in Leeds'. *Radical Statistics, 99*, 3–11.
Senge, P.M. (1993) *The Fifth Discipline*. London: Century Business. (First published 1990.)
Sheikh, S. and Teeman, D. (2018) *A Rapid Evidence Assessment of What Works in Homelessness Services*. London: Social Care Institute for Excellence.
Shelter (2014) *Can't Complain: Why Poor Conditions Prevail in Private Rented Homes*. Shelter. Accessed on 22/01/2021 at https://england.shelter.org.uk/__data/assets/pdf_file/0006/892482/6430_04_9_Million_Renters_Policy_Report_Proof_10_opt.pdf.
Shelter (2017) *BAME Homelessness Matters and Is Disproportionately Rising – Time for the Government to Act*. Shelter. Accessed on 09/06/2021 at https://blog.shelter.org.uk/2017/10/bame-homelessness-matters-and-is-disproportionately-rising-time-for-the-government-to-act.
Shelter (2020) *Black People Are More Than Three Times as Likely to Experience Homelessness*. Shelter. Accessed on 09/06/2021 at https://england.shelter.org.uk/media/press_release/black_people_are_more_than_three_times_as_likely_to_experience_homelessness.
Shelter (2021) *Covid-19 Protection for Tenants*. Shelter Legal. Accessed on 09/06/2021 at https://england.shelter.org.uk/legal/housing_options/covid-19_emergency_measures/rent_arrears_and_eviction.
Sherwood-Johnson, F. (2016) 'Discovery or construction? Theorising the roots of adult protection policy and practice'. *Social Work Education, 35*, 2, 119–130.
Siegel, D.J. (1999) *The Developing Mind: How Relationships and the Brain Interact to Shape Who We Are*. New York: Guilford Press.
Silva, C. and McGuire, M. (2010) 'Leading public sector networks: An empirical examination of interpretive leadership behaviours'. *The Leadership Quarterly, 21*, 2, 264–277.
Silver, I.A. and Nedelec, J.L. (2018) 'Ensnarement during imprisonment: Re-conceptualizing theoretically driven policies to address the association between within-prison sanctioning and recidivism'. *Criminology & Public Policy, 17*, 4, 1005–1035.

Simcock, P. and Machin, R. (2019) 'It's not just about where someone lives: Educating student social workers about housing-related matters to promote an understanding of social justice'. *Social Work Education, 38,* 8, 1041–1053.

Simcock, T. (2018) *Investigating the Effect of Welfare Reform on Private Renting, State of the PRS: Quarterly Report.* RLA Pearl. Accessed on 22/01/2021 at www.nrla.org.uk/research/quarterly-reports/2018/qtr-1.

Sinek, S. (2017) *Leaders Eat Last: Why Some Teams Pull Together and Others Don't.* London: Penguin Random House.

Skills for Care (2018) *A Guide to Adult Safeguarding for Social Care Providers.* London: Skills for Care.

Slasberg, C. and Beresford, P. (2017) 'Strengths-based practice: Social care's latest elixir or the next false dawn?' *Disability & Society, 32,* 2, 1–5.

Sloane, R. (2015) *Sleep with One Eye Open: Specific Safety Concerns that Homeless Males Face and How They Cope with Dangers.* Master's Thesis, Smith College. Accessed on 14/11/2020 at https://scholarworks.smith.edu/theses/696.

Social Care Institute for Excellence (SCIE) (2012) *Prevention: Safeguarding and Quality in Commissioning Care Homes.* Accessed on 09/06/2021 at www.scie.org.uk/publications/guides/guide45/prevention.asp.

Stacey, R. (2011) *Strategic Management and Organisational Dynamics.* New York and London: Pitman Publishing.

Stevens, M., Woolham, J., Manthorpe, J., Aspinall, F., *et al.* (2018) 'Implementing safeguarding and personalisation in social work: Findings from practice'. *Journal of Social Work, 18,* 1, 3–22.

St Mungo's (2018) *Dying on the Streets.* Accessed on 09/06/2021 at www.mungos.org/wp-content/uploads/2018/06/Dying-on-the-Streets-Report.pdf.

St Mungo's (2021) *Housing and Health: Working Together to Respond to Rough Sleeping during Covid-19.* Accessed on 09/06/2021 at www.mungos.org/publication/housing-and-health-working-together-to-respond-to-rough-sleeping-during-covid-19.

Stokoe, P. (2020) *The Curiosity Drive: Our Need for Inquisitive Thinking.* Bicester: Phoenix Publishing House.

Stonewall (2017) *LGBT in Britain: Hate Crime and Discrimination.* Stonewall. Accessed on 09/06/2021 at www.stonewall.org.uk/lgbt-britain-hate-crime-and-discrimination.

Stonewall Housing (2018) *Finding Safe Spaces.* Stonewall. Accessed on 09/06/2021 at https://stonewallhousing.org/wp-content/uploads/2018/09/FindingSafeSpaces_StonewallHousing_LaptopVersion.pdf.

Stringfellow, E.J., Kim, T.W., Pollio, D.E. and Kertez, S.G. (2015) 'Primary care provider experience and social support among homeless-experienced persons with tri-morbidity'. *Addiction Science and Clinical Practice, 10,* Suppl 1, A64.

Stuart, O. (2016) *Unconscious Bias Isn't Just Somebody Else's Problem: It's Also Yours.* London: SCIE.

Sumption, M. and Fernández-Reino, M. (2020) *Unsettled Status – 2020: Which EU Citizens are at Risk of Failing to Secure their Rights after Brexit?* The Migration Observatory, University of Oxford. Accessed on 22 January 2021 at https://migrationobservatory.ox.ac.uk/resources/reports/unsettled-status-2020.

Taylor, G. (2021) 'Commissioning and safeguarding'. Best practice seminar presentation, 13 January. Local Government Association. Accessed on 09/06/2021 at www.local.gov.uk/commissioning-and-provider-services-safeguarding-people-experiencing-homelessness-13-january-2021.

Teixeira, L. and Cartwright, J. (eds) (2020) *Using Evidence to End Homelessness.* Bristol: Policy Press.

Thacker, H., Anka, A. and Penhale, B. (2019) 'Could curiosity save lives? An exploration into the value of employing professional curiosity and partnership work in safeguarding adults under the Care Act 2014'. *Journal of Adult Protection, 21,* 5, 252–267.

The City View (2020) 'Coronavirus and homeless populations'. *The City View,* 13 March. Accessed on 27/04/2021 at www.thecityview.co.uk/coronavirus-homeless-populations.

Thomas, B. (2012) *Homelessness Kills: An Analysis of the Mortality of Homeless People in Early Twenty-First Century England.* London: Crisis.

Together Network (2019) *Relational Working and Homelessness: An Evidence Review Executive Summary*. Together Network. Accessed on 17/11/2020 at https://togethermc.org.uk/uploads/togetherMiddlesbroughAndCleveland/TN_Relational_Working_Exec_Summary_Web.pdf.

Torbay Safeguarding Adults Board (2011) *Serious Case Review Executive Summary Ms Y*. Accessed on 09/06/2021 at www.yumpu.com/en/document/read/27103363/ms-y-torbay-care-trust.

Tower Hamlets Safeguarding Adults Board (2020) *Thematic Review: Ms H and Ms I*. London: Tower Hamlets Safeguarding Adults Board.

Tunåker, C. (2015) 'No place like home?' *Home Cultures*, 12, 2, 241–259.

United Nations Human Rights, Office of the High Commissioner (2020) *OHCHR and Good Governance*. Accessed on 09/06/2021 at www.ohchr.org/en/issues/development/goodgovernance/pages/goodgovernanceindex.aspx#:~:text=About%20good%20governance%20and%20human,for%20the%20rule%20of%20law.

Valuation Office Agency (2020) *Local Housing Allowance (LHA) Rates Applicable from April 2020 to March 2021 – Amendment as Instructed by The Social Security (Coronavirus) (Further Measures) Regulations 2020*. Valuation Office Agency. Accessed on 09/06/2021 at www.gov.uk/government/publications/local-housing-allowance-lha-rates-applicable-from-april-2020-to-march-2021.

Voices of Stoke (n.d.) *Care Act Advocacy Toolkit*. Voices of Stoke. Accessed on 09/06/2021 at www.voicesofstoke.org.uk/care-act-toolkit.

Von Beuren, E., Klijn, E.-H. and Koppenjan, J. (2003) 'Dealing with wicked problems in networks: Analyzing an environmental debate from a network perspective'. *Journal of Public Administration, Research and Theory*, 13, 2, 193–212.

Ward, M. and Holmes, M. (2014) *Working with Change Resistant Drinkers: The Project Manual*. London: Alcohol Concern.

Watson, C., Nolte, L. and Brown, R. (2019) 'Building connection against the odds: Project workers' relationships with people experiencing homelessness'. *Housing, Care and Support*, 22, 2, 129–140.

Weal, R. (2020) *Knocked Back: How a Failure to Support People Sleeping Rough with Drug and Alcohol Problems is Costing Lives*. London: St Mungo's.

Webster, D. (2020) 'Benefit sanctions have failed: A comprehensive review is needed'. Accessed on 09/06/2021 at https://blogs.lse.ac.uk/politicsandpolicy/benefit-sanctions-have-failed-a-comprehensive-review-is-needed.

Wenzel, L. and Robertson, R. (2018) *What Is Commissioning and How Is It Changing?* Kings Fund. Accessed on 09/06/2021 at www.kingsfund.org.uk/publications/what-commissioning-and-how-it-changing.

Wheatley, M. (1996) *A Simpler Way*. Oakland, CA: Berrett-Koehler.

Wheatley, M. (1999) *Leadership and the New Science*. Oakland, CA: Berrett-Koehler.

Whiteford, M. and Simpson, G. (2015) 'Who is left standing when the tide retreats? Negotiating hospital discharge and pathways of care for homeless people'. *Housing, Care and Support*, 18, 3/4, 125–135.

Williams, E. (2020) *The Impact of DWP Benefit Sanctions on Anxiety and Depression*. Accessed on 17/11/2020 at https://blogs.lse.ac.uk/politicsandpolicy/benefit-sanctions-mental-health.

Wilson, W. (2019) *The End of Section 21 'No Fault' Evictions*. House of Commons Library Briefing Paper No. 8658. The Stationery Office. Accessed on 21/01/2021 at https://commonslibrary.parliament.uk/research-briefings/cbp-8658.

Wilson, W. and Barton, C. (2020) *Rough Sleeping (England)*. Briefing Paper 02007. London: House of Commons Library.

Winnicott, D.W. (1965) *Maturation Process and the Facilitating Environment*. London: Hogarth.

Wong, K.-F. (2003) 'Empowerment as a panacea for poverty: Old wine in new bottles? Reflections on the World Bank's conception of power'. *Progress in Development Studies*, 3, 4, 307–322.

Woodcock, J. and Gill, J. (2014) 'Implementing a Psychologically Informed Environment in a service for homeless young people'. *Housing, Care and Support*, 17, 1, 48–57.

Worcester City Council (2018) *Independent Review into the Death of an Individual Sleeping Rough – C*. Worcester City Council. Accessed on 09/06/2021 at www.healthwatchworcestershire.co.uk/wp-content/uploads/2018/07/Independent-Review-C-FINAL-160518.pdf.

Worcestershire Safeguarding Adults Board (2020) *Thematic Safeguarding Adults Review Regarding People Who Sleep Rough*. Worcestershire Safeguarding Adults Board. Accessed on 09/06/2021 at www.safeguardingworcestershire.org.uk/wp-content/uploads/2020/10/V0.6-2020-09-03-WSAB-THEMATIC-SAR-re-ROUGH-SLEEPERS-ACCESSIBLE-1.pdf.

World Health Organization (2021) *Constitution*. Accessed on 27/04/2021 at www.who.int/about/governance.

Young, L. and Horvath, T. (2018) *Promising Practice from the Frontline: Exploring Gendered Approaches to Supporting Women Experiencing Homelessness and Multiple Disadvantage*. London: Homeless Link.

Yukl, G.A. (2002) *Leadership in Organisations*. Saddle River, NJ: Prentice Hall.

Zimmerman, B., Lindberg, C. and Plesk, P.E. (2001) *Edgeware: Insights from Complexity Science for Health Care Leaders*. Irving, TX: VHA Inc.

Legislation

Care Act 2014
Care and Support (Discharge of Hospital Patient) Regulations 2014
Care and Support (Eligibility Criteria) Regulations 2015
Children Act 1989
Children (Northern Ireland) Order 1995
Children (Scotland) Act 1995
Equality Act 2010
European Convention on Human Rights and Fundamental Freedoms 1950
Health and Personal Social Services (Northern Ireland) Order 1972
Homelessness Act 2002
Homelessness Reduction Act 2017
Housing Act 1996
Housing Benefit Regulations 1996
Housing (Homeless Persons) Act 1977
Human Rights Act 1998
Immigration and Asylum Act 1999
Local Government Act 1972
Localism Act 2011
Mental Capacity Act 2005
Mental Health Act 1983
National Health Services Act 2006
Nationality, Immigration and Asylum Act 2002
Social Security (Coronavirus) (Further Measures) Regulations 2020
Social Services and Well-Being (Wales) Act 2014
Social Work (Scotland) Act 1968
Supported Housing (Regulation) Bill 2019/20
Vagrancy Act 1824

Case Law

Guiste v Lambeth LBC [2019] EWCA Civ 1758
Heart of England v JB [2014] EWCOP 342
Hotak v LB Southwark [2015] UKSC 30
N v ACCG & Ors [2017] UKSC2
Ncube v Brighton and Hove City Council [2021] EWHC 578 (Admin)
Nzolameso v City of Westminster [2015] EWCA Civ 1383
R v Bristol City Council ex parte Penfold [1998] CCLR 315 (QBD)
R (Antoniak) v Westminster City Council [2019] EWHC 3465 (Admin)

R (AW) v London Borough of Croydon [2005] EWHC 2950 (Admin)
R (Barrett) v Westminster City Council [2015] EWHC 2515 (Admin)
R (Daly and others, formerly MA) v DWP [2016] UKSC 58
R (Kimani) v London Borough of Lambeth [2003] EWCA Civ 1150
R (Limbuela) v Secretary of State for the Home Department [2005] UKHL 66
R (M) v Slough [2008] UKHL 52
R (S) v Swindon BC and Wiltshire CC [2001] EWHC Admin 334
R (SG) v Haringey [2015] EWHC 2579 and R (SG) v London Borough of Haringey & Ors [2017] EWCA Civ 322

Author Biographies

Fiona Bateman is a solicitor specialising in public law, health, social care and safeguarding responsibilities. She currently works with CASCAIDr, a legal advice charity, and as an Independent Chair of Safeguarding Adults Boards, a Safeguarding Adults Review author and lecturer at Brunel University.

Imogen Blood founded a social research consultancy, Imogen Blood & Associates, in 2009, which works with central and local government, national charities and housing and support providers to improve policies, services, strategies and practice with people experiencing multiple exclusion homelessness. A qualified social worker, she began her career working in hostels and as a prison drug worker.

Sharon Clint has 20 years' experience in the homelessness sector. Having worked in a broad spectrum of roles, she currently manages the Learning & Development Team for Groundswell UK. Sharon also benefits from having several years of personal experience of homelessness and uses her knowledge in this area to create training that focuses on equity and developing a deeper understanding of the issues faced by people affected by homelessness.

Adi Cooper OBE is the Independent Chair of two Safeguarding Adults Boards, Care and Health Improvement Advisor for London and the Safeguarding Lead (Local Government Association and Association of Directors of Adult Social Services) and Visiting Professor at the University of Bedfordshire. She has worked in adult social care for 30 years, including as a Director of Adult Social Services for nine years. She has contributed to national policy, service improvement and the Making Safeguarding Personal programme.

Paul England has worked in the field of leadership and organisational development for over 20 years, and now specialises in using complex adaptive systems theory to transform organisations and leaders.

Susan Harrison has over 35 years' experience working in operational and strategic roles in health, housing and social care in London and the South-East. Retired from full-time employment, she offers her time and skills in governance roles, project work and as a research ethicist. She is committed to the development of social science research evidence to support her practice.

Catherine Houlcroft is the principal project officer at the No Recourse to Public Funds (NRPF) Network. With expert knowledge of how immigration law intersects with entitlement to public services, she produces online publications for local authorities, delivers training and leads the Network's policy work.

Sione Marshall is an independent clinical psychologist. Sione is especially curious about the unconscious processes that enable as well as inhibit the effective application of psychologically informed approaches and environments across organisations. She currently works with Pathway, North London.

Karl Mason is a lecturer in Social Work at Royal Holloway, University of London. He has 15 years' experience as a social worker and managed a hospital-based homelessness team for three years. Karl's research and teaching focus on adult social care policy and practice, including the intersections with homelessness and housing.

Bruno Ornelas is an adult safeguarding consultant and trainer with a specialist interest in multiple exclusion homelessness and safeguarding. He has an MA in Safeguarding Adults Law, Policy and Practice and over 15 years of operational and strategic experience in leading and developing safeguarding and service delivery for people experiencing homelessness.

Michael Preston-Shoot is Professor (Emeritus) of Social Work at the University of Bedfordshire, England. He is a Fellow of the Academy of Social Sciences. His research has concentrated on law and social work practice, adult safeguarding and effective practice with adults who self-neglect. He is Independent Chair of Lewisham and of Brent Safeguarding Adults Boards, and Joint Convenor of the National SAB Chairs Network. He has authored Safeguarding Adults Reviews and completed sector-led improvement projects on adult safeguarding and homelessness and on the first national analysis of Safeguarding Adults Reviews.

Carl Price works as recovery coordinator for a national drug treatment charity in Birmingham. He has used his own lived experience of homelessness to champion co-production and trauma-informed practice in his professional work. In 2019, he won a Charity Film Award for his video 'Carl's Story' and has since appeared in other video and film projects highlighting the issue of homelessness.

Rebecca Pritchard is CEO of Surrey Care Association and a Trustee for Hestia. She has worked in service delivery, commissioning and policy roles in the homelessness, drug and alcohol treatment and social care sectors, starting as a volunteer alongside people with lived experience in 1989.

Tim Robson OBE has been the GP clinical lead for the Pathway Homeless Healthcare Team at University College London Hospitals (UCLH) since 2012. Tim set up Meadowell, a specialist GP service for the homeless, in Watford in 2003, and is a trustee for New Hope, a large charity providing services for the homeless in Watford that he helped found in 1990.

Nathan Servini is a mental health social worker and a sessional AMHP for the London Borough of Islington EDT. He joined Enabling Assessment Service London in 2015 following a 15-year career working as a mental health social worker AMHP/ASW based in the homeless outreach team in the London Borough of Camden.

Katy Shorten currently works for Research in Practice. Her role is to oversee the development and delivery of their annual learning programme. She also supports individual local authorities to promote and make best use of evidence-informed resources to support social care practice locally and nationally. Previously, she worked for Plymouth

City Council as a strategic commissioner, working to development systems and support across a range of areas, including multiple exclusion homelessness.

Kate Spreadbury is an independent social worker specialising in adult safeguarding. She currently leads Safeguarding Adults Reviews and works with practitioners and Safeguarding Adults Boards to promote good practice in all aspects of safeguarding. Kate is the lead author of *The Adult Safeguarding Practice Handbook* (Policy Press 2020).

Henry St Clair Miller is Head of NRPF, Refugee and Migrant Services, Islington Council. As part of the senior management team in the Housing Department, Henry leads work to end homelessness in Islington and to help residents from the refugee and migrant community achieve improved outcomes in their lives. Nationally, Henry delivers expert guidance and support to local and central government through the work of the NRPF Network.

Gill Taylor is the Strategic Lead for Homelessness and Vulnerable Adults for the London Borough of Haringey. She has 17 years' experience working in operational and strategic roles and is a specialist in practice improvement, partnership development and commissioning. In 2019, Gill authored an approach to reviewing the deaths of homeless people which has been adopted as best practice by MHCLG and the Local Government Association. Gill is committed to using her lived and professional experience to tackle the systemic inequalities which result in multiple exclusion homelessness.

Barney Wells is a mental health social worker and Director of the Enabling Assessment Service London (EASL). EASL is a social enterprise that supports projects that work with people experiencing homelessness by offering assessments, advice and training. Previously he worked in statutory services, including managing a specialist homeless mental health team.

Subject Index

Access to specialist support 56, 213, 218, 236
Accountability 14, 98, 128, 146, 186, 192, 193, 194, 196, 198, 201, 205, 206, 207, 208, 224
Acquired brain injury 34, 36, 43, 66, 176
Acute Trusts 117
Adult safeguarding principles 13
Adult Social Care/Services 18, 19, 20, 27, 34, 36, 99, 105, 126, 129, 133, 138, 163, 168, 170, 183, 205, 209, 216, 218, 221, 223, 225, 226, 231, 234, 238, 242, 244, 251
Adverse experiences 11, 16, 52, 73, 87, 179, 184
Advocacy 14, 25, 27, 52, 56, 57, 58, 96, 100, 103, 104, 105, 106, 108, 147, 148, 182, 220, 229, 234, 248, 250
After-care 109, 158
Age 60, 96, 119
Anti-discriminatory practice 146
Anti-social behaviour 23, 60, 142, 143, 168, 179, 180
Anxiety 73, 74, 76, 131, 134
Assessment 16, 17, 18, 28, 50, 51, 60, 61-70, 75, 77, 87, 89, 91, 95, 96, 97, 98, 99-107, 108, 110, 129, 137, 153, 159, 162-164, 181, 182, 183, 184, 215, 225, 236, 245, 246, 250, 254
Association of Directors of Adult Social Services 209
Assured Shorthold Tenancies 141
Asylum 27, 146, 158, 168, 170
Attitudes 24, 25, 27, 34, 37, 47, 194, 214, 222
Audits 19, 110, 146, 194, 202, 208, 210
Autism 180, 182
Autonomy 214, 220, 221, 226

Bias 46, 47-49, 60, 61, 78
Birmingham City Council 240
Birmingham Safeguarding Adults Board 240, 241
Brent 245
Bristol Creative Solutions Board 116-130
Budgets 114, 136, 148, 161, 213, 247
Bureau of Investigative Journalism 54, 81, 82, 190
Burnout 221, 222

Capacity-building 45, 198, 250
Care Act 2014 17, 18, 23, 25, 26, 27, 34, 35, 41, 59, 70, 96, 97, 98, 100, 101, 104, 107, 108, 109, 110, 114, 115, 119, 129, 131, 133, 148, 153, 154, 157, 158, 159, 162, 163, 164, 166, 170, 177, 182, 186, 187, 188, 196, 197, 198, 199, 207, 216, 218, 219, 224, 225, 226, 228, 249, 251
Care Act Toolkit 55, 110, 227
Care and Health Improvement Programme 21, 209
Care and Support (Discharge of Hospital Patients) Regulations 2014 98
Care and Support (Eligibility Criteria) Regulations 2015 110, 157, 176
Care and support needs 11, 17, 20, 26, 27, 28, 34, 35, 36, 41, 43, 51, 92, 95, 100, 104, 109, 110, 138, 153, 157, 159, 160, 163, 164, 165, 167, 176, 177, 181, 183, 187, 223, 225, 234, 240, 243, 254
Care/support plans/planning 17, 51, 74, 101, 105, 106, 108, 118, 184, 245
Case law 28, 67
Care lever 98, 140
Carer 100, 105, 108, 220, 233
Case conferences 247, 249
Cathy Come Home 33
Causality 80, 100
Charity Organisation Society 30, 31
Chartered Institute of Housing 140
Children Act 1989 153, 154, 156
Children (Northern Ireland) Order 1995 154
Children (Scotland) Act 1995 154
Children's Safeguarding Partnerships 200, 207, 211
Clinical Commissioning Group 117, 205
Coercion 105
Cognitive Behavioural Therapy 222
Colocation 181, 225, 231, 234
Commissioning 13, 18, 21, 57, 85, 90, 108, 110, 115, 130, 132, 135, 136, 148, 151, 167, 175, 185, 186, 188, 189, 205, 213, 229, 232-255

Communities of Practice 226, 227, 231
Community Safety Partnerships 12, 19, 175, 185, 200, 207, 211
Compassion 242, 253
Compassion fatigue 221
Complaints 138, 141, 241
Complex case panels 245
Confidentiality 63
Consent 37, 62, 103, 118, 119, 226
Constructionism 29
Contractual monitoring 136
Co-production 44, 115, 150, 233, 244, 246, 247, 251, 254
Coping 53, 58
Coronavirus Act 2020 175
Court of Protection 106, 107, 182
Covid-19 pandemic 11, 21, 22, 23, 32, 41, 77, 88-94, 106, 107, 126, 130, 141, 152, 153, 156, 158, 160, 165, 175, 186, 193, 196, 202, 237, 254
Criminal justice 45, 114, 151, 189, 205, 227, 234, 239
Crisis 33, 54, 63, 133, 140
Critical Time Interventions CTIs) 237, 244
Cuckooing 179

Data (homelessness/mortality) 79, 83, 84, 89, 114, 135, 136, 137, 151, 165, 179, 198, 199, 216, 238
Day centres 144
Decent Homes Standard 141
Decision-making 18, 46, 47, 48, 56, 58, 61, 62, 66, 67, 99, 110, 146, 154, 162, 171, 182, 183, 185, 216, 221, 222, 245
Department for Work and Pensions 240
Department of Health and Social Care 209
Dilemma 220
Disabled people/disability 55, 56, 60, 61, 96, 103, 144, 145, 146, 179, 183
Discrimination 11, 14, 34, 145, 146, 209
District Nurses 100
Diversity 11, 14, 144, 216, 232, 236, 255
Domains 88, 184-185, 193, 202, 230
Domestic abuse/violence 48, 134, 137, 144, 147, 163, 180, 207, 236, 250
Domestic Homicide Reviews 187
Drug-Related Deaths Reviews 187
Duty of care 168, 220, 221
Duty to enable 225
Duty to enquire (safeguarding alerts) 17, 25, 27, 66, 74, 96, 97, 101, 108, 114, 115, 119, 158, 160, 182, 183, 184, 241
Duty to protect 225
Duty to refer 182, 218
Dying Homeless Project 54, 81

Elected members 197, 204, 205, 210

Eligibility criteria 50, 97, 99, 120, 154, 157, 160, 161, 163, 182, 186, 226
Emotions/Emotional impact 75, 76, 216 220, 221
Employment 62, 81, 143, 166, 233
Empowerment 13, 66, 96, 118, 185, 207, 224, 243, 250
Enforcement 138, 168, 235
Engagement 46, 50, 85, 100, 115, 118, 119, 120, 126, 130, 131, 134, 148, 162, 166, 168, 183, 184, 214, 233, 235, 236, 245, 248, 252
England 79
Equality 95, 144-146, 207, 218, 233, 236
Equality Act 2010 14, 55, 96, 146
Escalation 70, 107, 182, 248
Ethnicity 61, 119, 144, 146
EU Settlement Scheme 145, 155, 168
European Convention on Human Rights and Fundamental Freedoms 18, 159
European Economic Area Nationals 155
Evaluation 60, 61, 75-77, 103, 194, 222, 232
Eviction 132, 141
Executive capacity/function 16, 43, 181, 183
Exempt accommodation 136, 137, 240, 241, 243
Experts by experience – see human stories
Exploitation 10, 114, 117, 137, 164, 169, 179, 180, 185, 200, 235, 237

Faith groups 137
Family and friends 191-192
Financial abuse 241, 248
Financial austerity/budget pressures 20, 36, 52, 55, 56, 82, 120, 132, 135, 136, 153, 161, 186, 204, 228, 232, 237, 239, 251, 255
Fire/Fire Service 108, 141, 180, 241
Friendship 57, 58
Fulfilling Lives Programme 147
Funding disputes 107

Gaming 34
Gender 60, 61, 96, 119, 146
Gender-based abuse 55
Governance 14, 19, 20, 21, 88, 93, 150, 185, 186, 188, 193, 195-211, 239, 240, 241
GPs 100, 192
Grief 190-191, 192
Groundswell 54, 55, 89
Guiste v Lambeth LBC [2019] 133

Harassment 146
Haringey Safeguarding Adults Board 174, 187
Healthwatch 207
Health and Personal Social Services (Northern Ireland) Order 1972 154
Health and safety 243
Health and Wellbeing Boards 12, 19, 185, 207, 211, 239

Subject Index

Healthy London Partnership 90
Heart of England v JB [2014] 102
Home Office 166, 168-170
Homeless Link 135
Homelessness Act 2002 228
Homelessness Code of Guidance 98, 102, 134
Homelessness Fatality Reviews 19, 174-194, 211, 254
Homelessness Reduction Act 2017 10, 20, 23, 132, 182, 218, 224, 236
Homelessness Partnership/Reduction Boards 12, 20, 207
Homelessness Strategies 228, 231
Homes England 240
Hospital admission 71, 84, 91, 99, 100, 129, 163, 176, 181
Hospital discharge 17, 24, 74, 77, 85, 91, 98, 182, 192, 225, 244
Hostels 26, 31, 32, 33, 41, 45, 48, 50, 88, 89, 103, 109, 129, 132, 135, 140, 147, 149, 150, 154, 178, 179, 180, 181, 192, 199, 235, 244, 253
Hotak v LB Southwark [2015] 96
Housing Act 1988 141
Housing Act 1996 18, 97, 98, 108, 109, 141, 142, 143, 153, 157, 158, 161, 186, 218, 224
Housing Benefit 20, 132, 135, 136, 138, 145, 240, 243
Housing First 11, 24, 33, 90, 147, 148, 149, 161, 237, 254
Housing (Homeless Persons) Act 1977 32, 33
Housing register 142-143, 150
Housing rights 32
Housing supply 20, 79, 142, 143, 144, 151, 220, 233
Housing support 91, 135, 151, 237, 239
Human rights 35, 81, 95, 96, 101, 107, 109, 111, 157, 159, 160, 162, 163, 169, 207, 208, 218, 237
Human Rights Act 1998 14, 18, 97, 182, 193
Human stories 10, 18, 21, 22, 40-58, 62, 65, 67, 69, 71, 72, 81-82, 86, 101, 103, 105, 116, 117, 122, 123, 124, 125, 128, 130, 148, 160, 163, 164, 166, 170, 177-181, 182-183, 188, 192, 205, 206, 207, 209, 211, 212, 213, 215, 223, 229, 231, 245, 247, 255

Immigration 79, 93, 94, 109, 133, 135, 145, 152-171
Immigration and Asylum Act 1999 154
Inclusion 14, 27, 51, 85, 249, 253
Independent Chairs 206, 207, 209
Induction 242
Inequality 81, 82, 83, 94, 198, 208, 209
Information-sharing 17, 25, 52, 97, 108, 122, 182, 183, 184, 203, 244, 248, 250
Institutional abuse 241

Intentionally homeless 23, 31, 33, 129, 133, 141, 186
Intervention 60, 61, 64, 67, 70, 71-74, 75, 77, 84, 91, 93, 94, 100, 103, 107, 120, 151, 163, 168, 176, 186, 212
Involvement of service users – see human stories

Joint strategic needs assessment 200, 239

Key performance indicators (KPIs) 245, 246, 247
Kings College 255
King's Fund 85

Leadership 195-211, 212, 224, 228, 243, 253
Learning disabilities 34, 43, 87, 135, 176
Learning Disability Mortality Reviews 187
Learning organisation 222, 230
Legal frameworks 61, 63, 95, 111, 132, 156, 200, 231
Legal literacy/options 15, 17, 104, 184, 213, 218-219, 231, 251
LGBTQ+ 10, 15, 24, 33, 55, 56, 61, 144, 146, 191, 209, 216
Lifestyle choice 15, 24, 27, 32, 34, 36, 37, 45, 103, 125, 181, 183, 190, 201, 215
Listening 40, 49-51, 72, 74, 76, 81-82, 93, 123, 185, 250
Liverpool City Council 253
Local connection 93, 108, 135, 143, 236
Local Government Act 1972 157, 158
Local Government Association 22, 55, 87, 209
Local Housing Allowance 139, 140
Localism Act 2011 139, 142
London Borough of Haringey 251, 254
London Multi-Agency Safeguarding Policies and Procedures 200

Making Every Adult Matter (MEAM) 147, 185, 217, 231
Making Every Contact Count 186
Making Safeguarding Personal 13, 35, 42-44, 97, 103, 118, 148, 205, 216, 219, 226, 229
MAPPA 140, 249
MARAC 249
Marginalisation 11, 55, 176, 196, 216, 219, 220
Mental capacity 16, 17, 36, 59, 64, 66-70, 72, 97, 98, 106, 134, 138, 181, 182, 184, 201, 235, 236, 251
Mental Capacity Act 2005 66, 68, 101, 102, 148, 182, 218
Mental health 10, 11, 16, 17, 24, 31, 34, 36, 42, 48, 49, 60, 61, 63, 65, 66, 68, 86, 87, 99, 103, 114, 115, 116, 117, 118, 128, 129, 131, 132, 133, 134, 135, 136, 143, 144,

Mental health *cont.*
149, 150, 164, 176, 179, 180, 181, 183, 184, 189, 192, 196, 201, 223, 245, 248
Mental Health Act 1983 65, 66, 70, 107, 109, 157, 158
Merseyside Safeguarding Adults Board 253, 254
Milton Keynes Safeguarding Adults Board 179
Ministry of Housing, Communities and Local Government 190, 209
Minority/Black communities 24, 33, 55, 144-146, 189, 208, 216
Modern slavery 163, 207
Multi-agency meetings/working 17, 19, 52, 74, 77, 88, 95, 97, 104, 115, 119, 120, 182, 183, 184, 185, 199, 201, 210, 221, 224, 234, 245, 248, 249
Multiple exclusion homelessness/multiple disadvantage 11, 12, 13, 17, 19, 21, 23, 26, 34, 40, 42, 43, 44, 53, 57, 80, 87, 99, 110, 114, 115, 130, 132, 133, 134, 139, 140, 144, 145, 146, 148, 150, 151, 174, 176, 185, 186, 188, 189, 193, 195, 196, 197, 200, 201, 202, 203, 204, 208, 210, 211, 214, 215, 234, 239, 255
Museum of Homelessness 54, 81, 190

N v ACCG and others [2017] 67
National Assistance Act 1948 26, 31
National Asylum Seekers Service 244
National Drug Treatment Monitoring Service 239
National Health Services Act 2006 157, 158
National Institute for Health and Care Excellence (NICE) 84
Nationality, Immigration and Asylum Act 2002 157, 159
Neoliberalism 28
New Right 33
NHS Continuing Health Care 109
NHS England 89
NHS Low Income Scheme 165
NICE 251, 255
No recourse to public funds 18, 20, 92, 109, 135, 145, 152-171, 179, 186
No recourse to Public Funds (NRPF) Network 159, 167, 168, 171, 237, 254
No Secrets 196
Non-commissioned exempt accommodation 136-138
Nzolameso v City of Westminster [2015] 108

Offending/offenders 114, 116, 131, 132, 135, 137, 140, 147
Optimism bias 246, 250
Ordinary residence 93, 108
Organisational culture 19, 115, 128, 130, 185, 193, 194, 201, 208, 212, 213, 214, 228-229, 231, 243, 249

Outcomes 11, 14, 17, 35, 45, 46, 85, 88, 94, 96, 99, 101, 102, 115, 116, 147, 153, 167, 168, 171, 174, 175, 182, 188, 192, 193, 194, 203, 206, 208, 235, 237, 238, 239, 243, 244, 245, 246, 247, 248
Outreach 16, 68, 90, 91, 97, 105, 148, 163, 166, 170, 205, 225, 247, 248
Outside Project 56

Partnership 13, 19, 43, 90, 92, 98, 115, 116, 121, 122, 124-126, 138, 151, 186, 188, 193, 195-211, 213, 223-227, 228, 231, 234, 235, 238, 247, 253, 255
Patterns 15, 16, 120, 129, 181, 183, 184, 215
Payment by results 239, 246
Peer support 46, 52, 55, 217
People with lived experience – see human stories
Personalisation/person-centred 14, 42, 59, 66, 77, 101, 114, 118, 123, 147, 151, 184, 212, 214, 216, 233, 236, 239, 246, 248, 250
Pharmacy 104
Physical abuse 128, 248
Physical health 11, 18, 24, 31, 42, 63, 82, 87, 99, 115, 117, 118, 128, 131, 133, 150, 164, 176, 179, 181, 189, 196, 223, 248
Place-based 251-255
Plymouth Alliance 244
Police 48, 105, 115, 117, 138, 205, 209, 229, 241, 248
Police and Crime Commissioner 207
Policy discourses/typologies 23-37, 57, 63
Policies and procedures 19, 61, 64, 79, 92, 125, 147, 164, 175, 185, 193, 200, 201, 202, 208, 210, 211, 219
Poor Law 31, 47, 54
Population health approaches 253
Positive risk-taking 45
Poverty 11, 14, 31, 32, 33, 34, 54, 55, 80, 82, 92, 176, 179, 214, 228
Power 40, 44-47, 48, 56, 58, 63, 123, 124, 215, 245-249
Prejudice 40, 46, 47, 48, 51, 58
Prevention 13, 17, 84, 96, 97, 100, 108, 114, 117, 152, 157, 161, 185, 187, 188, 193, 197, 198, 224, 226, 253
Prevention duty 132
Primary Care 89, 117
Priority need 133, 134, 135, 139, 158, 186
Prison 10, 17, 49, 55, 118, 126, 144
Private rented sector housing 139-141
Probation 115, 117, 225
Professional curiosity 14, 26, 50, 51, 57, 58, 59-78, 100, 125, 181, 182, 184, 222, 228, 250
Professional development 45, 250

Subject Index

Professional judgement 250
Professional/institutional/organisational abuse 45, 96, 109, 241
Proportionality 14, 97, 120, 186, 194, 224
Protection 13, 43, 56, 66, 97, 185, 197, 224, 226
Protection planning 96, 100, 105, 106, 107, 108
Psychological abuse 241
Psychologically-informed approach 59, 61, 64, 67, 77, 78, 119, 147, 213, 217, 222, 231
Public law principles 98, 111, 162
Public Space Protection Orders 31
Putting People First 216

Quality 136, 138, 139, 141, 149, 175, 181, 198, 208, 224, 238, 240, 242-244, 246, 247, 251
Questioning 78

R (Antoniak) v Westminster City Council [2019] 27
R (Barrett) v Westminster City Council [2015] 110
R (Daley and others, formerly MA) v DWP [2016] 108
R (Kimani) v London Borough of Lambeth [2003] 159
R (Limbuela) v Secretary of State for the Home Department [2005] 159
R (M) v Slough [2008] 109
R (S) v Swindon BC and Wiltshire CC [2001] 96
R (SG) v London Borough of Haringey [2015] 27, 103, 109
R v Bristol City Council ex parte Penfold [1998] 109
Race 60, 82, 96, 144, 146
Rapport 181
Recording 18, 51, 87, 97, 184, 250
Recovery 10, 11, 57, 58, 115, 131, 239, 247
Recruitment and retention 224, 238, 242, 243
Redbridge Safeguarding Adults Board 178
Referrals 18, 98, 117, 118, 120, 135, 136, 137, 162-164, 181, 182, 184, 225, 226, 243, 246, 247, 250
Reflective practice 69, 75-77, 78, 121, 122, 126-127, 146, 185, 191, 192, 193, 194, 210, 213, 221-223, 231, 250
Relationships 40, 50, 51, 52-53, 57, 58, 61, 64, 65, 66, 72, 74, 78, 85, 99, 105, 121, 124-126, 128, 129, 130, 147, 150, 162, 166, 168, 179, 191, 192, 193, 198, 204, 213, 214, 215, 218, 220, 228, 231, 238, 239, 248, 249, 252, 253
Relief duty 132, 133
Religion 60, 82, 96
Resilience 55, 81, 148, 180, 229, 230, 231
Resources 64, 74, 120, 135, 220, 225, 228, 236, 242, 247

Review 17, 18, 75, 101, 202, 208, 211, 232, 241, 254
Right to buy 142
Right to rent 145
Right to reside test 167
Risk 13, 14, 15, 16, 17, 19, 24, 25, 26, 34, 36, 37, 40, 47, 49, 50, 53, 55, 58, 59, 60, 61, 63, 65, 66, 68, 70, 72, 80, 88, 97, 98, 99, 101, 102, 103, 104, 105, 106, 107, 108, 114, 115, 116, 117, 121, 125, 126, 128, 129, 136, 143, 146, 150, 151, 156, 158, 159, 162, 163, 164, 169, 181, 182, 183, 184, 185, 186, 188, 190, 192, 195, 202, 210, 211, 215, 220, 221, 222, 225, 226, 228, 231, 234, 236, 240, 243, 246, 247, 250, 254
Risk management/mitigation 45, 97, 105, 127-129, 244, 250
Role conflict 220
Rough Sleeping Strategy 10, 12, 26, 54, 174, 177, 179, 196

Safeguarding Adults Boards 12, 19, 21, 25, 151, 174-194, 195-211, 219, 228, 236, 250, 254, 255
Safeguarding Adults Reviews 10, 11, 12, 14, 15, 16, 19, 24, 25, 26, 27, 28, 34, 37, 48, 87-88, 101, 103, 108, 116, 131, 132, 133, 134, 141, 146, 165, 174-194, 196, 198, 200, 201, 202, 205, 210, 211, 218, 224, 228, 229, 250, 254, 255
Safeguarding alerts 241
Safeguarding Children Partnerships 19
Safeguarding literacy 17
Safeguarding Toolkit 99
Safety 40, 41, 43, 52, 53, 80, 86, 92, 102, 134, 136, 137, 141, 150, 188, 216, 235, 238, 242-244, 247, 248, 251, 252
Sanctions 45, 143, 147, 150, 241
Scotland 26, 79
Sector-led improvement 208
Self-care 254
Self-neglect 19, 26, 27, 59, 63, 66, 70, 87, 115, 117, 119, 120, 125, 128, 129, 136, 176, 179, 183, 192, 201, 210, 215, 218, 219, 226, 236
Serious Case Review 215, 228
Severe Disability Premium 140
Severe weather 23, 32, 86, 181
Sexual abuse 48, 65
Sexual orientation 60, 96
Shelter 33
Shelters 31, 88, 89, 135, 144, 156, 191
Sisters Uncut 55
Six safeguarding principles 13-14, 95, 96-98, 118, 185, 203, 224
Social Care Institute for Excellence (SCIE) 243
Social housing 142-144, 186, 234, 240, 253
Social Impact Bonds (SIBs) 246, 247

Social isolation 17, 243
Social landlord 20, 136, 139, 141, 143, 241, 248
Social media 63, 64, 81, 90
Social Security (Coronavirus) (Further Measures) Regulations 2020 140
Social Services and Well-being (Wales) Act 2014 154
Social Work Education 215
Social Workers 62, 63, 64, 65, 69, 70, 75, 129, 138, 162, 215, 221, 224
Solihull Safeguarding Adults Board 180
Spare room subsidy 142
Specialist advice 18, 185
St Mungo's 135
Staffing 19
Stereotypes 190
Steven Hoskin 25
Stigma 40, 47-49, 55, 65, 140, 142, 213, 216
Strengths/Strengths-based approach 35, 36, 37, 100, 118, 119, 147, 187, 213, 217, 222, 228, 231, 250
Stereotypes 36, 51, 60, 190
Stress 213
Substance misuse/addiction/dependence/services 10, 11, 24, 32, 34, 36, 42, 43, 48, 53, 57, 60, 66, 84, 87, 89, 103, 104, 110, 114, 116, 118, 120, 129, 131, 132, 134, 135, 136, 143, 149, 150, 176, 179, 180, 181, 183, 189, 191, 192, 196, 201, 214, 215
Suicide/suicidal ideation 45, 83, 108, 176, 179, 180, 183, 253
Supervision 18, 45, 146, 182, 185, 213, 216, 221-223, 231, 242, 250
Support-exempt provision 243
Supported accommodation/housing 135-136, 180, 192, 199, 235, 240, 241, 243, 244, 253
Supported Housing (Regulation) Bill 2020/2021 137
Supporting People 27, 28, 132, 238, 239, 240

Targets 245, 246
Tenancy sustainment/management 91, 139, 149, 254
The Guardian 82
Think family 184
Thresholds 19, 182, 183, 234
Tower Hamlets Safeguarding Adults Board 180
Trafficking 163, 200
Training 70, 104, 123, 138, 146, 148, 175, 185, 198, 201, 210, 219, 222, 241, 243, 249, 250
Transition 17, 128, 129, 184, 185, 192, 207, 244-245

Trauma 11, 15, 16, 45, 50, 67, 73, 76, 81, 87, 99, 105, 106, 110, 118, 131, 143, 147, 149, 150, 151, 176, 179, 180, 183, 184, 190, 196, 217, 221, 222, 241
Trauma-informed working 45, 46, 148, 150, 213, 217, 231, 235, 245
Two-tier councils 205, 236

Unconscious bias/processes 14, 25, 36, 37, 51, 59, 64, 75, 78, 146
Unemployment 179
UNESCO 22
Universal Credit 20, 139, 140-141, 154, 155

Vagrancy 30, 31, 214
Vagrancy Act 1824 23, 30, 47
Values 208, 209, 220, 221, 228, 231
Veterans' charities 137
Violence 41, 45, 48, 61, 63, 65, 138
Voices of Stoke 55
Voluntary and community organisations/sector 46, 116, 151, 156, 205, 209, 213, 215, 223, 234, 239, 240, 247, 248, 249, 251, 254

Wales 79
Walsall Safeguarding Adults Board 178
Welfare benefits 45, 93, 186, 233, 234, 251
Wellbeing 18, 26, 35, 82, 83, 86, 101, 102, 110, 114, 125, 131, 141, 164, 181, 186, 212, 213, 216, 217, 219-223, 225, 226, 228, 230, 233, 236, 241, 251, 252, 253, 254, 255
Whistle blow 107
Whole person approach 49, 51
Whole system approach/change 12, 13, 14, 114, 116, 117, 119, 120-127, 128, 148, 185, 208, 211, 231, 233, 235, 249, 251-255
Wicked issues 195, 203, 204, 208, 211
Windrush 169
Winterbourne View 25
Women 10, 15, 24, 48, 55, 134, 137, 144, 145, 146, 147, 149, 179, 189, 216, 235
Workforce development 19, 37, 85, 146, 185, 193, 210, 212-231, 233
Workhouse Visiting Society 31
Working together 17, 72-74, 77, 107, 111, 121, 126, 181, 182, 183, 184, 218, 224, 226
Workloads/caseloads 52, 95, 161, 212, 225, 238
Workplace development 213, 252
World Health Organisation 82-83, 94
Wrap-around 13, 16, 90, 147, 149, 151, 183, 185, 186, 187

Author Index

Adlam 64, 81, 219, 220, 222, 235, 250
Albanese 131
Alcohol Change UK 15, 201, 214
Aldridge, R. 24, 131
Aldridge, R. W. 84
Anderson 227
Antonacopoulou 121
APPG 134
Appleton 115
Archer 55
Asmussen 11
Asthana 122

Baim 225, 226
Bampton 175, 199, 201
Barker 46
Barnett 144
Baron 217
Barton 23
Basran 140
Bassot 75
Bateman 102, 109
BBC 48
Bell 83, 94
Bellis 145
Beresford 35, 36
Bimpson 134
Bion 67
Birmingham Safeguarding Adults Board 207
Blood 132, 134, 136, 137, 141, 143, 150, 218
Boath 136
Boddy 63
Boobis 133
Booth 240
Bovill Rose 132, 135
Bradley 10
Bramley 42, 44, 80, 145, 238
Braye 198, 203, 207, 215, 218, 225, 228
Bretherton 24, 33, 65, 133
Brown, C. 36, 57, 191
Brown, G. 87

Brown, M. 221
Buck 236
Bureau of Investigative Journalism 81
Butler, I. 21
Butler, J. 190

Cambridgeshire Insight 140
Cameron, A. 15, 216
Cameron, E. 66
Camillus 195
Carr 51
Carroll 216
Cartwright 237
Centrepoint 216
CFE Research 147
Changing Lives 147
Charity Commission for England and Wales 137
Chiva 121
City and Hackney Safeguarding Adults Board 196, 199
Clark 115, 124
Cockersell 59, 61
Codling 66
Cole 142
Colomina 119
Connor 155
Cooper, A. 10, 98, 132, 134, 141, 202, 237, 248
Cooper, V. 31
Cordis Bright 147
Corner 110
Cornes 20, 27, 34, 36, 98, 99, 114, 225, 237, 239
Cream 21, 85, 186, 203, 205, 234, 236, 244, 247, 248, 249, 251, 252
Crisis 54, 63
Croley 32
Crowson 31, 33

Daly 220
Dear 247
DeCorte 195, 203, 204, 208

Department for Work and Pensions (DWP) 140
Department of Health 59, 78
Department of Health and Social Care 13, 24, 25, 26, 35, 95, 96, 100, 107, 118, 131, 176, 185, 196, 197, 198, 203, 204, 205, 206, 207, 216, 224, 225, 226, 242, 255
Dobie 133
Dobson 11, 23, 27, 28, 114, 115
Dominelli 63
Dorling 79, 141
Dorney-Smith 24
Downie 234, 237, 238, 244
Drakeford 21
Droy 205

EASL 67
Ecola 56
Elwood 219
Equality and Human Rights Commission 146
European Observatory on Homelessness 135
Evans 27
Ewbank 245, 249, 251, 253

Farran 253, 254
Fernández-Reino 145
Field 245
Finlayson 225
Fitzpatrick 23, 29, 40, 80, 212, 238
Flaherty 132
Foster 145
Fransham 141

Gallos 124
Garratt 132
Gibbs 75
Gill 214, 221, 222
Golden Key 130
Gousy 140
Gowan 23, 24, 25, 29, 31, 32, 33, 57
Graham 221
Grant 229
Greater London Authority 92, 94, 238
Greaves 142
Gregory 236
Groundswell 90, 132
Guthrie 216, 222, 226, 228

Hafford-Letchfield 51
Haigh 32
Hall 41, 89, 153
Hansard 153
Hattenstone 82
Health Education England 14
Health Services Management centre 233
Healthy London Partnership 91
Heffernan 81

Henderson 32, 57
Herman 52
Herring 35
Hewson 216
Holmes 14, 17, 18
Home Office 155, 158, 168
Homeless Link 66, 67, 134, 135, 136, 144, 147, 148, 149, 217, 234, 235, 236, 238, 251
Homelessness Code of Guidance 102
Horvath 235
Hough 245
Housing Benefit Regulation 240
Housing, Communities and Local Government Committee 152, 153
Housing First England 149
Housing First European Hub 147
Humphreys 29, 30, 31, 32, 33

Institute of Public Care 233
International Bureau of Education 207
Isle of Wight Safeguarding Adults Board 133

Johnsen 148
Johnstone 34, 37

Keast 204, 206
Kinman 229
Klijn 203
Knott 75
Kolb 222
Konradt 204
Koppenjan 203
Kowalewska 144, 146

Lambeth Safeguarding Adults Board 86
Lavelle 82
Lawson 35, 205
Leeds Safeguarding Adults Board and Safer Leeds 9, 11, 201, 207
Leverton 219
Levin 57
Levy 59
Lewer 32, 71, 88, 89
Lloyd-Smith 175, 199, 201
Loach 33
Local Government Association 43, 128, 152, 204, 205, 208, 209, 233, 235
Local Partnerships 156
London Borough of Brent 245
London Safeguarding Adults Board 200
Longmate 32
Lowe 208, 211, 239

Machin 115, 215
Maciver 235
Mackay 25

Author Index

Mackie 234
Maguire, J. 151
Maguire, N. 45, 46, 67, 222
Making Every Adult Matter (MEAM) 217, 225, 228
Mandell 204, 206
Manthorpe 24, 26, 32, 34, 66, 201
Marmot 83, 94
Marquet 122
Martin 221
Martineau 12, 24, 26, 34, 48, 87, 99, 114, 131, 132, 177, 201, 214, 215, 218, 224, 225, 228, 229
Maseele 23, 214
Mason, K. 10, 11, 18, 20, 26, 27, 32, 34, 35, 36, 133, 176, 186, 196, 215, 218, 224, 225, 226, 228
Mason, P. 247
Mattinson 142
Mayor of London 85
McCarthy 131, 132, 144
McClenaghan 82
McCulloch 31
McDermott 117
McGuire 204
MEAM 13, 17, 19, 114, 115, 145
Medicins Sans Frontiers 89
Mental Health Foundation 45
Menzies Lyth 64, 74
Merseyside Safeguarding Adults Board 254
Migration Observatory 155
Miller, C. 245
Miller, R. 115
Miller, R. M. 64
Ministry of Housing, Communities and Local Government 10, 12, 23, 26, 32, 54, 79, 89, 107, 134, 136, 138, 142, 149, 152, 153, 155, 161, 166, 174, 175, 179, 196, 234, 240, 242, 243
Ministry of Justice 17, 45, 144
Morris 47
Mullins 124
Museum of Homelessness 54, 81, 82

National Audit Office 89, 90, 153, 156
National Records of Scotland 79
National Network of Chairs of Safeguarding Adults Board 198, 199
Neale 36, 57, 191
Nedelec 45
Newburn 47
NHS England 85
NICE 14, 15, 16, 17, 85
No Accommodation Network 156
No Recourse to Public Funds (NRPF) Network 155, 161, 165, 166, 170
Nobel 57

O'Connor 117
O'Leary 24
Oakley 132, 135
Office of National Statistics (ONS) 10, 47, 54, 79, 83, 84, 141, 142, 155
Ollett 200
Ornelas 55, 99, 110, 227

Padgett 149
Parry 17, 18, 19
Parsell, C. 34, 37
Parsell, M. 34, 37
Passel 155
Pathway 23, 66, 69, 85
Pattison 131, 132, 144
Payne 29, 35, 36
Pereira 119
Petrovich 221
Phipps 214, 222, 223
Pleace 20, 24, 33, 65, 147, 186
Plymouth City Council 115, 244
Pochin 57
Preston-Shoot 11, 12, 14, 16, 18, 22, 24, 26, 27, 34, 35, 48, 52, 55, 88, 95, 100, 101, 103, 111, 114, 131, 132, 133, 134, 141, 146, 177, 179, 184, 186, 194, 201, 202, 208, 209, 210, 213, 218, 223, 224, 228, 229, 234, 236, 237, 244, 248, 249, 250, 251, 254
Psychology Today 47
Public Health England 11, 12, 14, 17, 84, 179
Pyper 23

Quilgars 147

Raisbeck 137, 240
Ramadass 203
Raman 119
Rawlings 194
Redbridge Safeguarding Adults Board 165, 166
Reeson 23, 31
Reeve 134
Regulator of Social Housing 240
Reid 78
Richardson 122
Ritchie 59, 64
Robertson, M. 132
Robertson, R. 232, 236, 245, 249, 251, 253
Rock 47
Rogans-Watson 23, 32, 34
Rollnick 64
Rowe 143
Rumlet 128, 130

Safeguarding Adults Executive Board 196, 199
Sanders 131
Satir 16
Scanlon, C. 64, 81, 219, 220, 222, 235, 250

Scanlon, K. 161
Schon 75
Scottish Government 84
Scragg 75
Scurfield 47
Senge 121
Shangold 53
Sheikh 249
Shelter 141, 144, 208, 216
Sherwood-Johnson 28
Siegel 74
Silva 204
Silver 45
Simcock, P. 115, 215
Simcock, T. 24, 140, 141
Simpson 17, 19, 24, 27, 34, 36
Sinek 121, 124
Skills for Care 249
Slasberg 35, 36
Sloane 53
Social Care Institute for Excellence (SCIE) 242, 251
St Mungo's 10, 92
Stacey 122
Stanley 217
Stevens 220, 221
Stokoe 61, 67
Stonewall 209
Stonewall Housing 61
Stringfellow 71
Stuart 36
Sumption 145

Taylor 238, 251, 252
Teeman 249
Teixeira 148, 237
Thacker 125, 222

The City View 88
Thomas 84
Together Network 52
Torbay Safeguarding Adults Board 215
Tower Hamlets Safeguarding Adults Board 9
Tunåker 57

United Nations Human Rights, Office of the High Commissioner 207

Valuation Office Agency 140
Von Bueren 203

Wagstaff 143
Ward 14, 17, 18
Watson 119, 214, 215, 220, 222, 224
Weal 186
Webster 45
Wenzel 232, 236
Wheatley 121, 124
White 10
Whiteford 17, 19, 24, 27, 34, 36
Whitehead 161
Williams 45
Wilson 23, 141
Winnicott 64, 75
Wong 56
Woodcock 214, 221, 222
Worcester City Council 178
Worcestershire Safeguarding Adults Board 9
World Health Organisation 82, 83

Young 235
Yukl 130

Zimmerman 121, 128